THE INTERNATIONAL JOURNAL OF ETHICAL LEADERSHIP

Volume 2
Fall 2013

The International Journal of Ethical Leadership
Case Western Reserve University
Editor-in-Chief: Shannon E. French, Inamori Professor in Ethics and Director, Inamori International Center for Ethics and Excellence
Executive Editor: Michael Scharf, Associate Dean of Global Legal Studies, John Deaver Drinko-Baker & Hostetler Professor of Law, and Director, Frederick K. Cox International Law Center
Managing Editor: Christian Frano, Assistant Director of Programs and Operations, Inamori International Center for Ethics and Excellence

Many thanks to former Managing Editor Kathleen Norman for her help with the early stages of this issue.

The International Journal of Ethical Leadership, Volume 2, Fall 2013

All new material © 2013 *The International Journal of Ethical Leadership*.

All rights reserved • Manufactured in the United States of America

ISSN 2326-7461

For additional information, please contact Managing Editor Christian Frano, caf59@case.edu or visit case.edu/provost/inamori

Contents

Letters
Message from the Editor, Shannon E. French — 1

Inamori Ethics Prize Recipients
David Suzuki (2012)
  Biography — 3
  "The Challenge of the Twenty-First Century:
    Setting the Real Bottom Line" — 6
  2012 Academic Symposium Transcript — 18

Yvon Chouinard (2013)
  Biography — 44
  "A Responsible Economy" — 47
  "What We Do For a Living" — 51

Articles
Chris Laszlo and David L. Cooperrider, "Business for a Prosperous and Flourishing World" — 62

Michele Hunt, "Vision of a Better World: *An Optimistic View*" — 67

Louise Rosenmeier and Peter Neergaard, "Exploring the Effect of The Ruggie Framework for Human Rights" — 74

Charlene Zietsma, "Is There Room for Ethical Leadership in Today's Business Environment?" — 90

Martin L. Cook, "Reflections on Courage (and Other Virtues): A Dialogue Between Ethics and Moral Psychology" — 102

David Hassler, "Habits of the Heart: Poetry and Democracy" — 115

Gregory L. Eastwood, "Moral Choices and Leadership" — 121

Duncan Gaswaga, "The Definition of Terrorism" — 136

Duncan Morrow, "Self and Other in Northern Ireland:
     The Challenge of Ethical Leadership in an Ethnic Conflict"   157

Talking Foreign Policy Transcripts   168

Contributors   262

Message from the Editor

Shannon E. French
Inamori Professor in Ethics and Director,
Inamori International Center for Ethics and Excellence,
Case Western Reserve University

We are very proud to bring you this second issue of the *International Journal of Ethical Leadership*. The mission of this publication is to spread awareness of the fact that every worthwhile human endeavor requires the application and embodiment of ethical leadership in order to succeed, endure, and produce positive outcomes for present and future generations. Our aim is to expand the transdisciplinary, international conversation that is ongoing around the question of what ethical leadership requires. We hope with each issue of this journal to highlight a wide range of perspectives on ethical leadership in theory and action around the globe. Our intention is not to endorse particular opinions, but to host a trusted forum for readers to explore a diversity of views.

Dr. Kazuo Inamori and the Inamori Foundation of Kyoto, Japan, founded the Inamori International Center for Ethics and Excellence at Case Western Reserve University in 2006 through a generous endowment. The mission of the Inamori Center is to foster ethical leadership on our campus, in our local community, nationally, and worldwide. The Center is dedicated to exploring ethical issues from a global perspective, to nurturing awareness and understanding of our common humanity through the study, teaching, and practice of ethics, and to creating internationally recognized programs and initiatives devoted to ethical inquiry in both practical and theoretical aspects. Our goal is to facilitate the development of leaders who will, in the words of Dr. Inamori, "serve humankind through ethical deeds rather than actions based on self-interest and selfish desires."

Each year, the Inamori Center at Case Western Reserve University presents the Inamori Ethics Prize, which recognizes an individual who has demonstrated exemplary ethical leadership on the global stage while trying to improve the condition of humankind. By honoring both the struggles and accomplishments of the recipients of the prize, the Inamori Center encourages deeper study of the true nature of ethical leadership.

These are the first six recipients of the Inamori Ethics Prize:
- Dr. Francis Collins, leader of the Human Genome Project and current Director of the United States National Institutes of Health (2008)
- The Honorable Mary Robinson, former (and first female) President of Ireland, former U.N. High Commissioner for Human Rights, and founder of the Mary Robinson Foundation for Climate Justice (2009)
- Mr. Stan Brock, conservationist and founder of the health care nonprofit Remote Area Medical (2010)
- Advocate Beatrice Mtetwa, Zimbabwean human rights lawyer and defender of social justice (2011)
- Dr. David Suzuki, Canadian environmentalist, author, award-winning broadcaster and documentarian (2012)
- Mr. Yvon Chouinard, American entrepreneur, leader in Corporate Social Responsibility (CSR), and founder of Patagonia, an outdoor clothing and gear company committed to ethical and sustainable practices (2013)

You will find in this issue a profile and essay by our 2013 Inamori Ethics Prize recipient, Mr. Yvon Chouinard, as well as transcripts of the 2012 prize recipient lecture by Dr. David Suzuki and the 2012 Inamori Ethics Prize academic symposium, featuring Dr. David Suzuki, Dr. David Orr, and Dr. Jeremy Bendik-Keymer.

We are immensely grateful to our gifted authors for their perceptive and thought-provoking contributions to this issue on topics relevant to many facets of ethical leadership, including integrity, sustainability, corporate social responsibility, human rights, international law, applied ethics, experimental philosophy, poetry and theories of democracy. We also are pleased to include in this issue transcripts of the public radio program "Talking Foreign Policy," which airs on the NPR affiliate WCPN in Cleveland, Ohio, and is hosted by Case Western Reserve University Professor Michael Scharf. This program features a roundtable of experts examining the ethical, legal, and social issues associated with current international events and the implications for world leaders shaping foreign policy.

At the heart of Dr. Kazuo Inamori's leadership philosophy is the simple but profound determination "to base every decision on *what is the right thing to do as a human being.*" Please join us as we seek a better understanding of what it is to live—and to lead—ethically.

David Suzuki
Recipient of the 2012 Inamori Ethics Prize

A passionate environmentalist, a global leader on issues of sustainable ecology and social justice, and a longtime activist working to address climate change, Dr. David Suzuki is a powerful voice on behalf of biodiversity, future generations, and the planet.

David Suzuki was born in 1936. His parents were first generation Japanese-Canadians whose parents immigrated to Canada from Hiroshima and the Aichi Prefecture, respectively. From an early age, Suzuki understood the imperative of conquering adversity with perseverance. In 1942, the Canadian government sent his father to a labor camp in Solsqua, sold the Suzuki family's dry-cleaning business, and interned Suzuki, his mother, and two sisters in a camp at Slocan in the British Columbia Interior. Suzuki's sister, Dawn, was born in the internment camp. David Suzuki did not speak Japanese like the other interned kids, so he went outside on his own and found solace in nature, an ability he attributed to his father's love of nature. Like many Japanese-Canadians who were interned and had family holdings confiscated or sold, Suzuki was both embittered and emboldened—seemingly intent on proving his worth to society beyond any doubt. Suzuki has stated, "The repercussions of Pearl Harbor were the defining moments in my life."

After the war Suzuki's family, like other Japanese-Canadian families, was forced to move east of the Rockies. The Suzukis moved to Islington, Leamington, and eventually to London, Ontario. Suzuki attended London Central Collegiate Institute, where in his last year of school he began his social activism and leadership by winning the election to become Student Council President. In 1958, Suzuki received an honors BA in biology from Amherst College of Massachusetts. In 1961, he earned his PhD in zoology from the University of Chicago. Early in his research career he studied genetics. From 1963 until his retirement in 2001, he was a professor in the genetics department and the Sustainable Research Development Institute at the University of British Columbia. Suzuki is currently a professor emeritus.

Suzuki began his environmental advocacy through broadcast media. He is a well-known media figure and has received much praise for his radio and television programs that explain the complexities of the natural sciences in a compelling and easily understood manner. Suzuki has hosted, directed, or produced over two-dozen series and documentaries focused on the ethics of environmental sustainability. From 1971 to 1972, he was host of *Suzuki on Science*, a children's science program. Since 1979, Suzuki has hosted *The Nature of Things*, a CBC television series that has aired in nearly fifty countries worldwide. Through this program, Suzuki aims to stimulate interest in the natural world, to point out threats to humanity and wildlife habitat, and to present alternatives for achieving a more sustainable society. Suzuki has been a prominent proponent of renewable energy sources and the soft energy path.

Suzuki is also a world-renowned personality in the environmentalist movement and in bioethics circles. In Canada, he tied for fifth place in a 2004 CBC Television poll of Greatest Canadians ever—interestingly, he was the first to make it onto the list while still alive. He has received the highest civilian honors possible for a Canadian: the Order of Canada and the Order of British Columbia. Suzuki is on the Global 500 Roll of Honor, compiled by the UN Environment Program. In 2009, he was presented with the Honorary Right Livelihood Award.

Suzuki's more recent championship of initiatives attempting to slow the damage caused by climate change has also brought him international attention. In 1990, he cofounded the David Suzuki Foundation to work with government, businesses, and individuals to conserve our environment by providing science-based education, advocacy, and policy work, and to act as a catalyst for the social change that today's situation demands. The foundation's main missions are transforming the economy, protecting the climate, reconnecting with nature, and building communities of individuals who live healthier, more fulfilled, and just lives.

His foundation has worked with the Ainu of Japan to protect salmon, as well as with the indigenous peoples of Columbia, and the Kayapo people of Brazil. Suzuki led a research project to explore the impact of a dam in Australia and worked with the Hesquiat people of Vancouver Island to restore a clam fishery. With each of these projects, his foundation partnered with community members to develop alternative models of economic and community development. In 1992, Dr. Suzuki and members of the David Suzuki Foundation team wrote the *Declaration of Interdependence* for the United Nations' Earth Summit in Rio de Janeiro. This *Declaration* was the seminal document that spurred efforts promoting peace, sustainability, global interconnectedness, reverence for life, and unity within the climate change community. It became the inspiration for the Earth Charter, whose adherents are still growing. Suzuki's climate change team has since expanded into the health arena, working with doctors to fight for clean air, while publishing energy solutions and lobbying successfully for Canada to sign the Kyoto Accord.

Informed by his experience as a Japanese-Canadian during WWII, Suzuki speaks out against racial discrimination and for minority rights. When Suzuki lived in the United States during the late 1950s and early 1960s, he was appalled by the treatment of African Americans there and joined the NAACP in an effort to demonstrate his solidarity with others who also experienced racism. Ultimately, he moved back to Canada when he could not foresee discrimination lifting in the United States. He has been consistently involved in the civil rights movement throughout his career, seeking justice and respect for all peoples of the Earth.

Suzuki's written work includes more than fifty-four books, nineteen of them for children. He has also authored over three hundred popular articles. Some of his more recent book titles include, *The Legacy: An Elder's Vision for Our Sustainable Future, The Sacred Balance: Rediscovering Our Place in Nature,* and *More Good News: Real Solutions to the Global Eco-Crisis.*

Suzuki's most recent film, *Force of Nature,* was the winner of the People's Choice Documentary Award at the 2010 Toronto International Film Festival. *Force of Nature* offers a glimpse into the events that shaped David Suzuki's life and career. The film weaves together scenes from the places and events that shaped Suzuki's life, with a filming of his Last Lecture, which he describes as "a distillation of my life and thoughts, my legacy, what I want to say before I die."

Dr. David Suzuki has dedicated his life to giving a voice to the voiceless and disregarded. He currently lives in Vancouver, Canada, with his wife, Tara Cullis. He is the father of five children. He has said, "however many years I have left, each one will be a gift."

The Challenge of the Twenty-First Century: Setting the Real Bottom Line

David Suzuki
Transcript of 2012 Inamori Ethics Prize Speech

I did not think I was going to get emotional tonight. Thank you so much for this incredible award.

When I learned that I had been selected for it, I was shocked, shocked that anyone knew about the work I was doing outside of our tiny country, Canada. Of course I was delighted to learn of the award because I discovered as I read, ethics was a part of the name of the award and that Dr. Inamori talks about love and the divine, words I am not used to hearing in the battles I have been involved with. And of course I am humbled when I learned of the teachings of Dr. Inamori and his philosophy. You know, someone like me is made possible by the work of countless people who supported me, starting with my wife and my children, who have helped me by enduring my many absences, who supported me and made a lot of my efforts possible. To do something like a television program, even writing a book, it takes dozens of people to apply their expertise to make these things possible, so I accept this award but on behalf of the many, many people who have made my life and efforts possible. Thank you so much.

I am grateful, as well, for this opportunity to share a few of my ideas with you. You see, I believe we are at a remarkable moment in all of human history. For decades, leading scientists of the world have been issuing increasingly urgent warnings that humankind is rushing along a path that is undermining the very life support systems of the planet. Let me give you one remarkable example. November 1992, this amazing document called "World Scientists Warning to Humanity" was released. And when you look at the back, 1,700 scientists from 71 countries in the world, including more than half of all Nobel prize winners signed this document. And let me just read you a few lines of what they said:

> Human beings and the natural world are on a collision course. Human activities inflict harsh and often irreversible damage on the environment and on critical resources. If not checked, many of our current practices put at serious risk the future we wish for human society

and may so alter the living world that it will be unable to support life in the manner that we know. Fundamental changes are urgent if we are to avoid the collision our present course will bring about.

They go on to list the various areas of that collision: the atmosphere, water resources, ocean, soil, forest, species, and population.

And then the words become even more bleak:

No more than one or a few decades remain before the chance to avert the threats we now confront will be lost and the prospects for humanity immeasurably diminished. We, the undersigned senior members of the world scientific community hereby warn all humanity of what lies ahead. A great change in our stewardship of the earth and life on it is required if vast human misery is to be avoided and our global home on this planet is not to be irretrievably mutilated.

Then they discuss five basic points that must be carried out immediately if we are to avoid the collision.

This is a frightening document. Scientists are not normally signatories of a document that is so strongly worded. But if this document was frightening, the response of the media around the world was terrifying—there was none. It may have hit the back pages of a few newspapers, but it certainly wasn't on the major television networks. Since that time, scientists have published dozens of scientific reports documenting the ecological devastation and rising sense of urgency about the collision that we are involved in. I sat on the board of the Millennium Ecosystem Assessment, the largest study ever done on the ecology of the planet, $24 million sponsored by the United Nations and the reports were absolutely devastating. We are having an enormous impact on the things that keep us alive. In 2005, we released our final reports in New York at the United Nations. Kofi Annan was there to introduce it. A day later, the Pope got sick—he died. And then there was a [Papal] succession, and that pushed everything, including the Millennium Ecosystem Assessment, right off the newspapers and the media. So it was a one-day wonder in the media, the largest study on the state of the planet. In the past two months, *Nature* has published a number of very important documents showing, among other things, human beings have become so powerful we are altering the very cycles of nitrogen, carbon, water, and the species that keep the planet habitable for animals like us, and in the last two weeks, a paper showed that in the past there have been periods of sudden change, ecological upset, that are irreversible and take us to a different place with species extinction. We are approaching that tipping point right now.

I believe that we have reached a point where what we do or do not do in the coming decade may very well determine the fate of all humankind. Now you may think that is rather hysterical or melodramatic, but consider this: One of the leading scientists in the United Kingdom, Sir Martin Rees, who is Britain's royal astronomer, was asked on BBC, "What do you think the chances are that human beings will be around by the year 2100?" And his answer sent a shiver up my back—he said, "Fifty/fifty." Fifty/fifty that our species will survive to the end of this century. Jim Lovelock, the man who coined the term 'gaia' to describe the web of life on earth, says in his latest book that 90 percent of humanity will be gone by the end of this century and Clive Hamilton, an eco-philosopher in Australia, has written a book called *Requiem for a Species,* and we are the species the requiem is for. Many of my colleagues are saying that it is too late, that we have passed too many tipping points to go back. To that I say, "Thank you for your report and your sense of urgency, but now please shut up and go away." There is no point saying it is too late. We are going to fight to the end anyway. But it is very, very urgent.

We first have to face the magnitude of the challenge that scientists are now documenting. You see, I do not think we have come to grips with the fact that we have suddenly become a 'force.' Human beings evolved about 150,000 years ago on the plains of Africa. For almost all of human existence, there were never a billion people. We reached a billion people early in the 1800s. I was born in 1936, when there were just over 2 billion people. The population of the planet has more than tripled in a single human life, in my lifetime. If you were to plot that on a graph in covering 150,000 years, the curve leaps straight off the page in the last pencil width of time. We are now the most numerous mammal on the planet, and every one of us needs air, water, food, shelter, and clothing, so just the act of living, because there are 7 billion of us, means we have a very heavy ecological footprint. It takes a lot of air, water, and land to support us, to keep us alive. But of course, we are not like rats or rabbits or mice; we have an enormous amount of technology used on our behalf. Just to come to Cleveland, think of the computers and phone calls and cars and planes, just to get my bottom from Vancouver to Cleveland. That's all technology used on our behalf. Look at your clothing, your food and where you live, your computers and cars, and you realize, technology is amplifying our ecological footprint. That technology that takes us to the depths of the ocean, to the tops of mountains, and into the center of the earth, we can now exploit for our purposes.

Ever since World War II, we have been afflicted with an incredible appetite for stuff. We love to shop. After that terrible tragedy of 9/11, George Bush's first speech to the American people included, "I want you to go out and shop." That wasn't a joke. The American economy is absolutely dependent on consumption, and all of the stuff that we buy and use, most of it is absolutely not necessary for our lives or livelihood. All of that comes out of the earth and when we are finished with it, we throw it back into the earth as waste and our ecological footprint goes much higher. And we now have a global economy that exploits the entire planet as a source of raw materials, as a place to dump our toxic waste. And that global economy hides the ecological and social impact of its activity. When you go to a store to buy a cotton T-shirt, I am absolutely sure very few of you ever ask, "Is this organic?" Cotton is one of the most chemically intensive crops that we grow and if you go to the Soviet Union, or what used to be the Soviet Union, around the Aral Sea, the largest cotton growing area on the planet, it has been devastated by large scale growing of cotton—the use of chemicals and the draining of the rivers to irrigate the crops. But we don't see that; we just want a T-shirt, and we pay our money, buy it, and put it on. Yet the very act of buying that shirt has repercussions that extend around the world. When you buy a car, how many of us ever say, "Gee, there are a lot of metals in this car?" Mining is one of our most destructive activities. "Where are all the metals that are in my car mined? And what was the impact of mining on the communities of that area on the local ecosystems?" We do not care about that; we just want a car that operates efficiently, we pay our money and out we go. The global economy now hides the ecological and social costs of the way that we live. When you add up these things—population, technology, consumption, and a global economy—we have become a new kind of force on the planet. We are altering the physical, chemical, and biological properties of the planet on a geological scale. There has never been a species able to do what we are now doing on the planet, and it has happened very suddenly. The Nobel prizewinner Paul Crützen says, "this should be called the Anthropocene era or epoch, a period in which humans have now become a geological force."

This is the fiftieth anniversary of the beginning of the modern environmental movement. In 1962, Rachel Carson published *Silent Spring*, all about the unexpected effects of pesticides. And when her book came out, there wasn't a single department of the environment in any government on the planet. Rachel Carson galvanized a movement that exploded in the coming years. In only ten years, by 1972, there was a global conference on the environment in Stockholm and the United Nations Environment Program was established. Now at every level of government, from the federal to the state to the municipal, there are committees and departments of the environment. Think of the laws that we have to protect water, to prevent pollution of the air, to protect endangered species, and forests. Millions of hectares of land have been now protected in reserves and parks. All were achieved through this massive movement of the 1960s and 1970s.

In the 1970s and 1980s, I was involved in a number of battles. We stopped a mega-dam to be built at Site C on the Peace River in Northern British Columbia. The Arctic National Wildlife Refuge in Alaska is where the Porcupine Caribou herd has their calves. Because the Alaskans want to "drill, baby, drill," periodically there are riders attached to bills to allow Alaskans to drill there, and we have mounted great campaigns and kept it from going into that area.

We fought and stopped a proposal in Canada to drill for oil in Hecate Strait up near the Alaskan panhandle. Brazil had a plan to build a series of mega-dams on the tributaries of the Amazon River and we got the World Bank to pull its loan and stop the dams.

These are great victories that we celebrated, but here we are thirty, thirty-five years later and every one of those issues is back on the agenda. We failed as environmentalists because we thought the victories meant that we were on a different path, but we didn't educate people about why we were opposing dams and drilling in critical areas. There was a bigger picture to be seen and a different relationship that we needed with the planet, but we did not achieve that, we did not shift the paradigm. We have failed in a fundamental way.

And I believe the great challenge that we face, the one that we have failed, is to change the human mind. The way we see the world is shaped by our values and beliefs. I realized how important that was many years ago when I did a film in a small village in Peru. The children in the village are taught from a very young age that in the mountain where their village is, is an apu. Apu in their language means god, and they believe that as long as that apu casts a shadow on their village, it will determine the destiny of everyone in that village. That is very different from the way our kids in British Columbia grow up in the Rocky Mountains and are taught there is a lot of gold and silver in there.

The way we see the world shapes the way we treat that world. Is a river the circulatory system of the land or simply an opportunity for energy and irrigation? Is a forest a sacred grove or just timber and pulp? Is soil a community of organisms or just dirt? Is another species our biological kin or simply a resource or opportunity? We have to see the world through different eyes.

The current paradigm through which we see the world is illustrated with what is often cited as the triple bottom line. Generally the triple bottom line is indicated by three circles of equal size. There is the economy, the environment, and society, and those three circles overlap. Where all three share an overlap, that is the sweet spot. If you focus in that part, then you get triple bottom line benefit to the economy, society, and the environment.

What kind of a vision is that? Are we suggesting that the economy is as big as society? Is society—us—as big as the environment? I believe that is the picture that is leading us down a very destructive path because the reality is there is one big circle, and that is the biosphere. That is the zone of air, water, and land where all 30 million species live. And within that biosphere are 30 million smaller circles of varying size representing the 30 million species that live within the big circle. But today one of those circles now occupies 40 percent of that area within that circle, and *that* is us. Scientists say that we are now using 40 percent or more of the net primary productivity of the planet, that is the sunlight captured by plants through photosynthesis that all life depends on in order to survive and flourish. Humans now have co-opted 40 percent of that net primary productivity of photosynthetic activity and that drives huge numbers of species to extinction. So, within the biosphere our circle is too big. Within the circle that is us, there should be a much smaller circle, which is the economy. That is the reality of the world that we live in.

We have to move from our current sense that the planet is there for us to use in any manner that we can, where everything we see is a commodity or resource, to visualizing ourselves as one species among a community of organisms dependent on the generosity of nature within that biosphere. The biosphere is our home and makes our lives and well-being possible.

In the real world, our lives and society are shaped by laws of nature. In physics, we know that you cannot build a rocket that will travel faster than the speed of light. There is a law of gravity, so we cannot build an antigravity machine. Entropy means that order inevitably becomes disorder or goes toward randomness. Those are realities that we live with; that is what is dictated by physics.

In chemistry, we know that there are principles and laws that regulate the kinds and rates of reactions that we can carry out and the kinds of molecules that are possible, limited by the atomic properties of the re-agents that we want to react. Chemistry tells us what we can or cannot do. And biology dictates and constrains our basic needs and reality. We are animals.

I gave one of the keynote speeches at the first Green Building conference in Austin, Texas, many years ago. There were a number of children in the audience, so I said, "Now kids, if there is one thing you remember from my message, please remember that we are animals." Man did their parents get mad at me! "How dare you call my Mary an animal! We are not animals, we are human beings!"

We think somehow that we are different from the rest of creation, that we have transcended being simply animals. But we are biologic creatures; we are mammals. We know that the most fundamental thing in our lives is air. The minute every one of us left our mother's body, we needed a breath of air. That first breath was to inflate our lungs and announce our arrival, and from that point on, fifteen to forty times a minute, we need air to the last breath we take before we die. We do not even think about it.

Try thinking about it for a minute. It's so easy, right? Two to three liters of air right down into the warm, moist organs that we call our lungs. Our lungs are made up of about three hundred million alveoli, little capsules. We need three hundred million to give us the surface area to come into contact with the air. If you flattened out all of the alveoli in our lungs in two dimensions, they would cover a tennis court. That's how much surface is all wrinkled up in our lungs. Each alveolus is lined with a three-layered membrane we call the surfactant that reduces surface tension so when the air comes into contact, it sticks. Carbon dioxide rushes out, oxygen and whatever else is in the air rushes in. Hemoglobin molecules in red blood cells grab the oxygen and with each beat of our heart, that oxygen is pumped to every cell in our bodies. And when we breathe out we do not exhale all of the air; if we did that, our lungs would collapse. About half of the air stays in our lungs. So the point is, you can't draw a line and say "the air ends here and I begin there." There is no line. It's in us, it's stuck to us, and it's circulating throughout our bodies. We are air. And the air that comes out of my nose mixes in the room and goes straight up your nose and when I tell this to kids, I see them go "Oh, yuck." I guess they think they have a bubble of air that belongs to Johnny or Mary.

We are air; it is our most vital need and we share that air not only with each other, but with all of life on the planet. In a wonderful thought exercise, the American astronomer Harlow Shapley said, "What happens to a breath of air?" How do you follow a breath of air? 98 percent of it is oxygen and nitrogen. Breathe in and it goes into your body. Breathe it out, and much of the oxygen never comes back out and some of the nitrogen stays in our bodies. But 1 percent of the air is an element called argon, which belongs to a class of elements called the noble gases which are so snooty, they won't react with anything else. They are inert gases. So argon is a good marker of the air. You breathe it in, it goes into your body. You breathe it out, it comes right back out. How many atoms of argon in one breath of air? Shapley calculates 3×10^{18}, that's 3 followed by 18 zeros. Take it from me, that's a lot of argon.

So if we take a breath of air that comes out of Bud's nose, very quickly through convection that one breath will mix in this room and every one of us will be breathing gazillions of argon atoms from that one original breath. But the door and windows are open, and eventually that breath will diffuse across Cleveland, across the United States, around the world and, according to Shapley, one year later, every breath you take, wherever you are, because air is a single system, every breath you take will have about fifteen argon atoms from that one original breath that Bud took a year before.

So on that basis, every breath you take has argon atoms that were once in the bodies of Joan of Arc and Jesus Christ, every breath you take has argon atoms that were in the bodies of dinosaurs sixty-five million years ago, and every breath you take will suffuse life forms with argon as far as we can see into the future. So air is not only a vital element, our most fundamental need, air should be sacred. It connects us to the past, the present, and on into the future. It is a connector for all life, yet we dump our most toxic substances into that air.

We are water. We are over 70 percent water by weight. We're basically a big blob of water with enough organic thickener added so we don't dribble away on the floor. We're losing water through our skin and our eyes and our crotch, we're losing water all the time. We drink water and that water comes from all over the world, and we think we're intelligent, but what do we do? We use water as a garbage can as we do with air.

As biological creatures, our most fundamental needs are dictated by our animal nature. We need air, we need water, we need food that comes from the soil, we need energy that comes from the sun. And we need biodiversity on the planet to deliver those sacred elements to us. Those are dictated by laws of biology. We cannot change those laws of nature. We live within it.

Other things are human creations. We draw borders around our property and I understand in Texas if someone comes onto your property, you can shoot and kill them; it's legal. Well, we take those boundaries very seriously.

We draw them around our cities, our states, our countries. And we will go to war and kill and die to protect those boundaries. But nature couldn't give two hoots about human borders. We have salmon that are born in Canada, in British Columbia, go out the rivers through the Alaskan Panhandle into the Pacific Ocean. They travel all the way over to Japan. Whose salmon are they? But we think, "Oh, when they're in our waters, they belong to us." Salmon don't care whether they're in Japanese, American, or Canadian waters. In the same way birds migrate from South American all the way to the Arctic, Monarch butterflies from Canada fly down to Mexico; fish, birds, they don't care. Even trees or plants don't care. Air, water doesn't belong to us. Dust travels from Africa on the high wind currents and drops on the United States. They don't stop at the border and say, "Oh, gee, I forgot my Visa." They come in because nature couldn't care less about human boundaries.

And then we create things like capitalism, economics, corporations, currency, markets—we created them. They are not forces of nature, we created them. Yet you talk to a neoconservative, Milton Friedman's disciples, and they seem normal until you say the word "market." And the minute they hear "market," it's "The Market, hallelujah; yes, praise the market; free the market, let the market do its thing." What kind of insanity is that? We created the damn thing. We can't change the laws of nature, but we sure can change what we created. You see, the only thing we can manage on the planet is us. We can't manage nature. We can't manage the air, the water. We can manage us and how we interact with it, and we can certainly change economic systems, currency, markets, any of those things, and we have to.

The economic system is a major problem. I've been watching the Republican National Convention and now the Democratic, and I don't know what planet these people are on. When protecting the air or the oceans, as I saw in the Republican Convention, becomes a one line joke, what kind of planet are these people living on? We're not facing up to the major challenge scientists have been warning us about for years. The biosphere is our home and it's finite.

Carl Sagan told us that if we were to reduce the biosphere, the zone of air, water, and land where all life exists, to the size of a basketball, the biosphere would be thinner than a layer of Saran wrap, and that's it. That's the home of us and thirty million other species and nothing can grow within the biosphere indefinitely, even though economists think that we can.

But in our focus on the economy, and the need to grow so the GDP has to be kept going up, we fail to ask the important questions. What is an economy for? Why has growth suddenly become the end? Growth is a means to something else. What is that something else? Growth shouldn't be enshrined as the good that we aim for; it's just a means to something else. Are there no limits? Are we happier with all the stuff? How much is enough? What are we leaving for our children as a result of our profligate growth?

We need to see the world in a very different way. Well, is that just some kind of hippy dippy dream, or is it possible? I believe that a paradigm shift is definitely possible and that we're seeing bits and pieces of serious shifts. I'm sure most of you have heard of the Kingdom of Bhutan in the Himalayan mountains on the border of India. The King of Bhutan said, "Hey, we're in the twenty-first century, we shouldn't have kings anymore; (or words to that effect) you need democracy and elections. I'm resigning as king. Now you go ahead and elect a prime minister." And they did. But the king said before he resigned, you know, the aim of government, the reason we have leaders like me or government, is not all about economic growth, it's about wellness and happiness. We should make wellness and happiness the goal, the very end to which we are operating, and on April 2, 2012, at the United Nations, he presented the vision of using wellness and happiness as the driving force of the way we govern people. Sixty-eight countries immediately cosigned. But what is happiness, how can we measure it? Bhutan has now established a working group charged with developing those measures and those indicators within the next two years, and I think that's a fundamental shift in the way we see the world.

I just came back from a month filming in Ecuador and Bolivia. Bolivia elected Evo Morales the world's first indigenous person as president, and he certainly talked a great deal about Pacha Mama, which is Mother Earth. We have to pay attention to Mother Earth. Ecuador is led by President Corea, who is an economist, trained in America. President Corea has revised the constitution of Ecuador to enshrine Pacha Mama in the constitution. That means Pacha Mama now has constitutional rights; trees, birds, fish, all have a right to exist and flourish.

Recently, a legal case was brought in southern Ecuador on behalf of the Vilcabamba River, under the constitutional rights of Pacha Mama, and the litigants won. While they cannot claim money, the river must be restored to the condition it was before it was impacted by a road builder.

Cuba, we all know that Fidel Castro in Cuba has been demonized in this country, which I think was terrible. Cuba has led the world of necessity in urban agriculture. Eighty percent of the food consumed in Havana is grown in the city of Havana, and it's a model for a new relationship with food. And there is much more to be learned from Cuba. But allow me to end with two stories.

My great teacher and mentor was my father. In 1994, he was eighty-five and he was dying, fortunately of a non-painful type of cancer. He knew that he was dying and he was not afraid; he was prepared for it. I moved in to care for him the last two months of his life, and that was one of the happiest times I spent with my father. We laughed, we talked, we cried. Every night my wife would come over with slides of trips that we took together and it was a joyous time. In all the time we were together, Dad never said, "Gee, do you remember that big house we had in London, Ontario," where we lived? "Do you remember that 1957 Buick I owned?" or, "Do you remember that closet of clothes that I had once?" That's just stuff. All we talked about were family, friends and neighbors, and things we did together. And my father said to me, "David, I die a rich man." Because his wealth was in his experiences, shared with people that mattered to him, and in that he was truly a wealthy man. We've got off on some weird tangent where we think that stuff is what gives us happiness and what gives us meaning in life. My father's death showed me that it is not that at all. It's our relationships that we have with each other and that brings us great joy and happiness.

I want to end with a story of my time in the United States. I was beginning my senior year at Amherst College in the United States in 1957. On October 4, we were stunned to learn that the Soviet Union had launched Sputnik. For those of you who are old enough to remember, the months and years that followed were really a terrifying time. Because as the American rockets were blowing up on the launch pad in full television view, the Russians launched the first animal in space, a dog, Laika; the first man, Yuri Gagarin; the first team of cosmonauts; the first woman, Valentina Tereshkova. America didn't say, "Oh my goodness, they're so far ahead of us. We can't afford to catch up to the Russians." America said, "We've got to catch up and pass them." And in 1961, John F. Kennedy said, "We're going to beat these guys to the moon." And it was a glorious time. Even a foreigner like me, all we had to do was say, "I like science." You threw money at us. Money went to universities and science departments. It was a glorious period. And look what happened. America is not only the first country but the only country to walk on the moon. And think of all of the spin-offs that nobody anticipated would come out of the space race—cell phones, GPS, twenty-four-hour news channels, and every year the Nobel prizes are announced, over fifty years later, most go to Americans because America said, "We've got to win this race." And they did everything they could and then wonderful things happened.

I believe that to take a challenge like climate change and say, "Oh, what are you talking about? It'll destroy our economy" is not the American way. And you can be absolutely sure if you make that commitment, decide this is a high priority, that you have no choice, all kinds of unexpected things are going to happen.

This is what Goethe said: "Until one is committed, there is hesitancy, the chance to draw back. The moment one definitely commits, then providence comes, too. All sorts of things occur to help one that would otherwise not have occurred. Whatever you can do or dream, you can begin it. Boldness has genius, power and magic in it. Begin it now."

That's the challenge I leave with you. Thank you very much.

2012 Academic Symposium Transcript

Participants: Shannon E. French, David Suzuki, Jeremy Bendik-Keymer, and David Orr

FRENCH: To begin our conversation, David Suzuki, you recently released a depressingly titled Op Ed piece that was called "The Fundamental Failure of Environmentalism." Has the environmentalist movement failed? In what sense?

SUZUKI: Well, this is not to denigrate in any way the history of the environmental movement. When Rachel Carlson published her book *Silent Spring*, there wasn't a single Department of the Environment in any government on the planet. That book began the movement that put the environment on the map, and think of the enormous growth in only ten years—the first global conference on the environment was held in Stockholm in 1972. At that time, the United Nations Environment Program was set up. We saw the rapid growth in interest and laws that were passed in many countries to protect air and water, limitations on pollution, protection of endangered species, and protection of millions of hectares of land around the world as parks or reserves. So this is not to deny the important role that the environmental movement has played, but I think that we failed to grapple with the underlying root cause of the destructive path that we are on. We fought against dams, mega dams, we fought against dangers of drilling for oil offshore, we fought against destruction of forests, but we never focused our message on the reason why we oppose such development, that we had to come to some kind of balance with the natural world that sustains us. We had to see ourselves as a part of a much bigger system rather than the species in charge, able to take it all over and manage it for our own purposes. This is often referred to as a paradigm shift. We must see ourselves in a different way, as part of the biosphere and we didn't succeed in that.

FRENCH: Jeremy, would you care to comment on that as well?

BENDIK-KEYMER: Yes, I mean, this came up in the radio show this morning, so apologies if this is the second time around. I was struck by how the very word environment involves this problem. The environment means the world around us, that's what it means in Latin or from Latin. In German, *umwelt*, it means the world surrounding us. So there's a picture there already of the duality, right? We're separate from the environment like a disembodied mind. The question is how do we relate to it? So I mean at some fundamental level we're not even thinking of our home—Earth—in the right way. We think of it already as something separate from us. So I do agree with that point.

SUZUKI: Sorry, David [Orr], but another aspect is that we think of environmentalism or the environmental movement as something special, so that we celebrate if there is a Green Party, and I'm saying what does it mean to have a Green Party? In Canada—until last year—we never had a Green Party in office in Parliament, so whenever there was a public debate, only the leaders of political parties in Ottawa were allowed to take part. So the Green Party leader wasn't there and all of the journalists acted as if, since the Greens weren't there, they didn't have to talk about the environment. So we have to get away from the idea that the environment is somehow a political football.

FRENCH: Or a separate issue as opposed to everyone's issue, we're all on the planet.

SUZUKI: Yes.

FRENCH: David, please, go ahead.

ORR: Humans are slow learners, [this] case notwithstanding. You know, Jesus, Moses, Buddha, Confucius, and so forth, lived thousands of years ago and we're still trying to figure out what they meant and what that means for how we live, and if you date the environmental movement from 1962 or whatever the [year of] Rachel Carlson's *Silent Spring*, that's a short period of time and I agree with David [Suzuki], we're still trying to mull this over. The problem we have is the timing. There is this remorseless working of big numbers. Carbon in the atmosphere and heat-trapping gases don't care a bit about any of us. They just do their work. We put them up there and we set in motion these effects that will occur, and if somebody were just saying before, if somebody says you don't believe in climate change, that is the wrong word. Nobody says you don't believe in the laws of gravity, and if they do there's a simple test for that: come to the top of the building and let's check it out. You know, you jump first. But we're still trying to mull this over. And one other comment here. I think that the environmental movement as a phrase in some ways is too big a phrase. If I break it up into the component parts, the green building movement is doing extremely well. My friend Gene Matthews here at Case has help to spearhead the movement here and elsewhere. Gene, is there anything else you wanted me to say? But the green building movement is doing extremely well. Jeremy is part of the environmental philosophy movement that is doing extremely well. David Suzuki has been a leader for years in getting us to think through all of the ramifications of this. So in some ways there are parts of this movement that are doing extremely well, but I agree with David's overall point that we have a long way to go.

FRENCH: Now let me ask what do you say to the optimistic person who says, "Well yes, I recognize the threat and the danger, but technology will save us. There will be some amazing innovation that will come up and they will figure out how to change the carbon or suck it out of the air or something, and we'll all be fine. We just need to let that happen."

SUZUKI: The problem with these technologies, powerful as they are, is that we don't know enough to recognize what the bigger implications are within the biosphere. So we opt for the immediate benefit of a new technology, for example, DDT. Great—kills bugs. Lots of studies done in labs and growth chambers show when you spray it on an insect and a plant, the [plant] flourishes and the insect dies. Oh, this is great. But the lab is not the real world. In the real world it rains, the wind blows, water flows, and you spray to kill insects on a field and you end up affecting fish and birds and human beings. I want to remind you, we didn't know that when you spray at very low concentrations of parts per million, then small organisms absorb that and are not killed, so at each level up the food chain you concentrate it. By the time you get to the fatty tissue in the shell glands of birds and the breasts of women, you have concentrated DDT hundreds of thousands of times. We didn't know about this phenomenon of biomagnification until eagles began to disappear and scientists tracked it down and discovered this. And this happens over and over again. CFC's: No one knew that CFC's would waft up into the upper atmosphere where chlorine-free radicals would be cleaved by ultraviolet light and break down ozone. I didn't even know there was an ozone layer up there when scientists began to say, "CFC's are destroying the ozone layer." When nuclear bombs were dropped on Japan, we didn't even know there was a thing called radioactive fallout that was found in the Bikini [Atoll]. So now that we have created the problem of climate change, we think we'll geo-engineer the planet in order to avoid the consequences—is madness. One of the things in Canada we are trying to do with excessive carbon is to simply capture it and put it back in the ground.

FRENCH: Carbon sequestration?

SUZUKI: Carbon sequestration. We have invested billions of dollars in this, but, you know, until a few years ago, it was assumed that life stopped at bedrock, that organisims went down a few yards and then it was sterile from that point on. But they kept getting drills that were going further and further down, contaminated with bacteria, and now we know there are bacteria that exist up to seven miles underground. These creatures are so different from any life forms we know on the surface of Earth, we have to create new phyla to define them. So they are very bizarre. They have been down there for millions and millions of years, and it's now estimated the weight of protoplasm underground is greater than the weight of protoplasm above ground. That's more than all the trees and birds and whales, because life goes down seven miles. And we have no idea what those organisms are doing down there. Are they involved in heat transfer, water movement, nutrient flow? We don't know anything about that. And we now want to pump millions of tons of carbon into the ground. I just think it's madness. We don't know enough.

FRENCH: So we can't fix the system if we don't know how it works?

SUZUKI: Exactly.

FRENCH: You wanted to jump in.

ORR: Well, in your question here, the word optimism appears, and since 1954 I have been a Cleveland Indians fan. And you know, the problem here is if you're optimistic in a way, because of what David [Suzuki] just said, you don't know enough. If you're in despair, that's a sin; you don't want to go there. And in between those two poles is something called hope. And the only legitimate position for us now is to be hopeful. And that is to believe you can change the odds that the optimist relies on, but hope in this case is a verb with its sleeves rolled up. It means if you're hopeful, you can't—as an optimist can or someone in despair—put your feet up on the table and have another beer, or whatever you drink, and you don't have to do anything. But if you're hopeful, you have to do something, you have to act, and I'm still a Cleveland Indians fan. It's been a long year.

SUZUKI: You know, this is not a Pollyanna hope. I think it's what we cling to in order to empower us to carry on. Many of our colleagues are now saying it's too late, that we have passed too many tipping points and can't reverse or restore things. I have followed their papers and I agree with what they say, but hope is what you have to cling to; if we can pull back and give nature a chance, she may be far more generous than we deserve. Let me give you an example of what can surprise us. The most prized species of salmon in the world is the Sockeye salmon. It's got that bright red flesh that we prize. The largest run of Sockeye salmon in the world is in the Fraser River in British Columbia. After white people arrived in BC, populations of salmon dropped—but now traditionally a 30 to 35 million run of Sockeye salmon was a good run. Three years ago, just over 1 million Sockeye salmon returned to spawn and I thought, "That's it. That's just not enough to sustain the species." One year later we got the biggest run of Sockeye salmon in a hundred years. Now that doesn't prove how stupid I am, because nobody knows what happened. Nature shocked us. And my hope rests on the fact we don't know enough to know whether or not nature has more surprises, but if we can give her a chance, I think all kinds of things are still possible.

FRENCH: Would you care to comment on hope, Jeremy?

BENDIK-KEYMER: I would like to go back to the techno-optimism, but that is a kind of Hail Mary pass hope. That's different than if you earn your hope by conscientiously doing what you know you're supposed to do, and you think, "you know, I need hope to go on to be able to do this." I mean, the thing that strikes me about the techno-optimistic line is it seems morally corrupt to me and for this reason: let's say my child wants to go into some area of the woods where there has recently been a landslide, and the question is about whether or not it's possible for engineers to get in there and to rebuttress the cliff. I don't send my child out into the woods expecting that there's a possibility that the engineers, who look like they may be able to do this, will just happen to get around to do this, let's say, by the end of the summer. Right? I need a *reasonable expectation,* and the techno-optimism you're talking about is not concrete yet. So what you'd really expect someone to say, who isn't corrupt mentally, would be to say, "Look, I really hope this singularity is coming, the moment where nanotechnology, genetic technology, biotechnology and information technology give us an entirely new, different fabric of being, but right now here are the real risks that we are facing, here are the real limitations we have, and here are the kinds of things that need to be in place if we're going to be responsible about this." And if the optimism comes to pass, great. But in the meantime, I have to be responsible for the risks that could happen. So the entire line of reasoning just seems morally corrupt to me. It doesn't seem conscientious.

FRENCH: Morally negligent.

BENDIK-KEYMER: Yeah, it sounds absolute to say that, but I really do think when you look at ordinary people who are conscientious, that isn't the way they think about things that are really serious coming down the pipeline.

FRENCH: And your example with your own child, you would never stake your own child's safety on this chance.

BENDIK-KEYMER: Not at all.

FRENCH: Do you want to jump in again?

ORR: I agree with that. I think there's an issue here of how we handle these questions. There are only so many options. One is you can go deep into denial. People can go into denial and countries can go into denial. We just don't want to see what is right in front of us. Staying out of denial, if you want to deal with this, then you have to confront hard possibilities. And that's tough for us as humans. We like optimistic people. And the way the US culture [is], it's hard for us to reckon with anything that might have a tragic outcome. It's easier in say, Europe and the Far East, where you have ruins that are testimony to human fallibility. We are a more ignorant species than we are smart for all the reasons that David [Suzuki] has said so well. So it's how do we handle tragic possibility. E. F. Schumacher, the great British economist, at the end of his books, he said if we pose the question, "Can humans survive?" And the answer comes back, "No," well then it's eat, drink, and be merry. If the answer comes back, "Yes," then it leads to complacency. His advice was better not even to pose the question, just get down to what's in front of you, what you can do here and now, and I think there's some real virtue in that.

FRENCH: I keep thinking of the mythology—that when they opened Pandora's box, all these terrible vices came out, but at the bottom of the box was hope, but you still had to deal with all the vices and the hope was just to give you the strength to address them one by one. And again, not to be complacent—I think you've all echoed that theme. I want to bring up a slightly different point; it's certainly related to everything we have been discussing. Jeremy, in your book *The Ecological Life*, you discuss what it means to be human. And you stress the importance of relatedness. And also in *Ethical Adaptation of Climate Change*, you talk about the importance of recognizing our ethical obligations to future generations. So I was thinking about that, and I'm wondering what is the obstacle here? Why is it difficult for people to take future generations into consideration in a meaningful way, and I think the work of all three of you relates to this, certainly Dr. Suzuki—you have talked about the importance of intergenerational work in this area, and I wonder if you could all comment on this aspect of the issue.

SUZUKI: Well, traditionally in Canada the aboriginal people speak of seven generations. When decisions were made by the tribes—major decisions—they would remember seven generations of their ancestors in the past, and on seven generations into the future, and what the repercussions might be. That's long-term thinking. We have become a very impatient animal. We want everything now. And from the political standpoint, children don't vote. So it's not because politicians are evil or stupid, but the nature of their game is that when you're elected, your primary concern is getting reelected and that means appeal to those people who are going to vote. Young people don't vote. For that matter can you imagine a politician in the United States saying, "I want to commit $10 billion to greenhouse gas reduction because of future generations." I mean, they'd be laughed out of the room because they aren't even born. In looking at long-term potential costs the economic system discounts the impact of what we do now on future generations. So we write them off or we consider them worth less, or our costs left to them are less. It all goes against the rights of future generations. So I'm trying to come up with legal means of holding our so-called leaders to account. I attended the Earth Summit in Rio in 1992, the largest gathering of heads of state ever in human history. I went back again this year on the twentieth anniversary. None of the leaders that were there in 1992 were there twenty years later. So they can sign all kinds of documents but they don't have to worry about whether they are followed through. We have to hold them to account. There's a group in Germany that's looking at a legal means to hold people to account for intergenerational crimes. There is a legal category called "willful blindness." If you're responsible for an area and deliberately avoid being informed of something vital to that field, you can be sued for that. I certainly think that politicians ought to be held accountable for their willful blindness.

FRENCH: Jeremy.

BENDIK-KEYMER: I agree with the basic point, right. Whether or not we can be oriented toward the future morally depends on our institutional structure, depends on our political systems and the way that they shape our economy. There is some evidence anthropologically that we have various kinds of short-term decision biases. There is a sense in which we have evolved to be somewhat near-term thinkers, but the other amazing thing about human beings is that we're capable—we're political animals, right?—we're capable of complex organization and of extending our minds beyond our communities through technology to vastly counteract our limitations. So it doesn't have to be very fancy, right? A seventh generation matriarch is a thousand-year-old thing up in upstate New York in the Onondaga nation, you know. So it's a question of political organization. So all I would add to what David [Suzuki] said is I just think first of all, politically, I do not understand how future children are not on the national political agenda in my country, which is this country. I mean this boggles my mind. We're supposed to be concerned with family values and we're not talking about putting our junk onto future kids, and it's not just junk, really, it's the risk of incapacitating them horribly. And usually the least powerful, right? The problem is what I call *presentism*. Like racism, presentism is caring more about yourself than about the equal and rightful demands of the future, more about your own generation than the future. The problem with presentism is it's a magnifier. It magnifies the effects on all the other forms of "isms." Right? Because usually the people who are subject to racism or sexism, in particular, are vulnerable. But presentism magnifies the situation so that in the future those vulnerable people who don't have access to power, resources, and so on, are more likely to get hurt as a result of what we're doing. So the first thing I would say, and then I'll just end it so David [Orr] can talk, is that this just has to be on the national political agenda and part of it should be an attempt to put, not just in law, but in institutions some way of hearing the voice or giving place to the voice of the future. I don't mean this in a fantastic way. I mean it has to be done through some thinking of rights and legality and internalization of economic burdens.

FRENCH: That you could, for example, bring a suit saying you have harmed future generations.

BENDIK-KEYMER: And that there's something like the State Department, some institution—boom!—that is tasked with doing that.

FRENCH: That has that focus. Yes, David Orr.

ORR: I don't have a lot to add to this. David Suzuki is the great spokesperson for future generations and Jeremy is one of the leading scholarly voices on this, but my training was in political science. If you read the US Constitution, the word posterity only appears one time and it's in the preamble. And there's no case law. Now if you go back, that was about seven generations ago, so if you go back those seven generations and you ask, "What would they have us do for the next seven generations from our time going forward?" They had no idea of what we could do to the planet, that we could unravel the biosphere the way that David has described so eloquently, with the implications that Jeremy has explained so clearly. So, now we know that our behavior can deprive future generations of life and liberty and property without due process, and that is a violation of the Fifth Amendment to the US Constitution and the Fourteenth Amendment, and so now we need to think of a legal movement. And I totally agree with my colleagues on the panel that this needs to be an issue morally driven of law. And then the perplexities begin. You say, "How do you represent the rights of future generations?" Well, in the case of—let's say brain-damaged people or people who are otherwise disabled—you appoint a court custodian, some representative that represents their interests as best they can be known, and so this is not an impossibility; it is a complicated thing. The last thing I would say is this. We hear a lot, aside from the original intent of the US Constitution, we hear a lot about the right to life. And if we take the right to life seriously, it isn't just about fetuses, whatever your opinion on abortion, it isn't just about that. It's about the people who live now, it's about the people and all the web of life who will exist in the future, and in a philosophy you can't pick and choose. Philosophies are not cafeterias, you pick a little of this and a little of that, then ignore the rest. You have to take the whole thing. And if life really is the oriented principal, then you have to take it seriously across the full range. That includes all life now, all life that could exist if we don't deprive it of its existence and property and freedom to live.

FRENCH: I'd like to stick with you for a moment, David Orr. You've been quoted as saying, "Sustainable development cannot happen in classrooms; it has to happen in the streets." And I was wondering, in what ways can we implement sustainable practices in urban communities without backlash or unintended ill effects? Can you comment on that?

ORR: Well, first is I didn't mean it when I said it. No, I think—I'm an educator and I teach at Oberlin College—and I think the issue for us is that we're visual creatures. We believe what we can see, touch, feel, experience. And we live in this realm where people like us talk about sustainability and so forth, and that's an abstraction, and abstractions don't move people. Well, they move people like us, maybe, ideologues and professors, but they really don't move the world very far. And so what you're doing here, and my colleague and friend David Beach, and so forth around Cleveland, it is to begin to make these ideas real so it becomes a main street reality. Just very quickly, in Oberlin we're trying to take a model in a city of ten thousand—we're thirty-five miles from downtown Cleveland—trying to take our assets as a community of ten thousand and bundle that together so that what we're calling The Oberlin Project includes food, law, policy, green building, green development, economic renewal, and so forth, and put them together into a package where the parts reinforce the whole thing. We've never done that before. That's never happened in the United States before, but it ought to begin to happen in little places like Oberlin and taking it viral throughout this particular region. There's a different economy trying to be born here. Many of you in the room are working seriously on this as educators and as city people and so forth, but this is where education becomes real, because mostly what we do, and back to the word "hope," to embody hope and to make, let's say the Cleveland metropolitan area or Northeast Ohio a laboratory of 'here's what you can do when the chips are down' and this 'rust belt region' began to go through a renaissance and did it sustainably, that's hopeful. And that begins to attract more people to begin to do that elsewhere. So, Shannon, the point here for me as an educator is to take these ideas and give them main street reality. You can talk about renewable energy, but the wind power and the full arrays that you're involved with here, that begins to be hope. People can see that and say, "Now I understand that," and begin to build the green jobs and green employment, that's something that people can begin to get their minds around at a scale that is comprehensible.

FRENCH: From the abstract to the concrete.

ORR: That's right, the concrete. You bet.

FRENCH: Would either of you like to comment on this further?

SUZUKI: Well, I'm not sure I'm going to answer the question but I became involved in environmental issues after Rachel Carlson's book, and basically we were fighting against things, fighting a dam, fighting the destruction of a forest, fighting pollution of the ocean.

FRENCH: Much a conservationist movement in some ways, too? Trying to conserve what was being destroyed?

SUZUKI: Of course. But what I feel now is that we can't afford to fight any longer because when you win there is always a loser, and we can't afford to have losers anymore. In British Columbia where I live, two of the big issues are fisheries and forests. And we have had all of these long battles so now we're trying to come together at a round table where all of the "stakeholders," people with different vested interests, come together and try to work something out. But what happens is that people come in and they have their turf; "I'm a commercial fisherman and I'm going to fight for my share," "I'm an aboriginal and this is my tradition," and you end up coming out with a compromise that's not really focused on the issue of genuine sustainability. So what I ask is, can we come together and forget our vested interest and start from a platform of what we agree. Because if we don't start with what we agree, then we're just arguing for our own special stakes. So my position is this: Can we not all agree that the absolute, most fundamental need is air? The minute we were born, we had to take a breath of air and from that point on fifteen to forty times a minute until the last breath before we die, we need air. So surely our highest priority as a species should be protecting air. That means when someone wants to dump something into it, you go, "Wait a minute now, that's the life-giving substance that maintains all terrestrial creatures." Air should be sacred so we deal with it in a different way. If you don't have water for more than a few days, you're dead. If you have polluted water, you're sick. So surely everybody has to agree, water is a fundamental need that we have to treat in a special way. And then every bit of our food was once alive and most of it was grown in the soil. So soil should be protected. Every bit of the energy in our body is sunlight fixed by photosynthesis, so photosynthesis is a priority. Can we not construct a platform of our most basic needs, biological, social, and spiritual? If we agree on that, then we ask, "How do we make a living?" or "How do we live?"

FRENCH: We have some violent agreement going on—yes.

ORR: And I agree with that. The perplexity, the difficulty, is how do you take those ideas—this is one for our whole generation—and then render that into an economy that works. And how we provision ourselves with food, energy, water, livelihood, health care, all of these things, in celebration in a way that we don't contaminate the fundamentals of life that David [Suzuki] describes so well. And I think for our generation, let me just leave this as a question for you young people in the audience, the most important task you can have is how do we begin to take all of the things that we want—clean air, clean water, and so forth—and begin to build an economy around that, and an economy, maybe small 'E' hints to a society of capital 'S,' so this seems to me to be the challenge of our time. How do we make this work? At two political conventions, economic growth is a huge item for both parties. And the question is, how do you grow the economy more? And I think the question for us is not one of growth but one of quality, and how do you ensure fair distribution of what there is, provide for long-term sustainability for future generations? But I don't want to gloss over this point, I think this is THE challenge. That is the heart of the challenge ahead of us.

FRENCH: Jeremy, I'd like you to comment, but before you do, I want to give a heads up. In just a moment I'm going to open the floor to questions from any of you. You will notice in the aisles we have microphones set up. I'm afraid because of the taping we can only take your question if you proceed to the microphone because otherwise the audio will be—we won't be able to hear it. So if you have a question in mind and would like to actually start to line up at the microphones, I will be doing that in just a moment. Jeremy, would you care to comment on this train of thought?

BENDIK-KEYMER: There is so much to say. I think it has been so eloquently said. I'd rather hear what the floor has to say, and I'll weave something in. The only thing briefly I would say is about David's initial comment, sorry, David Orr's initial comment—look you're talking about sustainability, and [it] is such an abstract word. You're talking about not just a new set of habits, but a new experience of tinkering and reexploring what it is to be practical. So I just think the very nature of it requires that you think of education as a kind of externship, as a kind of lab, as a kind of socially, community-embedded experiment, and that means breaking the—you know in theater you talk about breaking the fourth wall—well, you need to break the walls of the classroom. I don't want to say too much more because I don't think it's as impassioned as what was just said, but that's the logical implication of it. The university needs to be rethought around these interdisciplinary problems that are fundamentally practical and political, and so it needs to get—any kind of school—needs to get the students out in the community and also tinkering and working with stuff so that it's possible to see what a different kind of life is like, and what a political life is like. So yes, I agree with these points.

FRENCH: Well, it looks like we do have folks lined up, so I'm going to start over here, and if you could please, if you don't mind stating your name and then your question and then if you have a particular panelist that you'd like to direct it to, or if you'd just like the panel in general to respond.

AUDIENCE: Thanks. I'm Joe Conan from Cleveland. I was interested in your comments, any of you, on the net effect of religion on the future of this whole movement that you're talking about in our future. It seems on the one hand we have some religious people who are very impassioned about the future of the planet and I think on the other hand we see religion sometimes buttressing kind of a blindness that maybe we were talking about earlier.

FRENCH: Who would like to take that?

ORR: Thanks for the question. If you ask what the word environment implies, bringing a wholeness and so forth, and the root for the word religion means "to bind together." And so I think you can make a very good case that if you're concerned about wholeness or religion, wholeness, whole, holy, there's more than an ethnologic similarity here. There's the attempt to try to build a civilization where the parts do in fact hang together, in a way that's fair, decent, and just, and honors the sacredness of the creation, whatever your denomination or religious affiliation might be. Thanks for the question. I think that's a really good question.

FRENCH: Would either of you like to comment on religion and the environment?

SUZUKI: I'm an atheist. I don't have much comment about religion, I'm afraid, but I'll go with David [Orr].

FRENCH: Jeremy, do you have anything to say on this topic?

BENDIK-KEYMER: Yes, just two brief things. The one is that the core of piety—or if you don't call it piety you may call it whatever that relation is that binds you to the beings of your religion, or the being of your religion, or the nothingness of your religion—is a form of devotion, right? It engages the capacity inside the human being to be more than cynical and to be willing to give for something that's just not your egotistical self. So to the extent that religion really speaks thoughtfully to that, I think it has a very intimate connection with being able of thinking about future generations and the continuum of life. But the second thing to say is that the way that religion gets used in the public sphere I don't think is truly religious, because religion becomes hardened as a way of creating divisions or as a way of moving a platform around. But real religiousness involves a kind of attention to the meaning in front of you, whether it's a person you're talking to, something with which you vehemently disagree, or something that you have to do. It's not hardened. And so I think one has to distinguish between the use of religion, which is a false god or idol, and genuine religiousness, and I think genuine religiousness is a very powerful thing.

FRENCH: Okay, let's go over here now.

AUDIENCE: Hi. My name is Drake. Earlier, David, you said something about a project that you were working on in Oberlin involving a community and making this abstract idea more concrete in terms of a community. I'm sure a lot of individuals outside of Oberlin would love to be involved projects like this. How would you suggest individuals go about making this abstract ideal more concrete, more personal, rather than just pertaining to a community that they may or may not live in?

ORR: Let me link that question with the previous question. There is a joke some of you may have heard about a little girl—actually it was a true story I'm told—who decided to draw a picture of God, and her mother said, "Well, honey, nobody knows what God looks like." And she says, "Well, they will now." And I think in some ways, back on your question, to take this word 'sustainability,' it's the same kind of thing. What is it we are attempting to build? And so our intention in Oberlin is a joint enterprise with both the city and the college, we're a little city of ten thousand, the first college to accept African Americans and women and graduate them back in the 1830s and so forth, this is going to sound like an admissions pitch, it probably is, but the attempt is to give, to attempt to flush out this word 'sustainability' that gives it, you know, when you want to see what sustainability is, you go there, you see how food, the downtown redevelopment and education, the law and policy and these things hang together in very much the way that David [Suzuki] has described in terms of environment.

FRENCH: Here at Case Western we have The Fowler Center of Sustainability.

ORR: Yes, and Roger Saillant may be here, you already are embedded in this. The Cleveland metropolitan area, Northeast Ohio has become a hotbed of some awfully important innovation in terms of sustainability. The goal is to make this real. So the longer term goal here, long-term meaning a year or two, is to link up a network across the country and start our version of a grassroots movement, eventually trying to change the political dialogue at the very top, so we've got an office in Denver, we've opened an office in Washington, D.C., in cooperation with the New America Foundation, we have board of directors, and we're trying to feel our way toward that network, but contact me afterward or just email me at David.Orr@oberlin.edu and I'd be happy to pull you into the effort.

AUDIENCE: Can you repeat that email please?

ORR: It's just David.Orr@oberlin.edu.

AUDIENCE: Thank you.

FRENCH: And thank you for your question. Let's go now over to here.

AUDIENCE: My name is Zoe Conrose from Montessori High School, and I just had a question relating to a personal story that I had. I grew up in a town where there were radioactive materials located in a certain area. This generated a large portion of the people living in this certain area having cancer of various different types. I was closely related to some of them. I was wondering if you, I mean we're so interconnected, the earth and us, because it not only harms the environment but it harms ourselves to have this happen to us. How do you even justify that? I mean, how do you I don't know, I'm sorry. I just wanted to ask your thoughts on that. Thank you.

FRENCH: Go right ahead, Jeremy.

BENDIK-KEYMER: I'm sorry you had to…, it sounds like there was real loss involved, and I'm sorry to hear that. If I understand your question right, it's, "how can people put themselves in such a position that they—to use David [Suzuki]'s expression from a little while ago about the air—that they can just throw their garbage into the air that they breathe?" Is this the thought? Yes, so look, there are various different levels of explaining this, right? From thinking of humans as being shortsighted or errant or so on, but I think I agree that most of us are saying that the main problem has to do with the political structure of the society you're in and whether or not the citizens in the society we are in make our businesses and make our government be accountable to *humanity* and not just to human*kind*. To humanity—the virtue—where we understand that humans are just part of a continuum of life [alongside other living beings]. And…ultimately I think that's the simple one-line answer. [The pollution of our biosphere is] possible because citizenship has waned and because we're not empowered in the right way through knowledge, through educational systems, through a media that is generally helpful, and through business leaders who decide that over their dead body they're going to let business interests get underneath the citizens. That's where I would come at this issue.

SUZUKI: I think that politics simply reflects, that is how politicians act, will reflect the underlying values of society. I have spent a lot of my life when I was still an active scientist, lobbying every new minister of state for science and technology. They didn't know anything. They come in, we have to educate them, they get up to a certain point and then they get moved out and I start all over again. In order to deal profoundly with science and technology, we must have a society that is scientifically literate. In terms of the ecological issues we're talking about now, politicians will simply reflect society's values, and that affects the way that we treat the rest of the world. So we need to have a fundamental understanding that we are animals, and as animals, our biological nature dictates our most fundamental needs. I once gave a talk at the first Green Building conference in Austin, Texas, and there were a lot of children in the audience so I said, "Now kids, if you remember one lesson from my talk today, please remember we are animals." Man did their parents get pissed off at me! "Don't call my daughter an animal! We're human beings." You can see we think somehow we're different from the rest of life. If you call someone a snake or a worm or a rat or a pig or a chicken, these are all insults because we think that we are superior to them. We haven't come to grips with our basic biological nature which dictates our most fundamental needs. Politics is not going to be able to deal with that unless it's one of our basic cultural values. And we don't have that right now.

ORR: Your question is a really good question, and the points you make behind the question is really good, and I agree with my colleagues on the platform. Ultimately this comes down to a political system that can protect the least among us, and future generations, and that is a political revolution that we have not yet experienced. Another Texan, Sanford Levinson, who is a constitutional lawyer, is proposing another constitutional convention in this country to deal with issues like this, but this eventually is a matter of power and politics. And one last comment is, I worked for the last five or six years or longer with people in West Virginia where mountaintops have been cut off so we can get cheap coal. So of course that means the coal is not cheap at all. It just means that the costs are never fully paid for the damage you've done, and they're suffering all kinds of illnesses and so forth, and I think the issue in part is also one that Nelson Mandela had to wrestle with in his memoirs. He was imprisoned in South Africa and the wrongs were egregious, and yet he came out of that process without hatred, and led the revolution then in South Africa. I think there's a good bit of that attitude we've got to build into this because we have some suffering and pain and some egregious wrongs that are going to go on before we fix this, but thanks very much for the points you have made.

FRENCH: Yes, thank you for sharing your personal story. We appreciate that. I'm going to come back over here.

AUDIENCE: William Carter. I'm an emeritus professor of Environmental Health and Safety at the University of Findley. In all due respect to our sponsors, I would like to ask the question is capitalism as currently emphasizing growth antithetical to permaculture and sustainability?

FRENCH: Dr. Suzuki, would you care to comment on this?

SUZUKI: Yes. The problem we face is that we've come to think we're so smart and so important that we're going to dictate the conditions of the biosphere. I'm going to say this in my talk tonight, but we know that we live in a world that is shaped by laws of nature. In physics as David [Orr] says, we accept there is a law of gravity, there are limits to how fast a rocket can go, we accept that entropy is a reality. Chemistry determines the kind of chemical reactions and molecules you can create. We understand those are laws of nature. In biology it's the same. Our biological nature dictates that we have an absolute need for clean air, clean water, clean soil, sunlight, and so on. Other things like capitalism, currency, markets, economics, corporations, these aren't forces of nature, we invented them. But what do we try to do? Look at Copenhagen, where three years ago 192 nations met to deal with the atmosphere that doesn't belong to anyone. But they had 192 national boundaries and 192 economic agendas that they negotiated by trying to shoe horn nature into. Well it can't work that way. We think we're so important we can make the air conform to our country or our economic demands? That's what we're trying to do.

FRENCH: David?

ORR: Yes, I agree with that.

AUDIENCE: So far you've agreed with everything that David [Suzuki] said.

ORR: Yes, we were told to be agreeable, just stay away from controversy. You know, the issue here with capitalism is in part the laws of capitalism, if you start that with Adam Smith and *The Wealth of Nations*. That was 237 years ago. So the laws we take to be the laws of capitalism are 237 years old. The problem is they were trying to shoe horn those into a planet where it has evolved into 3.8 billion years, and that's kind of a tough assignment. And without getting in details, if I'm optimistic, I'm optimistic in part because of people like Ray Anderson, a friend of mine who died last year of cancer. But he started a company called Interface Carpet Corporation. And Ray decided that he wanted his supply to start with his supply chain, not Saudi Arabian crude, and then he wanted to give the customers a product that he would own, he would lease it and then get it back, remake it into new carpet, which meant he had to assemble the molecules in the way that he wanted, he could disassemble them and rearrange them, and then give it back, so you cut off the crude oil supply over here, it never went to a landfill where it otherwise would have stayed for 40,000 years. Jean Benyus, who will be here in several weeks, has developed a field called biomimicry. And to think of biomimicry, how, for example, she says spiders take dead flies and sunshine, and they make materials stronger than steel by five times, tougher than Kevlar, which makes bulletproof vests, ambient temperature, no fossil fuels made at or near of the body, biodegradable, no heat, beat, or treat, as she describes it: biomimicry. And nature does things, nature manufactures things, ceramics and so forth, much more intelligently than anything we can make. So there is a way here to begin to calibrate the way nature works with the way this human institution, capitalism, works. And then in the meantime, I think we have to figure out how to regulate capitalism for the good of the whole community. So no more deregulation of— let's say the banking industry and collapsing the global economy, as we had in 2008. And that was because of the repeal of legislation passed in The New Deal that had regulated banks and kept them out of certain kinds of activity. So I don't think we have an alternative to capitalism. I think we have a choice of whether we have a good capitalism and begin to encourage innovation in the way we make things and the way we provide livelihood or not, and on that I can be optimistic on Monday, Wednesday, and Friday; Tuesday, Thursday, and Saturday I'm not; and on Sunday I don't think about it.

FRENCH: And Ray Anderson was successful with his sustainable carpet model, it was not as though he gave up on profits and so forth, it was at both ends, correct?

ORR: He decided he was going to make it so that there was to be no waste product and to be powered by sunshine and so he began to make a company that was sustainable in every way you can think of at this point. And I think that there are other companies beginning to move in that direction, but it's called, it's a different kind of capitalism, that in the business world, the business school here, to where they had school courses in triple bottom line, and you have some of the leading thinkers and how you begin to shift corporations into this kind of mindset. And it turns out it's really weird. Because what appears to be just do-gooderism actually is pretty good for the bottom line. And so it's one of these ironic convergences of doing the right thing and doing the smart thing converge on the same kind of business enterprise.

SUZUKI: Well, the weird thing about current economic agenda, and I don't think it's inherent (it may be, I'm not an economist) is this drive for constant growth. What is growth? Why is growth suddenly an end in itself? In my country we hear we have to dig up the tar sands because that's going to be the economic engine of the country—we have to keep the economy growing. But nobody asks, "Wait a minute, what's an economy for? Are there no limits? How much is enough? Are we happier with all of this growth?" We are among the richest people on the planet. How much do we need? Why do we have to have more? We live in a finite world, the biosphere, the zone of air, water, and land, where all life exists. Carl Sagan told us if you shrink the earth to the size of a basketball, the biosphere will be thinner than a layer of Saran wrap, and that's it. Not just for us, but 30 million other species that share that space, and we think that we can grow our economy forever? Steady growth is called exponential growth, and anything growing exponentially will double in a predictable time. So if it's growing at 1 percent a year it will double in 70 years, 2 percent a year in 35, 3 percent in 24. We can predict the growth rate. Art Barlett, a physicist at Colorado, gave this story to me. I'm going to give you a system that is going to grow exponentially. We have a test tube full of food for bacteria, put in one bacterial cell which is going to divide every minute, that's exponential growth. So at the beginning there is one bacterium, in one minute there are two, two minutes there are four, three minutes, eight, four minutes sixteen, that's exponential growth. And at 60 minutes, the test tube is completely full of bacteria and there's no food left. So when is a test tube only half full? Well, of course the answer is at 59 minutes. So at 58 minutes it's 25 percent full, 57 minutes 12.5 percent full. At 55 minutes of a 60 minute cycle, it's 3 percent full. If at 55 minutes one of the bacteria says, "Hey guys, we've got a population problem," the other bacteria would say, "what have you been smoking? 97 percent of the test tube is empty and we have been around for 55 minutes." So at 59 minutes, they realize, "we gotta do something, Jack was right. We have one minute left." So what do you do? Suppose those bacterial scientists invent three test tubes full of food. So they're saved, right? They have quadrupled the amount of food and space! So at 60 minutes the first tube is full, at 61 minutes the second is full, and 62 minutes all four are full. So even if we found three more planets to live on immediately, it would only buy us two extra minutes. Every scientist I've talked to agrees with me, we're already past the 59th minute! People say, "How dare you say that. Look at our stores. We're living longer and healthier." Yes, we have created the illusion that everything is fine by using up the rightful legacy of our children and our grandchildren. That's how we're doing it.

FRENCH: I apologize for this, but I need to make a practical announcement. There are some Case Western students who may have to step out at this moment because they have classes, and I just want to give them one moment to do so discretely, and we appreciate them coming and attending for as long as they could, but we need them to continue their education, and so we will let them step out for one moment. Jeremy, did you want to comment on this? David Orr? Yes.

ORR: Let me get this straight. You went to Texas and said they were animals, you came here and compared us to bacteria. You know, one thought that comes to mind and it fits Case Western. You have some amazing capabilities here. David Cooperrider has been the leading scholar in something called appreciative inquiry. And as David Suzuki is talking, it strikes me that we need a national dialogue of that kind of tough stuff. And we need to get to the bottom of a lot of things very quickly, and Case has been a leader in that field, and I just want to point that out. There is a dialogue here that needs to be managed and there are some rules to carry out those kinds of dialogues. Just a thought.

BENDIK-KEYMER: I do want to say one thing. Growth is growth of an abstraction. I just think that's important to say. I have a colleague in Colorado who works on this problem philosophically, and I always think he's making this mistake. It does not necessarily mean growth of things, physical things; it means growth of value. Value can be *intensified* if it is regulated properly, right? So this is what costs are supposed to reflect. But the problem is, I mean I appreciate hearing stories of businesses that are starting to turn the corner on this issue, but the issue frankly is *macroeconomic*. The great business that does it [i.e. is environmentally respectful], that's great. Perhaps it will catch on, but it will not do anything if the incentives in the system say, "free ride and push it off onto the future"—if the incentives say, "I don't have to pay anything for taking away what the future deserves." So I mean, I agree with the general gist of [the turn to environmental business] but I wouldn't get too hung up on this growth thing. The issue is, are we regulating the economy properly? This is what David Orr was saying. We need to internalize externalities. Every economy, no matter how libertarian you are, has regulation for contract. We've decided it's not okay to sell human beings. These things can be done. We need the right kind of legal instruments to frame in the generation of wealth so that when wealth comes out and is registered as growth, it's quality, it's a quality that we can live with and hold up to ourselves in the morning as human beings and say, "You know what? This is all right." So I mean, I wouldn't emphasize too much the issue about growth but rather the issue that [what we have now is] a macroeconomic mess that we've let get out of our hands, and that's a *citizenship* issue. That's what I'm trying to say with the politics.

FRENCH: First of all, I want to just extend thanks to those of you who are waiting with the questions and standing there, but I mean, how can I interrupt this conversation. But you, sir, are next.

AUDIENCE: My name is Peter Hart. I'm a biologist here at Case Western. I was at the first Earth Day in 1970 when I was a sophomore in college, and I want to thank you all for making this one of the most stimulating discussions that I've heard since then. I think we need a lot more of this. We all try to think over the course of our lives how we can best invest our time in these issues, and I mean we're going back and forth about a lot of different issues, you know, we all do recycling because it maybe reaffirms our daily commitment, even though we may feel like it's a drop in the bucket, but I think certainly in my life I've tried to think about what are the most significant actors on the planet for the problems that we have, and if I might perhaps revisit the comment of my friend from Finland without raising the whole issue about capitalism per se, I'd just like to hear your comments on the implications of what I think is the most significant actors, and that is the emergence of certain multinational corporations, and particularly those, for example, those proposing extracting oil from tar sands, the current frenzy in the United States over using new fracking technology to extract natural gas, we're seeing a real boom of that around here. I can't help but think that these corporations, who have—despite the opinion of our Supreme Court that they're individuals—have largely outflanked the ability of government. We like to talk theoretically about ourselves as citizens and individuals, but in fact there are actors that are much larger than us who have successfully and persistently pursued the ability to outflank nations, states, governments, making it increasingly difficult to be optimistic about our political impact on these issues and making us increasingly discouraged about where do we act, in what arena do we act, in order to deal with these problems. Thanks.

FRENCH: Thank you for your question. Who would like to go first?

ORR: Corporations are nowhere mentioned in the US Constitution, so for people who like to talk about original intent, corporations do not appear in that document. Second thing, both Thomas Jefferson and Abraham Lincoln worried a great deal about corporations. In 1864, Abraham Lincoln assumed—just from what he had seen in the Civil War and corporations supplying guns and blankets to the Union armies—that corporations would eventually amass all the power and the public would be destroyed, and that was 1864, and he was a Republican. The issue in 1886 was that the Supreme Court was said to have given the legal rights of a person to corporations. In fact, the case shows that they didn't really do that, that was misreading of a portion called the Head notes to that decision. But it's a moot point because corporations have been assumed to have the same protections of due process that people have by the Fourteenth Amendment. Now you and I are people, we are mortal, we can be in one place at one time, our assets are limited, we die, we are ethical people in between, but corporations stand oddly against this backdrop of democracy. We don't know quite what to do with them, and that's going to be one of the huge issues: Are corporations persons, legal persons? You and I are legal persons. Are corporations entitled to the same rights you and I have? That is going to be one big issue. Mitt Romney raised it several months [ago] and the issue has been kind of inflammatory, but this is going to be a tough issue. How do we provision ourselves with all of the things that we need and corporations stand astride international politics in many ways beyond the reach of law in any given country, and so it is an issue, and I don't propose a solution for it. It is going to be a very tough political issue. They have corrupted, I think, American politics in some very fundamental ways and so forth, but you know the story as well or better than I do, so thanks for raising the issue. But I can't think of anything politically that would be more important than beginning to reorient corporate behavior to long-term public purposes and rather like corporations were at the start of this country at the writing of the Constitution in 1787. It is a tough issue because it's so legally embedded and it's going to be hard to disentangle all the issues and come to an equitable and fair solution that coincides with a decent long-term future.

FRENCH: You know, I have been letting all of the panelists comment on each question but I see the rows stacked up on each side, so I actually would like to see if we can fit in a few more questions before we run out of time here.

SUZUKI: Can I just make a partly tongue-in-cheek comment, but it would help be a big beginning if all corporate leaders would read Mr. Inamori's books.

FRENCH: Yes, well we agree with that here at Case Western Reserve. For any of you who are not familiar, the Kyocera motto is, "Respect the divine and love people." How's that for a corporate motto? Now I'd like to take this question please.

AUDIENCE: Hi. I'm Lee Batdorf from Cleveland Heights. This is for David Suzuki, but you're all welcome to speak to it unless she stops you.

FRENCH: Which I might!

AUDIENCE: My question is how are we going to find our way? As any environmental activist knows, it's a complicated thing to deal with environmental issues and talking with the public about it. In the last decade, I've noticed schisms developing what you could call the environmental movement, and I've noticed that Stewart Brand of Whole Earth fame has come out for nuclear power, among other technologies, and then I've read in a recent issue of *Wired* magazine about how not only is renewable energy not going to do the job, but nuclear of course is very expensive to do, and the solution is in fracked natural gas. And where do we go to find a coherent direction to pursue as individuals to make decisions of how to treat the environment in a way that seven generations from now there might be something left?

FRENCH: Thank you, and I think to continue as I was suggesting, David Suzuki, if you could reply and we'll take another question, we'll take one reply to each response to try to get a few more folks in.

SUZUKI: I wish I knew the answer. I think what we need is diversity of thought within the movement and certainly a lot of my colleagues are now looking to nukes as the answer. It doesn't make any sense to me. It makes no economic sense and we have major problems with the technology, even when it's in place, and Fukushima ought to be a big reminder of that. So we have to constantly be listening and open to the issues in environmentalism. Nobody has the absolute truth. But I think the most important issue is how do we stay in the game? We have to have sustainable activism and so many of my colleagues have just burned out, gotten involved in an issue and flamed out. I hate to say it, but a number of them have committed suicide because it is so very serious. We need to have sustainable activism, as well. For me the greatest gift that I received was one day, I would ignore my family, I was in the office working saying I have to do this, I have to finish a project, and one day I looked in the mirror and thought, "Who the hell do you think you are? You're one person out of 6.5 million people, 7 billion now. You think you're so important you're going to make a difference?" We're all just one human being and we do the best we can and hope there are enough people to add together so that collectively we will have an impact. Don't flame out is the important thing.

FRENCH: I've just been cautioned that we have time for two more questions. So, over here please, and apologies to those of you who have been waiting so patiently, and I hope that perhaps you can join us for some of our other events.

AUDIENCE: My name is Eric Schreiber. I am on the staff of the Cleveland Clinic, and you've almost answered the question with your great discussion about growth, Dr. Suzuki. I wish you could amplify on one thing Dr. Bartlett also mentioned in his talk on this the oxymoron of sustainable growth. We have heard from both conventions, as was pointed out—growth, economic models are based on growth. What's this going to look like? Any mathematician will tell you that all growth stops. What do you think the prognosis is for making a transition from economic models based on growth to different economic models that are not? Thank you.

SUZUKI: I'm not a futurist. I don't know, but I think you can look at Clive Hamilton, an eco-philosopher from Australia. His book is *Requiem for a Species* and we're the species the requiem is for. He simply traces what we've been talking about over the last forty years, and what has actually been done politically and it's pretty depressing. So the reality is we work as hard as we can in whatever areas, but I think it's going to take a crisis of monumental proportions. I thought when thirty thousand people died in Europe of heat one summer, that was it. I remember six hundred or seven hundred people died in Chicago of heat. I thought Katrina might be it, but it looks like there's going to have to be a massive crisis. I thought the 2008 economic meltdown might be it, but it's not going to move us the way we should be going.

BENDIK-KEYMER: Just real short, I've been trying to hold over the past questions; so I'll be short, again. I'm a gradualist about these things. I don't think you get the solution like this. You get bridge concepts to start hinging [what we're working on] toward something different. So again, growth is just an abstraction. I would suggest a phrase something like *intensification of value* as a hinge concept, and the real issue then is not the semantics of it, although maybe the semantics help. The issue is, is the macroeconomic system regulated properly in a way that is in line with justice, in the way that we no longer sell human beings because it is unjust to sell human beings? It's unjust to sell the future, it's unjust to externalize our costs on the future, so the issue, I mean you can change the language and talk about intensification of value, but the core issue is about *the macroeconomic frame*. So then, just to the last question, again in practical judgment, the issue is not always what's going to keep [our life] going forever or what's going to solve the whole problem [of our unsustainability], but *what's the first most important thing [to bring about]*, and then if we can get that thing in place, maybe we can see how the terrain looks different after it. So I do think there's one very simple important thing: The United States has to have a serious role in signing up for a binding global climate treaty, post Kyoto. It's a complete travesty that we have inhibited climate regulation, but if we could get behind climate regulation, China would have to start taking it more seriously, India would have to start taking it more seriously, and most importantly there would be a legal frame to start modeling for other sorts of ecological regulations that can only happen at the global level. So I think you know, as an environmentalist, if you have to recycle to keep your integrity going and to imagine a different lifestyle, go for it. But the main, number one thing is getting a global compact that has some enforceable power and that the United States and other major polluters are behind, and as citizens we need to say to every single one of our representatives, "Why aren't you talking about this?" So I think that's *the* thing. That starts [working on] the macroeconomic frame, and then you can start thinking about what the system would look like differently.

FRENCH: Please, if you could state your name.

AUDIENCE: Hi! I'm Hope Gerald from Shaker Heights High School, where I'm a junior and candidate of the IB—International Baccalaureate program. I had a question constructed for Jeremy, like no favoritism involved, but earlier you mentioned we have evolved into near-term thinkers as a society, but what specific factors, examples, areas of knowledge, or even ways of knowing do you have to back up your knowledge claim?

BENDIK-KEYMER: That's a great critical comment. You know what, there's a book by a guy named Matthew Ridley called *The Origins of Virtue*. It gives you the anthropological evidence on the extent to which we are near-term and to the extent to which we can counteract it. But I want to turn it over to my colleagues because they made some claims about how our economy now has made us short-term, and maybe they can fill that out a little bit.

FRENCH: Very briefly, if you would, gentleman.

ORR: One comment very quickly. Going back to the last point, if you were to go back to say the year 1750 in Western society and say, "Let's go out and watch the enlightenment happen," remember your history? Where would you go? The enlightenment was a letter from Montesquieu to Diderot and Thomas Jefferson in a hotel room in Philadelphia, and so forth. There was no place you could go to see it. And if you run the film forward by two hundred years and look back at our time, I think there's something like an ecological enlightenment beginning to emerge. You all are here because of it. A lot of the activity in Cleveland and Case and Oberlin and all over the world now is part of a global enlightenment and it is possible, it is just possible that we are further along in this process than we think or that we would be able to see from right now, in the same way that nobody in 1750 could have foreseen Thomas Jefferson and the Declaration of Independence and so forth and so on. It's hard to see good things unfolding when you're right in the middle of it. This prize and the work of all of you in the room and my colleagues and so forth, may be an indication, could be, just perhaps, maybe, possibly further along than it otherwise would look. Maybe.

FRENCH: May I give you the last word?

SUZUKI: No, that's fine for me.

FRENCH: Well, I want to thank you all for a wonderful discussion. I think everyone in the room is saying, "Don't make them stop." But it is my job to make it stop. But this is not the end of our events and I'm very sorry that we could not get to all of your questions, but I hope you will continue your engagement with us. As soon as we conclude here, our panelists will be walking over to our first ever Eco Showcase at the Kelvin Smith Library Oval, where they will be selling and signing copies of some of their more recent books, and the Eco Showcase is a wonderful opportunity for you to network and learn about environmental and sustainability work in our region. I also invite you all to join us this evening back right here in Severance Hall at 6:00 p.m. for the 2012 Inamori Ethics Prize ceremony, when we will actually put the medal around your neck, Dr. Suzuki, and we will hear David Suzuki's lecture, "The Challenge of the Twenty-First Century: Setting the Real Bottom Line." Now if you will, please join me in thanking our panelists for an amazing discussion.

On behalf of President Snyder and Provost Baeslack, I declare this academic symposium closed, and I thank you all for joining us.

Yvon Chouinard
Recipient of the 2013 Inamori Ethics Prize

As the founder of Patagonia, Yvon Chouinard is one of the most successful and ethical outdoor industry businessmen alive today. Business journalist Kristall Lutz recently described Chouinard as "THE pioneer in corporate social responsibility."

Yvon Chouinard was born in Maine in 1938. His father was a French-Canadian handyman, mechanic, and plumber. In 1946, he and his family moved from Maine to Southern California. At age fourteen, he became a member of the Southern California Falconry Club, and it was his investigations of falcon aeries that led him to rock climbing. To make adaptations for the way he was climbing, he decided to create his own reusable climbing hardware. In 1957, he went to a junkyard and purchased the equipment he needed to learn blacksmithing on his own, and eventually started a business producing climbing gear. This entrepreneurial venture sustained him while he climbed and surfed throughout California and the Western United States.

Chouinard became the most articulate advocate of the importance of the style and intention behind an ascent, which has become the basis of modern rock climbing. In 1974, he penned an essay with his then-business partner Tom Frost entitled, "A Word." In this work they present a challenge: "As we enter this new era of mountaineering, reexamine your motives for climbing. Employ restraint and good judgment. Remember the rock, the other climbers—climb clean." This philosophy is the foundation of Chouinard's subsequent leadership.

Over the course of the next thirteen years, through his innovative designs and grassroots efforts, Chouinard's company, Chouinard Equipment, became the largest supplier of climbing hardware. However, he realized that the use of his products by climbers was detrimental to the environment. In 1972, determined to end this negative impact, and building on his core belief to "climb clean," Chouinard introduced and patented new aluminum chocks that would not harm the rock. Whereas his best-selling pitons had caused harm to the cracks in the rocks in Yosemite, his new product line did not damage these surfaces. This was the first major business decision he made on behalf of the environment. It revolutionized rock climbing and led to the further success of the company, despite destroying the sales of pitons (formerly his most important and lucrative product).

Chouinard is most noted for creating the clothing and gear company, Patagonia. In 1970, on a trip to Scotland, he purchased sturdy regulation team rugby shirts and resold them with great success to climbers who had formerly climbed in thin thrift-store clothing. From this modest start, Patagonia developed a wide selection of rugged technical clothing. With Chouinard at the helm, Patagonia has been innovative in the quest to protect the environment, even when it hurt the company's bottom line; his goal is to, "create the best quality with the least impact." After realizing the terrible environment impact of the production of standard cotton, Chouinard committed Patagonia to the use of pesticide-free cotton beginning in 1996, thereby creating the organic cotton industry in California. Patagonia continues to lead the way in research and design in their recycled fabric department, and has been a leader for the apparel industry to emulate. Chouinard partnered with other companies (Gap, Nike, Walmart, Levi Strauss, Adidas) to create the Sustainable Apparel Coalition. This group embraces his efforts to set data-driven benchmarks for improving their collective environmental practices. Mary Fox, an executive in charge of Walmart's global sourcing, says, "I adore Yvon. When we went around together to get other companies on board, we code-named ourselves David and Goliath. Because in the realm of sustainability, we were David. Patagonia was Goliath" (*The Wall Street Journal,* 2012).

Recognizing that the financial success of the company provided the opportunity for his employees to achieve personal goals, Chouinard committed the company to fostering employee wellness and being an outstanding place to work. Patagonia has a cafeteria offering mostly healthy, vegetarian fare. The company also provides on-site daycare and flexible work schedules for employees. As Patagonia states, "We have never had to make a 'break' from the traditional corporate structure that makes businesses hidebound and inhibits creativity…we simply made the effort to hold to our own values and traditions." Chouinard's 2005 book, *Let My People Go Surfing,* explores the unique corporate climate at Patagonia. Chouinard is also the author of the 1982 book, *Climbing Ice,* and most recently co-authored *The Responsible Company* with Vincent Stanley (2012).

Chouinard's primary goal is protecting the environment. He gives financial incentives for employees to work on local environmental projects. In 1985, he instituted the Earth Tax, through which Patagonia has committed one percent of sales to grassroots environmental organizations, totaling millions of dollars. Chouinard went on to co-found 1% for the Planet, an organization through which other companies can make their own environmental donations. In 1989, he co-founded the Conservation Alliance with REI, Kelty, and The North Face. Now the group boasts over 170 member companies who give money to environmental organizations and engage in more work on behalf of the environment. In 1994, Patagonia began hosting "Tools for Grassroots Activists Conferences," where experienced activists train leaders in the environmental groups Patagonia supports through grants. In 2005, Patagonia built their own power plant out of solar panels that cover the parking lot and provide 10 percent of the power for their headquarters in Ventura, California. The company's current campaign, "Our Common Waters," focuses on human water use and related threats to biodiversity. Chouinard and Patagonia continually return the focus to their own impact on the planet, such as reducing their water footprint, and reporting their own water use. In 2009, Chouinard stated, "The reason I am in business is I want to protect what I love. I used to spend 250 days a year sleeping on the ground. I've climbed on every continent. I'm old enough to see the destruction."

Yvon Chouinard began a company while also inspiring a movement. In celebration of his leadership, he earned the prestigious David R. Brower Conservation Award in May 2007 from The Glen Canyon Institute for a lifetime devoted to conservation. The 2011 cover story in *Fortune* magazine on Chouinard declared Patagonia, "The Coolest Company on the Planet," and *US News* placed him among America's Best Leaders in 2009. He was also honored in 2007 by the National Forest Foundation for his contributions to the protection of public lands. In 2006, a jury consisting of outdoor and design journalists from leading European trade media awarded him the first Outdoor Celebrity of the Year Award.

In addition to his other accomplishments, Chouinard has made many famous and notable ascents. He currently lives in California with his wife of over forty years, with whom he has two children.

A Responsible Economy

Yvon Chouinard
Recipient of the 2013 Inamori Ethics Prize

In my quarter century of stupid stunts, I've had enough near-death experiences that I've accepted the fact that I'm going to die someday. I'm not too bothered by it. There is a beginning and end to all life—and to all human endeavors.

Species evolve and die off. Empires rise, then break apart. Businesses grow, then fold. There are no exceptions. I'm OK with all that. Yet it pains me to bear witness to the sixth great extinction, where we humans are directly responsible for the extirpation of so many wonderful creatures and invaluable indigenous cultures. It saddens me to observe the plight of our own species; we appear to be incapable of solving our problems.

I saw the birth of my first grandchild last year, and I worry about the future she faces. When I was born, the human population of our planet was 2.5 billion. When she will be just 38 years old, the population will hit 9 billion. Already, worldwide, Americans are using up over four planets' worth of resources. Hardly 'sustainable.'

The reason for this crisis is very simple. There are too many of us consuming too much stuff, and we demand that it be as cheap and disposable as possible. (Have you looked at the junk in an airline mail-order catalog recently? Does the world really need a special tool for cutting bananas?) No wonder we don't want to face up to the cause of our problems: It's us! We are no longer called 'citizens.' Economists, government and Wall Street call us 'consumers.' We "destroy, waste, squander, use up," and that's just Webster's. The sad truth is that the world economy revolves around our consumption. The stock markets rise and dip according to the level of consumer confidence.

And while we work harder and harder to get more of what we don't need, we lay waste to the natural world. Dr. Peter Senge, author and MIT lecturer, says, "We are sleepwalking into disaster, going faster and faster to get to where no one wants to be."

Can we even imagine what an economy would look like that wouldn't destroy the home planet? A responsible economy?

During the next two years, Patagonia will try to face and explore that question. We'll ask some smart people to write essays on that subject for our catalogs and website. We'll ask you to tell us where you see responsible economies cropping up. We'll use real-world examples, not a lot of pie-in-the-sky theories. Most of all, we're going to feel our way into how this question affects how we do business. Can Patagonia survive in a responsible economy? Stay tuned. It is the most ambitious and important endeavor we have ever undertaken. Our other environmental campaigns have addressed travesties such as the depletion of the oceans, pollution of water, and obstacles to migration paths for animals. But these are all symptoms of a far bigger problem; the Responsible Economy Campaign addresses the core.

Patagonia has worked for some twenty plus years to try to behave more responsibly. In 1991, Patagonia was growing at a rate of 50 percent a year, and we hit the wall in the midst of the savings and loan crisis. The bank reduced our credit line twice in several months, and the company ended up borrowing from friends to meet payroll and laying off 20 percent of its workforce on July 31, 1991. That's a day I still refer to as Black Wednesday.

We learned the hard way about living within our means. We had exceeded our resources and limitations. We had become dependent, like the world economy, on growth we could not sustain. I even thought about selling the company. But if I hadn't stayed in business, I never would have realized the parallel between Patagonia's unsustainable push for growth and that of our whole industrial economy.

After that day in 1991, we added a third point to our mission statement: It now reads, "Build the best product, cause no unnecessary harm, and use business to inspire and implement solutions to the environmental crisis."

Making things in a more responsible way is a good start, and many companies like us have started doing that, but in the end we will not have a 'sustainable economy' unless we consume less. However, economists tell us that would cause the economy to crash.

I think we at Patagonia are mandated by our mission statement to face the question of growth, both by bringing it up and by looking at our own situation as a business fully ensnared in the global industrial economy. I personally don't have the answers, but in the back of my simple brain a few words come to the fore, words that have guided my life and Patagonia's life as a company: *quality, innovation, responsibility, simplicity.*

I recently read a book about forty companies that have been in business for over two hundred years. I thought if those companies could exist that long, maybe they have some guiding principles that a responsible economy should follow. The common traits they all had were quality, innovation, and restrained growth. Coming from a background of making the very best, life-saving tools for the mountains, we applied the same philosophy to clothing. We have been innovators using technology not for the sake of inventing new products but to replace old, polluting, and inefficient products and methods with cleaner, simpler, and more appropriate technology. Every garment we make, for example, can be recycled now, unthinkable ten years ago. We are working together with forty other clothing manufacturers on what we call the Higg Index, which measures the environmental impact of textile manufacturing and which will be, in the end, public facing: You will be able to see the impact and history of a pair of jeans by pointing your smart phone at the bar code on their label. By choosing to consume more responsibly, perhaps we can relearn how to be citizens again and be part of the strongest force in society—civil democracy.

I have always believed that a design is perfected not when you can't add anything more but when you can't take anything away. The illustrator becomes an artist when he or she can evoke the same feeling with simpler line and form. Simplicity is the way to perfection. As a mountain climber, it pleases me to see the new generations of climbers soloing and climbing free routes on El Capitan in Yosemite that took us multiple days, fixed ropes, and many pitons to climb.

I enjoy manual labor and love using good tools that leverage the efficiency of my efforts. But not a tool or machine that takes away the pleasure of the labor. (I think of that airline catalog banana cutter which replaces a perfectly good tool: my knife.)

I think the simple life really begins with owning less stuff.

We are questioning what Patagonia can do, as a company making some of this stuff, to lead us into the next, more responsible economy. After we grew too fast in the nineties, we tried not growing at all. That resulted in stagnation and frustrated customers who often could not buy what they needed from us. You do not need a zero-growth economy. (In the same way you don't have to stop people from having babies in order to stabilize the population: People die, babies are born; you need a balance between the two.) What we are reaching toward is an economy that does not rely on insatiable consumerism as its engine, an economy that stops harmful practices and replaces them with either new, more efficient practices or older practices that worked just fine. An economy with less duplication of consumer goods, less throw-away-

and-close-your-eyes. We don't know exactly how this will play out. But we do know that now is the time for all corporations to think about it and act.

I hope Patagonia can find a way to make decisions about growth based on being here for the next two hundred years—and not damaging the planet further in the process. As my granddaughter grows up, I'll do my best to see that, just as I did and her parents did, she has a life in nature that she loves. Then she will want to protect it.

Property of Patagonia, inc. Used with permission.

What We Do For A Living

Yvon Chouinard
and Vincent Stanley

We are all still in the earliest stages of learning how what we do for a living both threatens nature and fails to meet our deepest human needs. The impoverishment of our world and the devaluing of the priceless undermine our physical and economic well-being.

Yet the depth and breadth of technological innovation of the past few decades shows that we have not lost our most useful gifts: humans are ingenious, adaptive, clever. We also have moral capacity, compassion for life, and an appetite for justice. We now need to more fully engage these gifts to make economic life more socially just and environmentally responsible, and less destructive to nature and the commons that sustain us.

This book aims to sketch, in light of our environmental crisis and economic sea change, the elements of business responsibility for our time, when everyone in business—at every level—has to deal with the unintended consequences of a two-hundred-year-old industrial model that can no longer be sustained ecologically, socially, or financially.

The co-authors have been involved in Patagonia since its inception nearly forty years ago. But it is not the purpose of this book to retell our company's history in detail. That story may be found in Yvon's book, *Let My People Go Surfing*.

This book, though it draws on our experience at Patagonia, aims to be useful to all people who see the need for deep change in business practices and who work in companies quite unlike ours. Although we mostly address companies that make things, or like us, design things made by others, this book is germane to all businesses that offer a service or to nongovernmental organizations (NGOs) and nonprofits that want to treat their people well and reduce the environmental impact of their operations. This book is for anyone who works, not just business leaders and managers. It is also for business students and other young people who want to engage their best, deepest self in the working life that stretches ahead.

You should know that at its beginning, Patagonia was meant to be not a risk-taking, environment-obsessed, navel-gazing company but an easy-to-milk cash cow. Yvon created Patagonia as an offshoot of the Chouinard Equipment Company, which made excellent mountain-climbing gear recognized as the best in the world, but very little money. Patagonia was intended to be a clean and easy company—desk jockey's work—in contrast to the ten hours a day sweat and toil of hammering out pitons with coal-fired forge or drilling and cutting chocks from extruded aluminum. The clothing business required no expensive dies to amortize and had a much broader customer base than a few dirtbag climbers. Who knew then that cotton could be as dirty as coal?

At Chouinard Equipment we were used to a life-or-death standard of product quality: you did not sell an ice axe without checking it closely for a hairline fracture or any other fault. Although we applied the same standard to rugby shirts (they had to be thick and tough to survive the skin-shredding sport of rock climbing), we knew that seam failure was unlikely to kill anyone. Patagonia was to be our *irresponsible* company, bringing in easy money, a softer life, and enough profits to keep Chouinard Equipment in the black.

Our responsibilities as businesspeople came slowly and almost involuntarily to light while we focused on the "real" work of designing our clothes and getting them made and sold. In the chapters ahead, we'll describe a handful of moments that stunned us into consciousness (including the discovery that cotton, our most commonly used natural fiber, turned out to be the most toxic) to illustrate how one step makes the next step possible—a simple lesson but key.

We can't pose Patagonia as the model of a responsible company. We don't do everything a responsible company can do, nor does anyone else we know. But we can illustrate how any group of people going about their business can come to realize their environmental and social responsibilities, then begin to act on them; how their realization is progressive: actions build on one another.

We used to think that because Patagonia grew out of a small band of climbers and surfers who have a special love for the natural world and a palpable need to be in it, feel a part of it, that we were somehow exceptional as a business. Twenty years ago, we didn't think we had much to say to the woman next to us on the plane who might wear a Chanel suit and pearls and fetch a copy of *Fortune* out of her Tod's handbag (we would have been accidently upgraded to business class to be anywhere near her). Now, though, we can think of a number of topics we might have discussed, from design to inventory control, to the implications of material shortages for long-term planning. We now know, from talking to all kinds of businesspeople, that Patagonia, if exceptional at all, is so only at the margins. As mice and men share 99 percent of their genes, so do Wal-Mart, BP, and Patagonia. Patagonia may seem different because its owners are committed to social and environmental change; and our company is privately held, not publicly traded, so we can take on greater risks. But our management requires the same set of skills, pursues the same opportunities, and faces the same competition and constraints as any other business.

We started as climbers and surfers, so our direct engagement with nature may have allowed us to recognize the environmental crisis earlier than others and begin to act on it more quickly. But eventually the crisis would be apparent to everyone in business. Soon we would trade stories with other businesses that acted out of environmental and social concerns. In the earliest days, we talked with the founders of Ben & Jerry's, The Body Shop, and Smith & Hawken. Later, conversations with REI, The North Face, and other companies in the outdoor industry led to the creation of the Conservation Alliance, a nonprofit that protects wilderness as habitat and space for recreation.

When we finally turned a cold eye to our own wasteful and polluting industrial practices, or those done in our name by our suppliers, we sought out and found other concerned companies willing to offer advice and help. Often they were huge, and included Levi Strauss, Nike, Timberland, and The Gap. We spoke with others farther afield, like the courtly carpet-tile manufacturer Ray Anderson, founder of Interface, whose spiritual epiphany upon reading Paul Hawken's *The Ecology of Commerce* led him to become, as *The Economist* noted in his obituary, "America's greenest businessman." It turned out we were not unique in our desire to become a more responsible business.

When we wanted to improve our quality without increasing our costs, we shared notes with Jack Stack, who with other employees had bought back the failing Springfield Remanufacturing Company from International Harvester and had made it successful through innovations in participatory corporate control (i.e., listening to front-line employees) and open-book management. Jack taught us that any successful business strategy had to engage the intelligence of the people on the floor as much as those at the top.

Along the way we've seen a tectonic shift in work culture in many businesses. During the past twenty years, Silicon Valley companies have turned old work rules on their head. Almost everyone is familiar with the free fitness rooms and free food. Fewer know that Google allows employees to spend 20 percent of their working time doing almost anything they like: We know, because some employees of Google Earth donate that time—and their technological expertise—to helping wildlands activists map migration corridors for large animals displaced by climate change and development.

We've seen the rise of the specialty bakers and brewers, and of organic farmers and farmers' markets, as well as the mainstreaming of what used to be called health foods. We've seen the introduction of Leadership in Energy and Environmental Design (LEED) standards revolutionize commercial construction by proving that greener building standards create healthier workspaces and that better-quality construction repays owners and investors over time.

There are many new businesses that are sensitive to their workers' needs and mindful of nature's vulnerability; and many older businesses have begun to come around. But none of us have done nearly enough.

Those who plan for the future of their businesses, in every industry, have to take into account the increasing scarcity of energy and water and their rising cost, as well as the rising cost of waste and its disposal. Every company—from Wal-Mart to the Cheese Board Collective, from BP to the makers of Fat Tire Ale, from Dow Chemical to Patagonia—is already at work, in some way, even inadvertently, to dismantle a creaky, polluting, wasteful, and increasingly expensive industrial system, and is struggling to create new, less life-draining ways to make things; we are all trying to get a new roof up over the economy before the old, sagging one caves in.

Every company faces questions from skeptical customers: Will your company's product hurt them or their children? Has your product hurt the workers who made it, or their community, or the ecology of the region where the product's components were drilled, mined, or farmed? Is your product worth its social and environmental cost? It may arguably have a social benefit that outweighs its cost; but everything we all do at work, unless you happen to sell organic seeds or night-soil compost, hurts the environment more than it gives back.

Your customers may not be eager to know what's wrong with your products, but if and when she finds out, she is likely to care. And she no longer need to tune into *60 Minutes* or *Mother Jones* to find out who's dumping chemicals or mountaintops into the local creek. Any citizen with a cell-phone camera and access to a blog can now sound this neighborly alarm. And others can spread it—and will.

This is not news to the businesspeople at work on one or more of four hundred new indexes to benchmark, and advance, their social and environmental practices in the outdoor, apparel, automobile, electronics, chemical, and other industries. No one wants to feel the heat of an unfavorable spotlight. Every company should be afraid, as is Wal-Mart, of teenagers, and what they will consider environmentally acceptable or socially cool as they come into adulthood. No one under forty has ever lived in a year without an Earth Day or thought the health of an ecosystem subordinate to the whims of a corporation.

Wal-Mart woke up after a survey by McKinsey & Company jarred then-CEO Lee Scott: 54 percent of customers thought Wal-Mart "too aggressive," 82 percent expected the company to be a "role model for other businesses," and 2 to 8 percent, as many as fourteen million people, had stopped shopping at Wal-Mart altogether because they were upset by things they had heard about the company.

Some companies begin to change their ways in order to protect their reputation. Others change to reduce their cost. Still others change because they see opportunities to create new markets, whether to satisfy customers who want healthy, organic food or purchasing agents for pubic institutions who have to meet new environmental mandates for everything from vehicles to cafeteria napkins.

Every company faces competitors who, through their own efforts to thrive, become more adaptive, nimble, and efficient, as well as less wasteful and harmful. A company that can make environmental improvements will attract more customers. Companies that do business globally have to choose whether to adopt the toughest European standards or divide up their production and make lower-quality goods for the rest of the world. The choice they make will not go unnoticed by the watchful eyes of NGOs and competitors.

Investors, especially large institutional investors like pension funds and universities, now allocate more of their portfolios to socially and environmentally responsible mutual funds, not just to pay ethical lip service or ward off demonstrations on campus. For all investors, including individuals who rely on 401(k) accounts to fund their retirement, faith in the Modern Portfolio Theory (MPT) of diversified investment to minimize risk has been sorely tested by gyrations of the past fifteen years. According to a new Harvard Business School study, socially responsible investments, which once underperformed more enticing opportunities like subprime mortgages, now over the long term out-perform the market as a whole.

No company has to rely solely on its own resources to attract responsibly minded employees, customers, and investors. Every company can work with other companies, often under the auspices of a trade association, to co-develop more responsible business standards, practices, and benchmarks: then share information to help everyone reduce industrial harm and waste. That levels the playing field on which companies can then compete in good faith.

Every company that thinks it's a good guy or wants to be—Patagonia, Interface, Stoneyfield Farms, etc.—has to make room in our little clubhouse for old villains who now don a white hat for at least part of the working day. They are legion. Nike, stung by public disgust over child labor in its contract factories, has become a global leader in the effort to improve workplace conditions throughout the supply chain and create at least minimally fair labor practices around the world.

After being criticized for polluting groundwater and sucking wells dry in India, Coca-Cola has committed to return its wastewater to the environment clean enough "to support aquatic life and agriculture."

Dow Chemical, former maker of napalm, has committed to finding alternatives to petroleum as a source for its chemicals. Dow has recently teamed with The Nature Conservancy on a five-year, ten-million-dollar exploratory project to develop methodologies that can assign dollar values to ecosystems. These new tools will allow Dow to evaluate the ecological costs of every business decision it makes. Moreover, Dow was awarded an A+ from the Global Reporting Initiative (GRI) for its 2010 Annual Sustainability Report. Both Coca-Cola and Dow have teamed with Kellogg's, DuPont, and others to develop "material-neutral" packaging (packaging is responsible for a third of all waste generated).

And Wal-Mart, the world's largest company, formerly committed to an exclusive strategy of low prices, regardless of environmental cost, has committed to use 100 percent renewable energy, create zero waste, and to "sell products that sustain our resources and environment."

Consumers, both individual and institutional, have become and will continue to be more demanding. Individual consumers are famously powerful for controlling two-thirds of the US economy. For local, state, and national government and public institutions, who all buy "in bulk," the Prius is succeeding the late Crown Victoria as the emblematic tax-exempt fleet vehicle (although the NYPD prefers the hybrid Nissan Altima).

Whole industries are changing. The conservative but troubled US dairy industry is now engaged in large-scale projects to increase the productivity and shelf life of milk without resorting to destructive factory-farm practices; to change cattle feed to reduce methane "burps" (a significant contributor to greenhouse gases); and to harvest cow patties for use as organic fertilizer.

The commercial construction industry ten years ago was no bastion of green: its old, fixed-budget business model, based on the low bid, drove down quality at every stage of design and construction. Every builder has requirements to build to code but no incentives to build in resource-saving systems that might cut the building owner's cost in the long run but not the short. Enter the LEED certification system for building to energy-efficient standards with less environmental harm. At the time it was introduced in 2000, only 635 buildings worldwide could comply. As of 2012, more than 40,000 LEED-certified projects have been built or are in the works.

LEED had educated building owners and managers to the long-term high cost cheap heating and air conditioning (and of cleaning a building with high levels of indoor pollution), as well as to the saving inherent in new materials and design. An initial 2 percent increase in cost of a new LEED-certified project incurs savings of ten times that amount over the life of the building. A LEED retrofit saves owners an annual ninety cents a square foot; they make their investment back in two years. LEED is becoming the standard for commercial properties and, in the process, changing the urban landscape. In big cities, for instance, look for more roofs planted with shrubs and herbs, which insulate, filter the air, reduce heating and cooling needs, and provide a garden haven for workers taking a break. Look for more of the kind of low-income housing built by developer Jonathan Rose, with more under-the-roof residential services and a lot more light: the gym of his new South Bronx project is located not in the basement but on the top floor.

Our own outdoor industry is changing as well. Its trade group, the Outdoor Industry Association (OIA), is developing an assessment tool called the Eco Index, for use by manufacturers to measure the social and environmental impacts of every one of their products. Patagonia's Jill Dumain has been part of a working group of twenty companies that for two years met weekly by conference call to develop the relevant criteria. They benefited from participation by Nike, which had invested seven years of work and six million dollars to create its Environmental Apparel Design Tool (which, for internal use, grades the impact of the company's products as bronze, silver, or gold).

The Eco Index measures impacts of manufacturing, packaging, and shipping, as well as customer care and use, recycled content, and recyclability. It allows a company to manage its entire supply chain to improve water use and quality, lower greenhouse gas emissions, and reduce toxic chemical use and waste, as well as monitor and improve pay and working conditions on the mill or factory floor.

The OIA group decided to adopt a policy of full transparency and created an advisory council that voted on all decisions. OIA also hired a consultancy firm called Zero Waste Alliance to form a collaborative framework and methodology that would work for a broad range of participating companies—some small, others quite large (among them REI and Timberland, in addition to Nike).

OIA's Eco Index council is now at work on the second stage, which will allow more than a hundred companies to provide open-source tools to benchmark their practices and measure improvements through their business reporting systems. Our hope is that within five years the Eco Index will become consumer-facing (as is Berkeley professor Dara O'Rourke's Good Guide rating system), so that a customer can scan a Quick Response (QR) code on a pair of jeans to see ratings of that product's social and environmental impact.

OIA has made the Eco Index both transparent and scaleable. As a result, the much larger Sustainable Apparel Coalition, whose members produce more than 30 percent of the clothing and footwear sold globally, will benefit from OIA's work, shaving much time from the development of its own assessment tool.

Patagonia owes its role in the larger coalition to our relationship with Wal-Mart over the past several years. When their executives first approached us to learn more about our environmental practices, we were, from the owners to the rank and file, skeptical and bemused. How could we help them or them help us when our two companies were so vastly different? There was the question of scale: we grossed four hundred million a year, while they grossed four hundred billion. There was the question of business culture: Southern California versus rural Arkansas; high quality and strong aesthetics versus rock-bottom prices and pallet racks. There was the question of values. We knew ours; what did Wal-Mart value?

By the time they approached us, in 2008, Wal-Mart had gone through a gradual environmental awakening. Shaken by its declining reputation, and a historic volume of lawsuits aimed at a single company, Wal-Mart at first adopted some basic environmental improvements of the sort corporations usually have their PR departments tout to the press. But removing excess packaging from deodorant sticks, concentrating laundry detergent in small bottles, and installing auxiliary power units in their trucks to reduce idling time turned out to save them millions of dollars. The more material they shaved from packaging, the less energy they used, the more money they made. The more carbon they removed from their operations, the less money they wasted. The word "sustainable," at first the province of the PR staff, became a business by-word.

Wal-Mart's currently low-idling truck fleet is the world's largest. If Wal-Mart were an economy, it would be bigger than Switzerland. Because its material needs—for operations but especially for products—are so great, and because it runs stores around the world, in China, India, and Brazil, as well as in Europe, Wal-Mart is in a position to understand the resource restraints to be faced over the next decade. The company understands how essential it is to reduce its environmental impact if it is to continue to do business on a habitable planet.

Patagonia's talks with Wal-Mart led to a shared David and Goliath enterprise. Yvon and John Fleming, Wal-Mart's Chief Merchandising Officer, co-signed an invitation written on joint letterhead to attend the "21st Century Apparel Leadership Consortium" to be held in New York three months hence. They sent it to sixteen of the world's largest apparel companies. One sentence on the invitation, printed in boldface, read like the crack of a ruler on the wrist:

During the course of one half day session, we expect to achieve consensus on the need for a universally accepted approach for measuring apparel sector sustainability, and to establish a strategy for ongoing collaboration to create and implement that standard.

The invitation's final sentences, printed in italic, laid out its raison d'entre:

Creating a sustainability standard will improve the welfare of our workers, communities, consumers, and environment far more effectively than the fragmented, incremental approaches that characterize existing efforts. Together we are better. We hope you will join us.

Join us they did. The invitees, during their meeting in New York, agreed to become the Sustainable Apparel Coalition. The coalition members, working by consensus, drew on the work of OIA's Eco Index to define its social and environmental benchmarks. The coalition has now launched into development of an open-source assessment tool to be shared by participants. It is our hope that this index, like OIA's, can be converted eventually into a consumer-facing rating that will allow a customer to hold a smart phone or to read an individual rating—and compare the impact of one pair of jeans to another.

Similar efforts are underway in other industries, with over four hundred indexes in effect or being considered that measure the impacts of everything from appliances (Energy Star ratings) to electronics (EPEAT) to automobiles. It's too early to tell, but these indexes could create a revolution in the way we buy: they certainly give us information we need to be good citizens as well as informed buyers.

Every company has business partners—suppliers, dealers—with a stake in its success. These partners have also begun to adopt and develop, voluntarily or not, a more responsible business model for their own companies. Companies, suppliers, and retailers all need to help each other. As your company is responsible for everything done in its name, so are your partners responsible for your part of *their* social and ecological footprint. As Patagonia is responsible for the labor practices of Maxport, the factory in Hanoi that sews our Super Alpine Jacket, so REI is responsible for the environmental footprint of the Patagonia jackets it sells in its stores. How so? REI can't tell Patagonia how to make jackets, but it doesn't have to buy from us either. If it cares about reducing the environmental footprint of the jackets sold on the floor, REI can influence us to improve our practices or buy from someone else who will. And they should. As Wal-Mart has discovered, 90 percent of the product's environmental impact is determined at the design stage; it is the designer in Los Angeles who determines most of the harm to be done in Guangdong.

Every company now has to work to win the minds and hearts of its employees; to earn their trust, loyalty, commitment, and to engage their intelligence to help figure out, before the old economy caves, how to put up that new roof (built out of renewable or recycled materials, to LEEDS standards, with a garden to reduce energy costs). To earn employee commitment and trust begs more of a company than providing competitive pay and benefits and enacting humane employment policies. Employees who grew up in the 1980s or later view it as their birthright to make the best use of their intelligence and creativity, not always for the highest pay.

Not everyone can satisfy his heart's desire working for your company. But everyone does want to feel useful, at or, better yet, enlivened by what they do all day long. No one wants to be ashamed to name the company he works for. No one wants to leave her values at home when she leaves for work in the morning.

People will argue about what makes the world a better place to live (and for whom), and over what each of us would like to see more and less of in the world. It is hard to imagine anyone rejoicing over the generally accepted landscape of only a decade ago: a suburban monoculture of tilt-up malls, cracker-crumb housing, pandemic obesity, cheap distractions, and expensive services—all at the expense of nature. It's as though we'd handed Satan a hard hat and asked him to refashion our earth according to his plan.

A word about a word we've chosen to use as little as possible: *sustainability*.

It's a legitimate term that calls us not to take more from nature than we can give, we do harm nature more than we help it. We have no business applying the word sustainable to business activity until we learn to house, feed, clothe, and enjoy ourselves—and fuel the effort—without interfering with nature's capacity to regenerate itself and support a rich variety of life.

We are a long, long way from doing sustainable business on a planet that now numbers seven billion human beings, including the growing, appetitive (though often socially and environmentally conscious) middle class emerging in China, India, Mexico, Brazil, and Russia. Everything we make does some damage. To produce enough gold to make a wedding band, for instance, generates 20 tons of mine waste. Closer to home: a Patagonia polo shirt is made of organic cotton from an irrigated field, whose cultivation requires nearly 2,700 liters of water, enough to meet the daily needs (three glasses a day) of 900 people. Each polo shirt, in its journey from the cotton field to our Reno warehouse, generates nearly 21 pounds of carbon dioxide, 30 times the weight of the finished product. Along the line, it generates three times its weight in waste.

No human economic activity is yet sustainable.

Twenty years ago, we at Patagonia felt compelled to include in our mission statement an industrial equivalent of the Hippocratic oath, "cause no unnecessary harm." There are degrees of harm. Our polo shirt harms less than one made of chemical-intensive, conventionally farmed cotton, which may be no cleaner than coal. Our polo would be more sustainable if it were made, as are our jeans, from less thirsty, dry-farmed cotton. But even that polo would take its toll on the natural world, through its use of energy, its carbon emissions, and its waste scrap.

Still, it makes a difference to do less harm, and lessening harm makes it possible to begin to imagine restorative and even, through biomimicry, regenerative practices for the future. It makes a difference, where harm is done on an industrial scale, to make improvements on an industrial scale. It makes a difference for businesses, as well as consumers, to use fewer materials and less energy and water, and generate less waste. To make the difference we need to restore the planet to health, or to allow the planet to restore itself to health, we need to make big changes and make them fast. But it would be irresponsible not to pursue every improvement, to take action, where we can.

Many companies are doing something to behave more responsibly to the earth and the commons. And every company that learns to take a responsible step without faltering gains confidence to take the next. "Responsible" seems to us the apt, more modest, word to use while we walk the path that, we hope, leads to a place where business takes no more from nature than what it can replace.

From The Responsible Company, *by Yvon Chouinard and Vincent Stanley. Property of Patagonia, inc. Used with permission.*

Business for a Prosperous and Flourishing World

Chris Laszlo
Associate Professor,
The Weatherhead School of Management,
Case Western Reserve University
and
David L. Cooperrider
Fairmount Minerals Professor of Social Entrepreneurship,
The Weatherhead School of Management,
Case Western Reserve University

Americans have tended to ignore green and social investments, often seeing them as obstacles to jobs. President Barack Obama's failed support for Solyndra[1] and his lackluster green energy policies only reinforce this notion. Yet research shows that the economic potential of America is greater than commonly thought in areas such as clean energy, sustainable agriculture, green buildings, and emission-free transportation.[2] The question now is whether the path to prosperity through a clean and green economy can be business-led, rather than dependent on government or the non-profit sector. Such a scenario would represent a bipartisan opportunity to strengthen our economy. China and Germany's massive investments in renewable energy—along with rapidly growing green industries worldwide—suggest that it is fast becoming a matter of national competitiveness.

Sure, everyone feels overwhelmed by global challenges such as climate change and growing social inequality. Next to death, the apparent damage we are doing to ourselves and to the planet—not to mention future generations—is one of the hardest problems we face. Yet there is plenty of evidence that large but under-exploited business opportunities exist, from vertical farms that can help feed increasingly urbanized populations[3] to $20

---

1. For several ABC News stories on Solyndra, see http://abcnews.go.com/Blotter/Solyndra/.
2. "Reinventing Fire," *Rocky Mountain Institute*, accessed March 25, 2013, http://www.rmi.org/ReinventingFire.
3. Owen Fletcher, "The Future of Agriculture May Be Up," *Wall Street Journal*, October

e-Readers designed for low income consumers[4] who could most benefit from literacy and education.

The key to generating such business innovation is to promote environmental and social well-being as smarter rather than just greener. Profitable and scalable businesses that are good for people and the planet already exist. They fall into two categories: big mainstream players offering solutions to global challenges as part of a broad business strategy, and small and mid-size companies who compete based on sustainability performance. Both types of companies offer exciting support for the business-led optimism that Bill Clinton touted in a recent *Time* cover article.[5] By creating value for society and the environment, these firms create even more value for their customers and owners.

Big mainstream companies finding profitable solutions to global challenges can be found in every sector from agriculture to waste management. Through its Smarter Planet and Smarter City[6] initiatives, IBM is working to provide health care, roadways, power grids, and food production with "instrumented, intelligent, and interconnected" products and services.[7] Says CEO Sam Palmisano, "We are looking at huge problems that couldn't be solved before. We can solve congestion and pollution. We can make the grids more efficient," he says. "And quite honestly, it creates a big business opportunity."[8] Recent headlines announced the launch of WaterWatchers,[9] a new mobile app, which harnesses the power of crowdsourcing. Not a day goes by, it seems, where someone at IBM does not come up with a way to turn social and global issues into a business opportunity to create sustainable value.

Small and mid-size firms are making sustainability a unique differentiator for their customers. Tennant Company is a Minneapolis-based floor cleaning

---

15, 2012, http://online.wsj.com/article/SB10000872396390443855804577602960672985508.html.

4. "How a $20 tablet from India could blindside PC makers, educate billions and transform computing as we know it," *Digital Doyennes*, accessed March 25, 2013, http://www.digitaldoyennes.com/post/35557184592.

5. Bill Clinton, "The Case for Optimism," *Time*, October 1, 2012, http://www.time.com/time/magazine/article/0,9171,2125031,00.html.

6. "Smarter Cities for Smarter Growth," *IBM*, http://www-935.ibm.com/services/us/gbs/bus/html/smarter-cities.html.

7. "Let's Build a Smarter Planet," *IBM*, http://www.ibm.com/smarterplanet/us/en/?ca=v_smarterplanet.

8. Jeffrey M. O'Brien, "IBM's grand plan to save the planet," *CNN Money*, http://money.cnn.com/2009/04/20/technology/obrien_ibm.fortune/.

9. "IBM Taps Big Data to Help Solve Water Challenges Across South Africa," *PR Newswire*, http://www.prnewswire.com/news-releases/ibm-taps-big-data-to-help-solve-water-challenges-across-south-africa-199547491.html.

equipment maker that uses ionized water to powerfully clean commercial floors without chemicals. "Chemical free cleaning" might seem risky business for a company with $745 million in sales, yet its stock has outperformed the Dow Jones Industrial Index by a three to one margin since 2006, when it first launched its chemical free strategy.[10] Clarke is a highly successful Chicago-based mosquito control company that won the 2010 US Presidential Green Chemistry Challenge Award for a new larvicide that replaces traditional organophosphate chemistries and is approved for use in certified organic farming.[11] Patagonia is a leading producer of outdoor clothing and gear with a loyal following of customers and employees who identify with its radical environmentalism. The company encourages people to "buy less stuff," makes goods that last longer and can be recycled, and uses materials that are produced more sustainably than competitor products.[12] Another favorite example is Fairmount Minerals. "Do Good, Do Well" is more than a mantra at this sand mining company. Since it was named the #1 corporate citizen in America in 2005, the company has become the fastest growing company in its industry—and its employees are on fire with a sense of purpose, high engagement, and a spirit of innovation. Similar overseas ventures hint at the upcoming battle for sustainable businesses: Natura (Brazil), Simpa Networks (India), Triodos Bank (Netherlands), and Icebreaker (New Zealand) are among the new breed of companies that are outperforming their peers.[13]

Sustainable innovations are what allow companies to offer environmental, health, and social benefits without higher product prices or inferior quality. The 'no-trade-off' approach to solving rising global and local problems could be the powerful economic engine of our time, much as post-war reconstruction was in the twentieth century. Business can now use the profit motive as a force for: (1) ending extreme poverty and meeting the needs of the underserved; (2) creating energy and food security; (3) reducing conflict and promoting peace; (4) advancing environmental regeneration; (5) upholding human rights and the empowerment of women; and (6) realizing global

---

10. "Top BSCs trust ec-H2O™ technology," Tennant Company, http://www.tennantco.com/am-en/Pages/Company/NewsArticle.aspx?itemid=we-stand-behind-ec-h2o.
11. "Sustainability, "Clarke Company, http://www.clarke.com/index.php?option=com_content&view=category&layout=blog&id=77&Itemid=59.
12. Patagonia, http://www.patagonia.com/us/home.
13. Fairmount Minerals, see http://www.fairmountminerals.com; Natura (Brazil), see http://en.wikipedia.org/wiki/Natura; Simpanetworks (India), see http://simpanetworks.com; Triodos Bank (Netherlands), see http://www.triodos.com/en/about-triodos-bank/; Icebreaker (New Zealand), http://us.icebreaker.com/on/demandware.store/Sites-IB-US-Site/default/Home-Show.

health, especially for our children. By providing value for society and the environment, the private sector has the opportunity to create even more value for its investors, as new market forces drive demand for solutions to these problems.[14]

"We have it in our power to begin the world again," Thomas Paine told his contemporaries at the start of America's democratic revolution. The same can be said of the role of business today in building a better world.

Sustainability innovations are already leading to entire new business models, such as those cited above, including IBM's Smarter Planet and Tennant Company's H2O chemical-free cleaning. Some are no more than promising ideas, but in many cases hint at the coming revolution in meeting consumer needs based on caring for people and the planet. They include electric car batteries with a five hundred mile range, ATMs that dispense clean water in even the most remote areas of the world, and solar cells sprayed on roads and rooftops to power our energy needs.[15]

All have the potential to change the world in a way that is good for people, good for business, and good for America. They offer a positive view of America's future based on sustainability leadership. To move this agenda forward, a number of initiatives are in the works, including the Global Prize for Business as an Agent of World Benefit, conceived at Case Western Reserve University, as well as the Pentagon's recent call for a national strategy of sustainability.[16] These and many others have the ability to change our narrative about having to choose between economic prosperity and a clean, green, sustainable future.

As Chuck Fowler, CEO of Fairmount Minerals, says, the mindset is not "do well, do good"—for that is the typical pathway of philanthropy (you can't give back until you do well, like a Gates or a Rockefeller). For Chuck that pathway is completely reversed to "Do Good. Do Well." It turns the

---

14. Chris Laszlo and Nadya Zhexembayeva, *Embedded Sustainability* (Stanford: Stanford University Press, 2011).
15. "IBM speeds push for 500-mile EV battery," see http://news.cnet.com/8301-11386_3-57417588-76/ibm-speeds-push-for-500-mile-ev-battery/; Ariel Schwartz, "Solar-Powered Water ATMs Provide Clean Drinking Water To The Thirsty," *Fast Company*, September 2011, http://www.fastcompany.com/1782224/solar-powered-water-atms-provide-clean-drinking-water-thirsty; Maria Trimarchi, "How Spray on Solar Panels Work," http://science.howstuffworks.com/environmental/green-tech/sustainable/spray-on-solar-panel.htm.
16. Global Prize for Business as an Agent of World Benefit at Case Western Reserve University, see http://www.openideo.com/open/business-impact-challenge/concepting/; Jim Dwyer, "A National Security Strategy That Doesn't Focus on Threats," *New York Times*, May 3, 2011.

equation around and requires heretical thinking, sustainable innovation, and solid, effective management. "For once you commit to building a better world through good business" says Chuck, "you always find a surprising, exciting way to do it through win-win imagination and innovation, and that's what leads to differentiation and success."

Vision of a Better World: *An Optimistic View*

Michele Hunt
DreamMakers

It is time for a new story for the future of humankind. People yearn for a vision that is inclusive and born out of our universally shared human values. Now more than ever we need a vision that inspires us to overcome our fears and compels us to recreate our institutions, businesses, organizations, and communities, into places that enable people and the planet to flourish. I believe the plethora of conflicts, chaos, confusion, and environmental degradation we witness today are symptoms of obsolete thinking and old systems breaking down under the weight of a growing awareness that radical, fundamental change is needed. The assumptions and archetypes on which we have built our societies are not sustainable. People are yearning for a new and better world. We are ready for a vision that transcends the artificial boundaries, classifications, and divisions we have constructed throughout history. On a very deep level people are beginning to understand that human beings have far more in common than they differ. We are discovering that there are deeply held values that resonate with most of us. I believe the technological innovations we are creating at a dizzying speed are driven by our hunger to:

- Connect with others
- Be heard
- Participate—contribute our talents and gifts towards something that matters to us
- Be recognized
- Learn and grow
- Live in harmony with each other and the planet
- Love and be loved

This profound shift in consciousness is rippling across our world, resulting in people creating new visions of how we can live, work, learn, and play together and how we view life. Unprecedented numbers of people are collaborating together to address global issues like poverty, AIDS, clean water, and education. The number of social networking groups innovating to solve big problems and create value in our world is astounding. The rapidly evolving social networking technology has enabled a movement that has become a powerful force for social, environmental, and political transformation, and it is unstoppable!

This new culture is most evident in young people. They are fundamentally different than past generations. Technology has given them easy access to a vast amount of information, the opportunity to learn and grow unfiltered and unencumbered by gatekeepers and boundaries, and the ability to connect and communicate numerous times a day with people all over the world. They understand the power of connections; they are linking with likeminded people to make change happen. Several months ago I had the privilege to give a keynote address at the Junior Enterprise Worldwide Conference in Brazil. There were over two thousand twentysomething entrepreneurs from Brazil and Europe in attendance. The theme of their conference was *One World One Network*. They are a part of a network of young people who have entrepreneurial enterprises working to solve real world problems. This generation shares a 'can do' attitude and are not afraid to take risks. They are not seeking or following the norm, they are creating it. They are redefining the definition of success. Profit is not their single aim; quality of life, social justice, environmental justice, and creating economic value appears to fuel this generation's passion. They see making a difference in the world and making money as inextricably connected.

There are compelling reasons for leaders of businesses, organizations, and institutions to catch up with this movement. Businesses in particular have a critical need to attract and retain the best and the brightest people to be successful. This requires businesses leaders to create environments that value people, foster participation and collaboration, and create a mission that is worthy of peoples' commitment. This will also require a different business model, one that does not fit neatly within our current interpretation of capitalism. Simon Mainwaring's book *We First* proposes a compelling argument why we must alter the current free market system from destructive capitalism to sustainable capitalism. He offers a new vision and specific ideas to "transform the entire private sector, corporations and consumers alike, into a force for global renewal." Mainwaring believes that "*We First* is neither anti-capitalist nor anti-wealth. It is pro-prosperity." He defines prosperity as "well-being for all" and believes that in the long view serving everyone's interest also serves our own (Mainwaring 2011, 5).

There are a growing number of companies and consumers that share this vision of prosperity. One powerful example is Patagonia, founded and led by

Yvon Chouinard, the 2013 recipient of the Inamori Ethics Prize. Patagonia exemplifies the business model of "doing well by doing good." In the book *The Responsible Company*, co-authored by Yvon Chouinard and his nephew Vincent Stanley, Vice President of Patagonia's wholesale division, they share their philosophy and practices. Patagonia is known for their commitment to the environment and they understand the need to create positive places for people to work. Another example is GOJO Industries, the inventors of Purell hand sanitizer and the leader in hand hygiene products. GOJO is in the business of "Saving lives and making life better through well-being solutions." They are committed to social and environment sustainability. "Sustainability is a purpose-driven commitment for GOJO," according to Joe Kanfer, CEO and Chairman. In addition to delivering both social and environmental benefits, GOJO's sustainability practices are contributing to its economic success via greater efficiencies, reduced costs, product innovation, and sustained growth, as illustrated by the company's annual double-digit growth over the last several years—all proof that integrating sustainability into a company's business strategy can deliver bottom-line benefits. To learn more see GOJO's Sustainability Report.[1]

There are numerous small businesses and entrepreneurs developing products and applications to engage consumers in this movement. Some Internet gaming developers are beginning to use social gaming to solve real-world problems. Zynga, the world's largest social gaming company, is developing games for the greater good. Zynga's 2012 revenues were $1.28 billion, with more than approximately 311 million monthly active users playing its games. In 2012 Zynga launched Zynga.org, the social impact arm of Zynga. The mission of Zynga.org is to help make the world a better place through games. They recently formed a partnership with Water.org to bring fresh water to real communities worldwide. They also inspired 1 million of their players to contribute more than $13 million through Zynga games. The money went to several non-profit organizations, including Direct Relief International, Save the Children, Habitat for Humanity, St. Jude Children's Research Hospital, Water.org, Wildlife Conservation Society, and World Food Programme.[2] There are also innovative mobile phone applications that enable consumers to become ethical shoppers. Barcoo, developed by a group of young Germans, is a free application that allows customers to point their mobile phones at the barcode on products while shopping to check prices, test reports, health,

---

1. The report is available at http://www.gojo.com/sustainability.
2. See http://www.zynga.org.

green, and sustainability information. They even make information available on the companies' social responsibility and the treatment of their employees.[3]

This evolved idea of making money by doing good is infectious and rapidly spreading to people of all ages and nations. We are seeing the emergence of conscious consumers, conscious employees, and conscious communities. People are making deliberate choices about the kind of businesses they want to work for. A growing number of consumers are using their purchase power to support ethical companies. Local governments and communities are becoming selective about the kind of companies they allow into their communities. We are seeing new constructs emerging: social businesses and social entrepreneurs are blurring the definition of for-profit and non-profit organizations. These examples are only the tip of the iceberg.

It probably has become apparent that I am an unapologetic optimist. My optimism does not come from idealistic notions of utopia or Pollyannaish sensibilities—it comes from my experience. I started my career as one of two of Michigan's first female probation officers to supervise adult male felons on probation in Detroit. I served as director of Michigan's only halfway house for female felons, and later became Michigan's first female deputy warden, leading programs for rehabilitation in an adult male prison. I served on the leadership team of a Fortune 500 company, served in President Clinton's administration, and I have owned my consulting company since 1995. In all of these experiences I have seen people transform their visions of hope into reality against tremendous obstacles. I have come to understand that people are extraordinary and capable of achieving the seemingly impossible.

Let me share a personal story. I worked for Herman Miller, a Fortune 500 global office furniture company, for thirteen years. This experience powerfully shaped my belief that when people mobilize around a compelling shared vision that is born out of their deeply held shared values and they are liberated to contribute their gifts, amazing things can happen. Herman Miller was ahead of its time—under the visionary leadership of Max De Pree, CEO and Chairman, we discovered it was possible to innovate for the greater good and be profitable. This bedrock principle led Herman Miller to phenomenal success. I had the privilege of serving on Herman Miller's senior leadership team for eight years as the Corporate Vice President for People. When Max first gave me this title I objected; I felt it was frivolous and a little corny. When I expressed my concerns, Max told me "People ought not to be regarded as human resources; money, facilities and equipment are resources—people are

---

3. See http://www.barcoo.com/en/w.

the heart and soul of this company." It took time for me to understand the deep meaning and awesome responsibility inferred by that title.

After many years of success, Herman Miller was challenged with an alarming number of global competitors, who were making our products faster, cheaper, and better. The world had changed but we had not; we learned the hard way that nothing fails like success. We had become arrogant and complacent—a sure sign of atrophy. Max De Pree was a wise, insightful leader and he called for a total company renewal that engaged every team in the company to help define the company's vision and values. The results were surprising and challenging. The people of Herman Miller wanted "to be a reference point for quality and excellence" in the world. The values they identified were:

- **Participation & Teamwork:** People had the right and responsibility to contribute their gifts to achieve the vision, and business goals, within the boundaries of our values.
- **Shared Ownership:** Employees had right to share in the risk and rewards of the business.
- **Valuing Uniqueness:** People were encouraged to bring their whole self to work and to contribute their uniqueness to help achieve the company's goals.
- **Family Social and Environmental Responsibility:** Work, family, and communities are inextricably connected. Our goal was to develop innovative solutions to support these important stakeholders.
- **Learning Organization:** Continual learning was a shared commitment.
- **Financial Soundness:** While essential, however, it was not the single aim of our work. It is the result of our commitment to our vision, values, and goals and our collective efforts.

Max then challenged us to change and align everything to serve the company's vision, values, and goals. We again engaged every team in the organization in a highly participative process to meet this challenge. We listened, learned, and we changed. After eighteen months Herman Miller was prospering again. The people in our organization were our greatest innovators and collaborators. The results were amazing; the people of Herman Miller collectively achieved the following:

- *Fortune*'s Most Admired Company
- Best Products by *BusinessWeek*

- One of *Fortune*'s top 10 Best Companies to Work For
- Best Company for Women
- Best Company for Working Mothers
- The Best Managed Company in the World—by the Bertelsmann Foundation.
- Most Environmentally Responsible Corporation—from *Fortune* and The White House
- A return to double-digit growth; we even enjoyed two stock splits in the following three years

Having the courage to include family, social, and environmental responsibility in our values brought out the good in us—and the best in us. These sets of values helped us to see the connections between the products and services we provided, and families, communities, and the environment. It helped us understand our responsibilities beyond profits. We became acutely aware that we were a part of a greater chain of events and a part of greater whole. Personally, it was an exciting, beautiful, and deeply fulfilling way to work.

Our commitment to our vision and values resulted in great benefits to everyone who was a part of the Herman Miller family. We attracted the best and the brightest people—not because we paid the most, but because of our commitment to the quality of life for all our stakeholders and our communities. People were proud to work at Herman Miller and like Peter Ducker always reminded us, "Your people are your greatest recruiters and public relations." Local governments and communities were constantly in pursuit of Herman Miller, wanting the company to expand into their communities. In the long view, we learned that leading with vision and values was not only the right thing to do, it made good business sense.

I was blessed to have worked at Herman Miller. Max De Pree believed "we must become, for all involved, a place of realized potential" (1989, 74). I experienced a very evolved form of leadership and saw the tremendous benefits of true inclusive capitalism at work. It helped to prepare me for the transformative times we are living through today. In the face of all the chaos, confusion, and ambiguity, I feel hopeful.

The growing number of people connecting to solve problems and create value in our world is becoming a global movement that is driving deep fundamental positive change. It is impossible to calibrate the impact this emerging mindset and the rapidly increasing technological developments will have on governments, businesses, and civil societies in three to five years; I believe it will be enormous. This is a historical game-changer never before realized in the history of humankind.

I used to think that the issues in our world were of such enormous magnitude that only the most optimistic, visionary people could even dream of tackling them; issues like grinding poverty, hate, prejudice, environmental degradation, and pervasive conflicts. But the 'pockets of hope' that I have seen have taught me a great deal about what is possible. One young man in a Puerto Rico community in Chicago expressed his view of the future.

> There are all of these pockets of hope developing all over the world; pretty soon there will be so many pockets of hope, that there will no longer be pockets—it will just be.

I believe most people feel on some level that the timing is right for the next stage of the evolution of humankind. We now have the tools to help us to see that we are all connected, interdependent, and part of a greater awesome system.

> A human being is a part of a whole, called by us the universe, a part limited in time and space.
>
> He experiences himself, his thoughts and feelings as something separated from the rest, a kind of optical delusion of his consciousness. This delusion is a kind of prison for us, restricting us to our personal desires and to affection for a few persons nearest to us.
>
> Our task must be to free ourselves from this prison by widening our circle of compassion to embrace all living creatures and the whole of nature in its beauty.
>
> Albert Einstein (1950)

These hopeful visions of our future are not impossible dreams—they are insights into the capacity of human potential. If we look around at the amazing things we have created, they were all considered impossible by the status quo at some time in their development. I believe the seeds that hold a vision for better world lie within each of us—waiting for the right time and conditions to germinate, grow, and flourish. I believe this is our time to create a better world.

References

De Pree, Max. 1989. *Leadership is an Art*. New York: Doubleday.

Einstein, Albert. 1950. Letter of 1950, as quoted in *The New York Times* (March 29, 1972) and *The New York Post* (November 28, 1972).

Mainwaring, Simon. 2011. *WE FIRST: How Brands & Consumers Use Social Media To Build A Better World*. New York: Palgrave Macmillan.

Exploring the Effect of The Ruggie Framework for Human Rights

Louise Rosenmeier & Neergaard
Consultant
Climate Change & Sustainability Services, KPMG
and
Peter Neergaard
Professor emeritus,
Copenhagen Business School

Introduction

In June 2011, the UN Human Rights Council endorsed the 'Protect, Respect, and Remedy' Framework (also referred to as the Ruggie Framework), which marked the ending of the six-year mandate of John Ruggie as the UN Secretary-General's special representative for business and human rights. The framework rests on three pillars:

1. The state duty to protect against human rights abuses by third parties, including businesses, through appropriate policies, regulation, and adjudication;
2. The corporate responsibility to respect human rights, which means to act with due diligence to avoid infringing on the rights of others; and
3. The state duty to create access to effective remedies, judicial and non-judicial, for victims.

This paper will focus on the responsibilities of companies. As stated by Dovey and Morrison, "we are entering an interesting and important time in the development of human rights in business. Real progress has been made....Very few businesses would state 'human rights are not our concern,' and a growing number are actively engaging the issue" (2007, 8). This paper will also address how and why Danish companies embrace the corporate responsibility of respecting human rights according to the second pillar. A human rights due diligence (DD) process is proposed as a means for companies to become "aware of and address the human rights harm they cause"

(Ruggie 2010). A DD process will differ across sectors and according to the size of the company, but should, according to Ruggie, contain at least the following four elements: 1) human rights policy, 2) assessing impacts, 3) integration, and 4) tracking performance.

This paper will address three research questions:
- What institutional pressures affect the Danish corporate approach to human rights?
- How can different contingencies contribute to explaining the behavior of different firms in their approach to human rights?
- How responsive are Danish companies in terms of implementing the Ruggie framework?

Theoretical perspective

Institutional theory is one of the building blocks of this paper, as it is useful in explaining how companies react to demands for human rights issues in the institutional environment. The theory departs from the assumption that institutionalized practices are adopted in order for an organization to gain legitimacy in the market place. "Institutionalization involves the process by which social processes, obligations, or actualities come to take on a rule like status in social thought and action" (Meyer and Rowan 1977, 341). By ruling on (permitting) some actions and ruling out (forbidding) others, the institutional setting is important in defining what is considered to be legitimate (Ostrom 1991; Pedersen et al. 2012). A distinction is often made between three types of isomorphic pressures defined as "a constraining process that forces one unit in a population to resemble other units that face the same set of environmental conditions," (DiMaggio and Powell 1983, 149). In coercive pressure, the main argument is that organizations must respond to the external demands, rules, and regulations in order to ensure political influence and legitimacy. The pressure to conform stems from regulating bodies and holders of critical resources. Mimetic processes are an organizational response to uncertainty in which organizations imitate each other. An organization will often look to an industry leader or a successful peer when faced with insecurity about an issue. Normative pressure stems from professionalization of the organization, i.e. similar educational background, training, and job functions, leading to similar company structures and practices (DiMaggio and Powell 1983).

Institutional theory has often been applied in studies of corporate social responsibility (CSR) (Doh and Guay 2006; Pedersen et al. 2012; Matten and Moon 2008). Matten and Moon (2008) argue that there are important national differences in CSR approaches, depending on the institutional context; as part of their argument, they discuss implicit and explicit CSR.

In Europe, the welfare state or government has been perceived as the prime provider of social welfare and benefits (Matten and Moon 2008). This has, according to the authors, contributed to a situation where European companies have been more reluctant to explicitly claim social responsibilities. Implicit CSR is therefore dominant in Europe, whereas explicit CSR is dominant in the United States, because of the different role of the government. However, they argue that there has been a recent rise in explicit CSR in Europe, which is a response to changes in the institutional environment.

The four steps in the DD process suggested by Ruggie will be used in the analysis (Ruggie 2010). These will be combined with the four steps outlined by Mamic (2005) in his study of global supply chain management. Mamic has a managerial perspective, proposing a management system for implementing a Code of Conduct (CoC). The combination of Ruggie (2010) and Mamic (2005) therefore enables a framework, rooted in the UN framework and the human rights DD process and combined with the necessary managerial steps for corporate management of implementation, which will be relevant when assessing the current state of human rights in Danish companies.

Similar to Ruggie's DD process, Mamic (2005) presented four steps to ensure efficient implementation and management of a CoC: 1) creating a shared vision, 2) developing understanding and ability, 3) implementing code in the organization, 4) feedback, improvement, and remediation. However, the second step in each of the respective models differs in scope and makes it necessary to split this step into two. This implies that assessing impacts (Ruggie) and developing understanding and ability (Mamic) will be respectively applied as prioritize and building capacity. Figure 1 presents the theoretical framework. The title of each step (i.e. setting the tone, prioritize, building capacity, walking the talk, and knowing and showing) is derived from the Business & Human Rights Initiative's DD guiding tool (2010).

Step 1: Setting the tone

The first key step is to develop a statement or policy (Ruggie 2010). This should clearly communicate the company's commitment to all stakeholders (Business & Human Rights Initiative 2010). At this point, it should also be considered how the policy should be implemented in the organisation: if it should be part of the company's mission or value statement, a stand-alone policy, or part of the CSR/sustainability policy.

Human rights are not an isolated part of CSR, and will most likely influence various issues such as working conditions, community relations, corruption, and environmental considerations (Buhmann et al. 2011). Ruggie (2010) emphasizes that no rights should be judged as inferior prior to an impact assessment; however, for the context of this paper, human rights will include both human rights and labor rights. The reasoning behind this is rooted in the close connection between the two. In the UN Global Compact (UNGC), human and labor rights are treated as separated entities, however, this separation is often difficult to make, as the two are highly interrelated. Labor rights are basically human rights applied to the workplace. Thus, in this paper, human rights are defined as including the four principles of labor rights from the UNGC: the freedom of association and the effective recognition of the right to collective bargaining, the elimination of all forms of forced and compulsory labor, the effective abolition of child labor, and the elimination of discrimination in employment and occupation, as well as general working conditions (hours, wages, safety).

Mamic's first step, creating a shared vision, entails the process of demonstrating a commitment and is an overall aim of the CoC, much similar to formulating a human rights policy. Stakeholder consultations and involvement—especially of suppliers or contractors who will have to carry out the standards—are central to this development. Stakeholder involvement is emphasised as a means to facilitate problem-solving and consensus building (Freeman 1984), and interested stakeholders play an active role in setting the norms, and should therefore be consulted to determine their expectations and how companies can meet them.

The conceptualisation of CSR—and human rights—and in particular, stakeholder involvement, is therefore vital in this phase. Companies undoubtedly already have many existing polices addressing human rights e.g., hiring schemes, health and safety, product safety. This initial step will, in most cases, not mean a complete overhaul of systems, but rather an assessment and systematisation of existing policies (Ruggie 2010).

Step 2: Prioritize

The second step in the human rights DD process is about assessing impacts, which means identifying the business areas where the company has an impact on human rights (Business & Human Rights Initiative 2010). The framework is very explicit about not deeming any human rights inferior prior to a risk assessment, but identifying the risk areas and prioritizing actions to mitigate them. The UN framework uses the concept 'sphere of impact,' arguing that a company's responsibility is valid whenever its activities have a potential or actual impact on human rights. Ruggie outlines three factors that determine the scope of the responsibility to respect human rights: the company's own activities, the company's relationships (with suppliers, contractors, customers, and governments), and the country and local context of operation (and its social, economic, and political factors) (2009).

Companies cannot be responsible for all human rights violations, but should thoroughly assess the contingent factors: its activities and industry, its supplier relations, and the context of its operations, to ensure that the risk areas will be addressed by the policy. A contingency approach seems valid in determine the relevant factors (Husted 2000; Galbraith 1973) and the different contingencies will be elaborated later in this paper. The impact assessment is crucial as a means between creating the human rights policy and setting up the appropriate systems for compliance.

Step 3: Capacity building

Resting on Mamic's second step, developing understanding and ability, this phase is about disseminating awareness, understanding, and implications of the human rights policy to all relevant internal and external stakeholders. It is thus about building internal capacity through communication and training of the relevant parties (Mamic 2005). Besides merely disseminating the content and principles of the policy, the implicated parties should also gain an understanding of why the issue is being addressed, what the implementation will mean for the specific employee, and how senior management has committed to it.

This step therefore encompasses the importance of building capabilities and knowledge throughout the company, in order for the policy implementation to be efficient and effective (ibid.). Due to the focus on companies' capabilities for taking on a more systematic approach to their work with human rights, it is relevant to introduce the resource-based view (RBV) of the firm (Wernerfelt 1984; Penrose 1959; Barney 1991). RBV argues that sustainable competitive advantage derives from resources and capabilities that are valuable, rare, imperfectly imitable, and nonsubstitutable (Barney et al. 2001). These resources can be viewed as bundles of both tangible and intangible assets.

Building capacity and ensuring training and communication throughout the company on a continuous basis ensures that the new policy will be disseminated to all relevant parties. It further ensures that all relevant parties have the sufficient knowledge and capabilities to act in accordance with the human rights policy.

Step 4: Walking the talk

This is the actual implementation step, where the human rights policy and its priority areas are put into practice. This is ultimately about assigning responsibility and resources to the different business operation and functions, and setting up relevant systems for compliance. Assigning responsibility to a specific person or department and having them drive it through the organization can be an initial starting point for a full corporate integration (Business & Human Rights Initiative 2010).

Although there might be some overlap between capacity building and integration in terms of dissemination, the difference lies in disseminating knowledge and training—i.e. capabilities—and disseminating the actual policy and systems for this. The capabilities mentioned above are therefore a necessary prerequisite for disseminating the policy and having people adhere to, comply with, and execute it. Coherent with the contingency argument above, Mamic (2005) reveals some features upon which the appropriate structure is contingent: size of company, existing reporting arrangements, budgets, organizational structure, and history and culture of the company. Creating a company culture that adheres to this new policy also involves a consideration of aspects such as recruitment, hiring practices, and incentive and appraisal systems, in order to ensure compliance through all functions—regardless of their individual risk level (Ruggie 2010).

Step 5: Knowing and Showing

Finally, in order to account for how the companies address their human rights impacts, they should be prepared to communicate this externally. This is especially evident for companies whose operations or operating contexts pose risks to human rights, and it is recommended that they report formally on how these risks are addressed (Human Rights Council 2011). It is therefore useful to revisit the impact assessment in determining what to report, as it highlights the highest risks to human rights, which will most likely be the area of greatest interest to various stakeholders (Business & Human Rights Initiative 2010). Internally, compliance and monitoring of performance in relation to the policy are critical for its functioning and effect. Without a proper data collection system the company will not be able to discover and act upon noncompliance incidents (Mamic 2005).

Hess introduced the three pillars of social reporting: disclosure, dialogue, and development. Through stakeholder dialogue the corporation identifies the necessary changes, alters its behavior and responds appropriately, and discloses new information reflecting the advanced corporate behavior, which starts the process over again (2008).

It is essential that the data collected is representative of the risk areas of the company and thus in coherence with the human rights impacts. The performance of a company is not only relevant for internal compliance, but constitutes an increasingly important factor in the external stakeholder dialogue and evaluation of a company. Reporting, and reporting on all relevant aspects—not just the favorable ones—is critical in order to provide a full picture of the company, and it further encourages stakeholder interaction and ultimately corporate moral development.

The theoretical framework is summarized in figure 1.

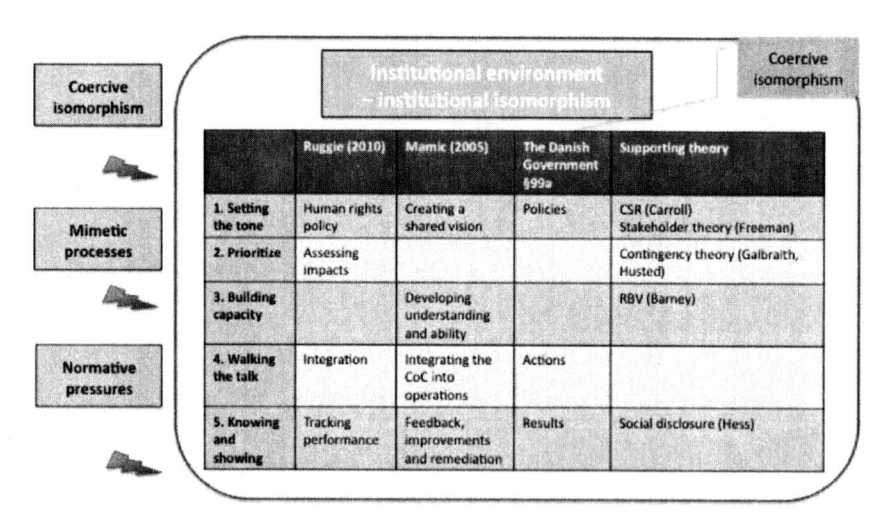

Figure 1 Theoretical Framework

Methodology

The research has been designed as mixed methods research, combining both quantitative and qualitative techniques (Johnson and Turner 2003).

The primary qualitative data set is composed of two groups of interviews. The first is composed of explorative interviews with Amnesty International and The Danish Confederation of Danish Industries (DI), which served to supplement the analysis of the institutional environment. Amnesty was chosen due to its status as an influential NGO focusing on human rights, and could therefore provide the more critical aspects on the current corporate approach to human rights. DI provided the business angle on human rights. As a strong industry organisation, DI also guides and assists companies on CSR issues—among these human rights. DI was therefore useful in highlighting the challenges and concerns businesses have regarding human rights. The interviews were semi-structured.

The second qualitative dataset was interviews with four selected companies, which provide a deeper understanding of the considerations and influences behind their human rights approach, and broaden the focus to include other potential factors contributing to the specific focus on human rights. The companies were selected as best in class from the sample of reporting companies (see below).

A quantitative survey of a selected sample of Danish companies' human rights reporting provides a representative picture of the current reporting practices and approaches to human rights. In December 2008, the Danish parliament introduced an amendment to the Danish Financial Statement Act, obligating all private as well as public enterprises to include information about their work on CSR in their annual reports. The law took effect with the 2009 financial year. The law applies to all companies in accounting class D (approx. 175 companies), which have securities traded on a regulated market in EU/EEA member states. Companies in accounting class C (approx. 1,250) shall report if they exceed at least two of the following criteria (DCCA 2010):

- Total assets/liabilities of 19.2 million Euro
- Net revenue of 38.3 million Euro
- An average of 250 full-time employees

Companies must account for CSR in three ways (DCCA 2010):
1. Policies: The company must disclose information on standards, guidelines, strategies, etc., that describe the company's work on CSR.
2. Actions: The company must describe how the CSR policies are translated into action and related management systems, evaluations, certification schemes, etc.
3. Results: The company must provide information on the achievements from the CSR work, as well as expectations for the future (if any). However, the company is not required to assess the financial results of CSR.

The quantitative analysis is based on a sample from a survey on CSR reporting for the first year of mandatory reporting (Neergaard and Pedersen 2010). The sample constitutes 10 percent of large Danish companies in accounting class C (125 companies) and D (17 companies). The companies were randomly sampled from the gross lists of the Danish Commerce and Companies Agency's list of those accounting classes (for more information on the methodology see Neergaard and Pedersen 2011).

In 2011, a similar study was made, but with a focus on tracking the changes and improvements. In order to ensure a longitudinal study, this report is based on the same sample of companies as in 2010 (Neergaard and Pedersen 2011). From 2009 to 2010, 5 companies dissolved and another no longer falls under the legal requirement due to a decline in its turnover. The total population of the 2011 survey is therefore 136 companies (Neergaard and Pedersen 2011). Of the 136 companies, 119 reported on CSR, meaning that 17 companies did not comply with the law. Of those 17 companies, 15 do not work with CSR, bringing the number of companies working with and reporting on CSR down to 104 companies. Among these, 74 had policies on CSR and 31 had policies regarding human rights. These 31 companies compose the sample for the second part of the analysis—the quantitative analysis of the companies' current human rights approach.

In order to explore the effect of contingencies explaining the behavior of companies, the 31 companies are grouped into two, depending on the risk level of the operational context. One group—the low risk—(13 companies) operates primarily in Denmark or Western Europe. The other group—the high risk—(18 companies) operates globally and in developing countries associated with a higher level of human rights risks.

Findings

The findings will be reported according to the research questions addressing the institutional pressure, the contingencies explaining the behavior of different firms, and how responsive Danish firms are in terms of implementing the Ruggie framework.

Institutional pressure

The most compelling institutional pressure in terms of broader CSR issues was the Financial Act §99a, which sought to make companies conscious of the responsibility they hold and seems to have encouraged a more structured, extended, and explicit approach to CSR. Reports on its effect showed an increase in both the quantity and quality of social reporting and also in terms of human rights reporting. According to a global survey conducted by KPMG, CSR reporting among the hundred largest companies in the thirty-four countries studied has increased from 53 percent in 2008 to 64 percent in 2011. For Denmark alone, the development over the three years showed a remarkable increase from 24 percent to 91 percent (KPMG 2011). This drastic increase can be attributed to an increased public attention to CSR, but more likely to the effect of the Financial Act. Looking at human rights and labor standards alone, there is a significant increase in companies reporting these actions. These figures have increased from 16 percent in 2009 to 38 percent in 2010 for human rights, and from 16 percent to 35 percent for labor standards. Thus, as the figures for both the quantity and quality of the reports are increasing, this could indicate the positive influence and effect of the act.

The four company interviews further confirmed the influential character of the act, as three of them had found it necessary to strengthen and elaborate on their (partly) existing initiatives. The act has therefore not only been coercive in terms of companies disclosing CSR information, but also in terms of advancing the foundation of the disclosures. This is perceived as a vital element in a more explicit CSR approach (Matten and Moon 2008). The UN framework, despite its incorporation and support from both national and inter-governmental institutions such as the Danish Government, DI, Amnesty, the EU, and OECD, was not perceived as a distinguished external pressure by the companies interviewed. This can be ascribed to the newness of the framework and the fact that the businesses were unsure what compliance would entail. The trend among Danish companies in terms of human rights has hitherto been highly standardized and generic, this is also confirmed through the analysis of the human rights reporting (see next section).

Through mimetic processes and normative pressures, the UNGC has reached an almost mandatory role when working with CSR. In 2009, 13 percent of the companies studied were members of UNGC. In 2010, the number increased to 20 percent (DCCA 2011). Despite its six principles concerning human rights, these rights are primarily interpreted as pertaining to the working environment and health and safety. This implicit approach to the 'core' human rights is rooted in the regulative Danish context, where the state has strongly enforced these rights, and where company initiatives have not been needed. Both Amnesty and DI further emphasised that there is a resistance among Danish companies to explicitly claim social responsibilities and that the companies would rather ensure their own house is in order without necessarily having extensive systems or procedures in place and without explicitly having to report these activities. The act, and now the UN framework challenge this, as greater efforts are required to disclose the activities, and more importantly, to be fully aware of and control the impacts of their business. Nonetheless, although Danish companies are more inclined to implicitly work with human rights—whether by not disclosing information or by the lack of formal policies in place—the UN framework has now imposed on all companies that through DD they must be capable of documenting their impacts and actions. As this advances, it is most likely that these efforts will be included in the social disclosures, which will serve as an inspiration for other companies that will then mimic the efforts, and the UN framework will slowly become institutionalized.

How different contingencies contribute to explain company behavior

From the analysis of the samples reporting on human rights, it quickly became apparent that the extent of human rights efforts varies greatly. By dividing the sample into two groups (risk and non-risk), depending on the geographical context of their business operation, it was possible to draw some general patterns and differences in how human rights are approached.

The entire risk group had a human rights statement (step 1), whereas this was only the case for approximately 40 percent of the companies in the non-risk group. Without exception, working environment and health and safety were the most frequently mentioned issues for both groups. From the analysis it is apparent that the human rights work is highly contingent upon the industry and geographical context. This implies that some of the risk-group companies were more explicit about the first six principles of the UNGC and listed these in terms of the company's commitment. The non-risk group is not facing issues regarding freedom of association and collective bargaining for employees or eliminating child labor, as these are ensured through national legislation. This group therefore placed less emphasis on explicating how the issues were connected to their business.

Stakeholder dialogue is essential in order to target efforts and gain feedback and knowledge from stakeholders concerning specific issues. The ability to determine the expectations of the stakeholders is important to companies. An open dialogue was emphasised by a larger part of the risk group than by the non-risk group (61 percent and 23 percent) and was for the latter primarily dealt with in terms of employees. This can be seen as a reflection of the 'safe' environment of operation in the non-risk group, where the understanding of standards of business conduct is more even across the business and stakeholder groups.

In terms of assessing impact, building capacity, integrating and involving management, and implementing the necessary systems and procedures to ensure policy execution, the risk group was leading the way (steps 2–5). The risk group generally showed a more tailored and integrated approach to all five steps of the analysis, through company-specific tools, various training methods, and a higher degree of transparency in terms of reporting on results. Given the context of their operations there is also a much higher urgency for these companies to take on a more proactive and extensive human rights approach than for the companies in the non-risk group. A few companies in the risk group stand out, those who have systematically assessed and defined their risk areas; have created extensive human rights policies; have numerous systems, procedures, and actions in place; and who openly report about their progress and performance.

The nature of human rights makes reporting results and achievements a more complicated matter than, for example, environmental issues, which have been on the public agenda for several years, and which might be more tangible and easier to collect data about (step 5). Yet, when looking closer at the sample, the majority of the companies were able to report on their results. The reported results generally adhered to the described policies and actions, but depending on the industry and context of the company, however, they primarily included a narrow range of indicators concerning occupational injuries and accidents. The limitation of primarily reporting and dealing with accidents means that a large group of stakeholders are not receiving the information they are most concerned about, and have no chance of engaging in a constructive and fact-based dialogue with the company. Thus, a more explicit focus and dedication—especially from the risk group—concerning other human rights perspectives that they face in the global world (child and forced labor, unionized employees, etc.) would provide a clearer and more correct presentation of the company, and will also be required by the UN framework. As Hess and Dunfee (2007) argue, when information is left out, stakeholders might get the impression that the company is trying to hide something, thus, although it might be difficult, the companies should strive towards including *all* information on *all* the initiatives and actions they take, even if these have not yet proved successful. The risk group should focus greater attention on addressing their policies towards the governance gaps that exist between the states, i.e. the non-enforced laws or regulations concerning freedom of association, child or forced labor, working hours, etc. As the risk group works in a remarkably different context than the non-risk group, this should be clearly reflected through their reporting, too. Although, as we have seen, differences do exist between these two groups, there is definitely room for improvement and greater focus on measuring the effect of the numerous manuals and policies the risk group have in place. That being said, the analysis showed that a few of the leading companies are actually very far ahead in terms of having addressed their risk areas, developed tools for mitigating the effect of these areas, and the ablility to track their performance.

Thus, Ruggie's claim that most companies already work with human rights without necessarily being aware of it and that a human rights DD process does not necessarily force companies to start from scratch, is confirmed in this analysis. However, there is still a significant need for a more systematic approach to human rights, and to fully recognise the areas impacted. The use of risk evaluations and impact assessments were only seen in a few cases, however, with mandatory reporting on CSR, it is most likely that the companies will work towards improving their reports from year to year, and seek inspiration from some of the leading companies. The wide use of the UNGC could also positively affect the number of companies explicitly claiming human rights responsibility, as the compulsory UNGC Communication of Progress (COP) report ensures that progress and initiatives are described.

How responsive are Danish companies in terms of implementing the framework?

Respecting human rights have, prior to the effectuation of §99a, been an implicit notion of how Danish companies do business, but §99a was able to foster a more explicit approach to overall CSR, and herein also to human rights (Matten and Moon 2008). However, as mentioned, the human rights issue is still primarily interpreted as working environment and safety, and as such does not explicitly target the various other rights. The interviews with the front runner companies disclose that only one company planned to initiate a DD process in 2012, the remaining companies had no concrete plans as to when and how to address the framework. It seems to be rooted in a common misinterpretation of the framework as something companies sign up for or choose to embrace if it is applicable to their activities. There also seems to be a general level of confusion concerning its extent, and the intimidation of suddenly being held accountable for a much broader range of human rights issues than those previously considered. The hesitance towards the framework can further be seen in the context of the general assumption that it might not be relevant to the specific business area, or that human rights are already managed through the focus on working environment and safety. This reinforces the implicit approach to human rights, and the perception that by virtue of the Danish regulatory environment, the companies are well aware and familiar with how to deal with human rights. However, this is not the case, and especially the risk group must recognize the distinct conditions they operate under, where the corporate responsibility in some cases is the only institution protecting human rights. The indecisiveness towards implementing the framework is therefore a response to uncertainty, to a lesser extent due to how this task should be accomplished, but more in terms of what it will imply. Only one company is ready to embrace the framework in 2012 due to normative pressure. Thus, the responsiveness and preparedness for Danish companies are relatively low at this point but it is evidently rooted in insufficient knowledge of the content and scope of the framework.

Conclusion

No doubt, human rights are important for Danish companies to respect and it has always been a concern which they have inherently dealt with. The unfamiliarity with having to explicitly and actively target issues such as employees' right to organize and collectively bargain and forced labor and child labor can be attributed the Danish or European origin of a state-regulated system enforcing these rights.

However, as the playing field is changing and an increasing amount of companies operate globally, there is a need for a more managed and explicit approach. As the situation is now, the companies are not particularly concerned about the UN framework, and a precondition for changing this seems to be the creation and expansion of a normative base that can build the necessary capacity to fully comprehend the framework's implications. Particularly, it is important to change the perception of the framework as something that should be adopted, to what it really is: a common baseline for companies' human rights responsibility. The institutional field of CSR in Denmark is currently changing towards a more explicit notion, and in line with this, the UN framework has created an expected standard of conduct where companies worldwide are obliged to take a more explicit responsibility for human rights. The UN framework does not imply that companies should improve or advance on human rights disclosure, however, in light of §99a and the increasing transparency of companies' CSR activities, a few frontrunners of disclosure can potentially inspire and guide other companies' internal work with human rights, and as thus be a step towards institutionalising the full palette of human rights issues that companies have an impact on. As both Danish and national initiatives are currently encouraging and integrating the UN framework in common guidelines and institutions, its presence will be indisputable, and eventually win over the hesitating Danish companies in its institutionalization.

References

Barney, Jay. 1991 "Firm Resources and Sustained Competitive Advantage." *Journal of Management* 17 (1).

Barney, Jay, Mike Wright, and David J. Ketchen Jr. 2001. "The resource-based view of the firm. Ten years after 1991." *Journal of Management* 27: 625. DOI: 10.1177/014920630102700601.

Buhmann, K., L. Roseberry, and M. Morsing. 2011. *Corporate Social and Human Rights Responsibilities Global, Legal and Management Perspectives*. New York: Palgrave Macmillan.

Business & Human Rights Initiative. 2010. *How to do Business with Respect for Human Rights: A Guidance Tool for Companies*. The Hague: Global Compact Network Netherlands.

DCCA (Danish Commerce and Companies Agency). 2010. "Corporate Social Responsibility and Reporting in Denmark: Impact of the Legal Requirement for Reporting on CSR in the Danish Financial Statements Act." Accessed 8/15/2012. http://www.eogs.dk/graphics/publikationer/CSR/CSR_and_Reporting_in_Denmark.pdf.

DiMaggio, Paul, J. and Walter W. Powell. 1983. "The Iron Cage Revisited: Institutional Isomorphism and Collective Rationality in Organizational Fields." *American Sociological Review* 48.

Doh, J. P., and T. R. Guay. 2006. "Corporate Social Responsibility, Public Policy, and NGO activism in Europe and the United States: An Institutional-Stakeholder Perspective." *Journal of Management Studies*, 43: 47–73.

Dovey, Kathryn and John Morrison. 2007. "Opening Perspective on the Case for Human Rights in Business." In *Embedding Human Rights in Business Practice II*. United Nations Global Compact and the Office of the UN High Commissioner for Human Right.

Freeman, R. Edward. 1984. *Strategic Management: A Stakeholder Approach*. Boston: Pitman.

Galbraith, J. 1973. *Designing Complex Organizations*. Reading, MA: Addison-Wesley.

Hess, David. 2008. "The Three Pillars of Corporate Social Reporting as New Governance Regulation: Disclosure, Dialogue, and Development." *Business Ethics Quarterly* 18 (4).

Hess, Davis and Thomas W. Dunfee. 2007. "The Kasky-Nike Threat to Corporate Social Reporting. Implementing a Standard of Optimal Truthful Disclosure as a Solution." *Business Ethics Quarterly* 17.

Human Rights Council. 2011. "Report of the Special Representative of the Secretary-General on the Issue of Human Rights and Transnational Corporations and Other Business Enterprises, John Ruggie: Guiding Principles on Business and Human Rights: Implementing the United Nations "Protect, Respect, and Remedy" Framework."

Husted, Brian W. 2000. "A Contingency Theory of Corporate Social Performance." *Business Society* 39 (1).
Johnson, B., and L. A. Turner. 2003. "Data Collection Strategies in Mixed Methods Research." In *Handbook of Mixed Methods Social and Behavioral Research*, edited by A. Tashakkori and C. Teddlie. Thousand Oaks, CA: Sage Publications.
KPMG. 2011. "KPMG International Survey of Corporate Responsibility Reporting."
Mamic, Ivanka. 2005. "Managing Global Supply Chain: The Sports Footwear, Apparel and Retail Sector." *Journal of Business Ethics* 59 (1).
Matten, Dirk and Jeremy Moon. 2008. "'Implicit' and 'Explicit' CSR: A Conceptual Framework for a Comparative Understanding of Corporate Social Responsibility." *Academy of Management Review* 33 (2).
Meyer, John W. and Brian Rowan. 1977. "Institutionalized Organizations: Formal Structure as Myth and Ceremony." *American Journal of Sociology* 82 (2).
Neergaard, Peter and Janni Thusgaard Pedersen. 2010. "Kvantitativt studie af virksomheders efterlevelse af årsregnskabslovens § 99a: og deres generelle regnskabspraksis." Center for Corporate Social Responsibility, Copenhagen Business School.
Neergaard, Peter and Janni Thusgaard Pedersen. 2011. "Kommunikation af samfundsansvar: Kvantitativt studie af virksomheders erfaringer med årsregnskabslovens § 99a for regnskabsåret 2010." Center for Corporate Social Responsibility, Copenhagen Business School.
Ostrom E. 1991. "Rational Choice Theory and Institutional Analysis: Toward Complementarity." *American Political Science Review* 85 (1): 237–43. DOI: 10.2307/1962889.
Pedersen, E. R. G., P. Neergaard, J. T. Pedersen, and W. Gwozdz. 2013 "Conformance and Deviance: Company Responses to Institutional Pressures for Corporate Social Responsibility Reporting." *Business Strategy and the Environment.* DOI: 10.1002/bse.1743.
Penrose, E. T. 1958. *The Theory of the Growth of the Firm.* New York: Wiley.
Ruggie, John. 2009. "Business and Human Rights: Towards Operationalizing the 'Protect, Respect, and Remedy' Framework: Report of the Special Representative of the Secretary-General on the Issue of Human Rights and Transnational Corporations and Other Business Enterprises, John Ruggie." UN Document A/HRC/11/13. www2.ohchr.org/English/bodies/hrcouncil/docs/11session/A.HRC.11.13.pdf.
Ruggie, John. 2010. Business and Human Rights: Further Steps Toward the Operationalization of the 'Protect, Respect, And Remedy' Framework: Report of the Special Representative of the Secretary-General on the Issue of Human Rights and Transnational Corporations and Other Business Enterprises, John Ruggie." UN Document: A/HRC/14/27. www.reports-and-materials.org/Ruggie-report-2010.pdf.
Wernerfelt, B. 1984. "A Resource Based View of the Firm." *Strategic Management Journal* 5: 171–80.

Is There Room for Ethical Leadership in Today's Business Environment?

Charlene Zietsma
Associate Professor, Ann Brown Chair of Organization Studies, Schulich School of Business, York University

Introduction: The Need for Ethical Leadership

As the Occupy movement signifies, there is a growing demand around the world that corporate leaders must behave more responsibly, and that more equality is required in the distribution of societal benefits. The slogan of movement members—"We are the 99 percent"—signifies the frustration felt by the 'ordinary' majority, which has seen a long-term slide in their economic well-being at the same time as the top 1 percent of society's wealthiest individuals has experienced significant increases in net worth. Furthermore, the anger experienced by those suffering from the many ill effects of the global financial crisis, which began in 2008, has been fueled by fury over the apparent lack of penalties for the architects of the financial crisis. Indeed, several of the firms who took government bailouts continued to pay exorbitant bonuses to the very executives that guided the firms into trouble, while hundreds of thousands lost their jobs around the world. The Occupy movement quickly became an international phenomenon, as 82 countries experienced protests and over 600 communities experienced protests in the US alone.[1]

While the financial crisis galvanized public cynicism and disgust with corporate immorality, demands for ethical leadership, defined as "the demonstration of normatively appropriate conduct…and the promotion of such conduct to followers" (Brown, Treviño, and Harrison 2005, 120), have been building for some time (Mendonca and Kanungo 2007). Scandals and blatant corporate greed at the expense of society have been revealed in recent years at firms such as Enron, WorldCom, Arthur Anderson, AIG, Lehman Brothers, Bre-X, Barings Bank, and tobacco companies. Unethical behavior by executives does not appear to be limited to "a few bad apples" (Bakan 2004); experi-

---

1. Information about the Occupy movement was gathered from Wikipedia: http://en.wikipedia.org/wiki/Occupy_movement. Accessed March 29, 2013.

ments with 179 top executives and 203 financial controllers in the US found that 47 percent and 41 percent of them, respectively, would artificially inflate profits (fraudulently) to increase their odds of promotion (Brief, Dukerich, Brown and Brett 1996). When *Harvard Business Review* surveyed its readers, 80 percent of them indicated the companies they worked for had unethical practices (Morgenson 2004, A-12). Unethical leadership is widespread, even outside of business: three dozen school officials and teachers in Atlanta were indicted for helping children cheat in standardized test scores in order to improve their schools' performance on the tests, earning bonuses as a result (Brumback 2013). A program of research by McCabe and colleagues over a number of years has found that across academic disciplines in universities and colleges cheating is widespread, but business students cheat more than others (McCabe and Treviño 1993; 1997; McCabe, Treviño, and Butterfield, 2001). Even among graduate students, the percentage of cheaters remains high: 56 percent of business students and 47 percent of nonbusiness students admitted to cheating in the prior year, usually perceiving that others were doing it, so they should too (McCabe, Butterfield, and Treviño 2006, 298).

Why do we see such unethical behavior in general, and in business in particular? After all, businesses are designed to create societal value by enabling the efficient production and distribution of goods and services. A business that creates value for its customers is a business that will continue to have customers in the long run.

Economic Self-interest Seeking as a Damaging Focus of Attention

Yankelovich (2007) and others claim that problems with business ethics make visible broader cultural problems associated with the rise in power of free market capitalism or market liberalism since the 1960s and 1970s, and the assumption, based in economics, that self-interest seeking is normatively good because it is economically efficient. Changes in values "have promoted a strikingly self-centered form of individualism that encourages people to look out for themselves even at the expense of others" (Yankelovich 2007, 14). While Adam Smith's version of capitalism had an explicitly moral component, this morality has faded into the background as the guiding capitalist logic seems to be more rooted in the directives of Milton Friedman, which focus simply on the business of business as profit-seeking within the confines of the law (Friedman 1970). Most business decision making models taught by business schools and used in companies focus purely on profit seeking (Bauer and Derwall 2011). In North America, business executives owe fiduciary duties to shareholders, which have been interpreted broadly as requiring executives to maximize profits. However, as Yankelovich argues, "The typical shareholder is a thirty-two-year-old fund manager who couldn't care less about your stock and will dump it in a nano-second if your quarterly profits fall by pennies a share" (2007, 15).

Many studies have shown how this economic logic, focused on business efficiency if not profit maximization, has been applied to multiple sectors, including health care (Arndt and Bigelow 2000; Reay and Hinings 2005), arts and culture organizations (Allmendiger and Hackman 1996), and previously nonprofit activities (Tracey, Phillips and Jarvis 2011), as a matter of survival. When this logic, based on economic self-interest, has become pervasive within society, is it any wonder that individuals feel it is only rational to pursue narrow economic self-interest themselves? Self-interested behavior, given its valorization in the media, popular culture, business schools, and elsewhere, seems to be the only rational way to avoid being a sucker when others are likely to take advantage of you when seeking their own self-interest.

As companies increasingly chase profitability in a self-interest seeking world, a vicious competitive spiral to the bottom occurs in many sectors. Many consumers, seeking their own interests, focus on purchasing at the lowest price, which favors retailers and suppliers with scale economies. As these retailers and suppliers gain more business, they increase their scale further, driving out smaller competitors and creating a set of goods that are increasingly homogeneous and commodity-like (Shell 2009). As retailers gain power, they increasingly squeeze suppliers to reduce the wholesale prices of their goods each year. Because retailers are facing 'hypercompetitive' environments with other retailers, they pass savings onto consumers (and pay their own employees low wages to keep their prices low) in order to maintain their growth through volume.

As pricing pressures increase, suppliers cheapen the quality of their goods and pay their employees less in order to meet the price points that the powerful, hypercompetitive retailers are demanding. As the quality and price of goods go down, consumers buy the same items more often, replacing items that break or that are so cheap they are virtually disposable. In addition, as the quality of goods goes down, consumers experience satiation from getting a good deal, rather than from the products themselves. In order to experience satiation, they must continue to get good deals, and because they are experiencing declines or stagnation in their real purchasing power (due to wage pressures), they continue to focus on low-priced goods, but must engage in buying more often in order to feel satiated. On the consumer side, we end up with overconsumption of cheap goods—goods which overfill landfills and don't make people happier. The television show *Hoarders* shows the ridiculous extreme to which this overconsumption can go.

On the business side, there is another dark consequence to this cycle. The concentration of power in the hands of the megaretailers and their megasuppliers creates a political force that subverts the democratic process. These large firms donate to political candidates, lobby politicians, and control so much economic activity that passing regulations that curtail these firms' activities is next to impossible. Indeed, Noam Chomsky has suggested that democracy is radically incompatible with our existing form of capitalism, as "control of government is narrowly concentrated at the peak of the income scale, while the large majority 'down below' has been virtually disenfranchised."[2] What this means is that Friedman's profit-maximization within the law is practically and ethically hollow. There are very limited opportunities to create laws that protect societal interests.

Is There Room for Ethical Leadership in a Highly Competitive Business Environment?

While the paradigm of profit maximization dominates, there are countervailing trends in today's business environment that favor more ethical leadership of companies. When considering a firm's external environment, trends that support ethical leadership include the increasing effectiveness of social activism, market incentives associated with socially responsible positioning, the impact of ethical or socially responsible investment, and the nascent but growing trend for companies to actively discourage investment from investors who focus on quarterly profits above all else.

The Trend Toward Increasing Social Activism

Easier access to information means that corporate behavior is now more visible than ever. Reductions in the cost of communications, and the democratization of communication through the internet and social networking, means that activists are able to share the job of monitoring companies and spread the news of transgressions to a larger audience. For example, when CNN recently covered the Steubenville, Ohio, rape trial in a way that was

---

2. Chomsky, N. 2013. "Will Capitalism Destroy Civilization?" *Truthout* Op-Ed: March 7. Accessed March 31, 2013. http://www.truth-out.org/opinion/item/14980-noam-chomsky-will-capitalism-destroy-civilization.

perceived to be excessively supportive of the rapists and dismissive of the victim, activists created an online petition demanding an apology that attracted over a quarter of a million signatures within a few days.[3]

Because of increasing transparency and activist targeting, there are more likely to be substantial reputational penalties for unethical or socially undesirable behavior, especially for firms that are large and generally have strong brand images, as these are the firms that are disproportionately targeted. Activist targeting can have an impact in several ways. First, it can increase managers' awareness of the moral content of issues, a first step in applying ethical leadership (Mendonca and Kanungo 2007). Second, it can create market sanctions: moral misconduct may preclude access to certain markets or may damage a carefully cultivated brand image. For example, mining companies with poor reputations for dealing with communities or environmental concerns may be unable to obtain rights to mine in certain countries. Third, because the managers of targeted firms often have very positive views of the firm's identity (and by reflection, their own), they may be distressed by public critique and may work to reduce it. Fourth, when these large firms change their behavior by, for example, adopting new supply chain standards or stakeholder engagement practices, other firms tend to follow, either because other firms are benchmarking best practices, or because the targeted firms later pressure the industry association or the government to change practices and/or regulations to level the playing field (Winn, Zietsma, and McDonald 2008).

The Trend Toward Market Incentives Associated with Socially Responsible Positioning

While market incentives, such as price premia associated with good ethical behavior, may also be available, there is evidence that many consumers will not pay a substantial premium for ethical or green goods (see, e.g., Devinney 2011; Gershooff and Irwin 2011). Because investing in highly ethical practices takes time and energy, it may be seen as irrational to invest heavily in ethical leadership. Yet, anecdotal evidence suggests that ethical leadership helps to build a positive brand image for differentiated companies, and there are numerous examples of firms that have taken an ethical stand and have strong financial performance, even if customers don't explicitly acknowledge they are buying because of ethics. Companies like Tom's of Maine, Timberland,

---

3. Two high school football players in Steubenville, Ohio, were found guilty in an incident where they repeatedly raped an unconscious girl and posted footage of the assault on the internet. The petition was found at: http://www.change.org/petitions/cnn-apologize-for-your-disgusting-coverage-of-the-steubenville-rapists. Accessed March 29, 2013.

Starbucks, Apple, Ben & Jerry's, and Trader Joe's (Hawthorne 2012) obtain substantial price premia because of their strong brand images, part of which is based on their ethical stance. Furthermore, when ethical companies like these change hands, acquirers seem to pay a significant acquisition premium (Hawthorne 2012). Many of these firms earn superior returns.

The Trend Toward Increasing Ethical/Socially Responsible Investment

As of 2010, approximately 12 percent of professionally managed investments in the United States were invested in ethical or socially responsible investments.[4] Socially responsible investment specialists select investments based on social and environmental screens, file shareholder resolutions to attempt to influence firms' social performance, engage in policy work, and invest directly in high impact community development initiatives.[5] While the performance of investment funds varies widely, a number of ethical or socially responsible investment vehicles perform at the top of the industry, and it appears one can invest with one's conscience and not pay a significant financial penalty. Given that societal expectations for social and environmental performance seem to be growing over time, increasing the risk associated with irresponsible or unethical corporate behavior, investment returns for socially responsible investments are likely to improve relative to investments in irresponsible firms in the future. The availability of capital that is actively supporting ethical leadership should increase the supply of ethically-led firms.

The Trend Toward Seeking Investor Alignment

There is a nascent but growing trend for companies to actively state that they will be making decisions based on longer term criteria more consistent with their social values, rather than focusing on short term profits. In doing so, they are actively warning short term investors to sell their stock or to not invest in the first place. Unilever is a high profile example of a firm that eschews company-provided earnings guidance, and that warned investors that the company would be managing to the mission rather than for short term results.[6] Unilever's profitability has been very strong. When a Starbucks investor expressed concern that the firm's support of gay marriage would hurt its sales at its annual general meeting, CEO Howard Schultz stated "Not every decision is an economic decision…The lens in which we are

---

4. http://en.wikipedia.org/wiki/Socially_responsible_investing. Accessed Mar. 29, 2013.
5. http://www.huffingtonpost.com/amy-domini/want-to-make-a-difference_b_834756.html. Accessed March 30, 2013.
6. Keynote address on responsible capitalism by Unilever CEO Paul Polman at Schulich School of Business, February 15, 2013.

making that decision is through the lens of our people. We employ over 200,000 people in this company and we want to embrace diversity of all kinds." Pointing to the 38 percent return on investment that Starbucks was earning, Schultz encouraged the investor to sell his shares if he felt he could do better elsewhere.[7] Stories like this one, and like Unilever's Lifebuoy soap campaign to reduce childhood deaths due to diarrhea in developing countries, are promoted virally through social media by supporters not affiliated with the companies.

Beyond these high profile examples, a broader trend is taking shape in the form of Benefit Corporations, or B-Corps, or their like in other countries, as well as a variety of mission-driven social and sustainable enterprises. A B-Corp is a firm which is required by law to create societal value along with shareholder value, by considering how its decisions affect employees, the community, and the environment.[8] The relatively new organizational form is growing, with approximately 670 B-Corps certified in 24 countries by early 2013.[9] Investors in B-Corps are explicitly aware that the social mission is important, and profits will not dominate the organization's purpose. Indeed, Hart (2011), in describing what he calls third-generation (sustainable) corporations, claims that profit maximization is not a purpose at all, but an outcome.

> It is now becoming clear that the best way to maximize profits over the long term is not to make them the primary goal (Mackey 2009). Profits are like happiness: a by-product of other things like having a strong sense of purpose, meaningful work, and deep relationships. Those who focus obsessively on their own happiness are usually narcissists—and end up miserable. Third-generation corporations, therefore, understand that you make money by doing good things rather than the other way around. (Hart 2011, 653–54)

Effects of Ethical Leadership on Employees

While external trends provide avenues and rationales for engaging in ethical leadership, it is clear that employees also benefit from their involvement in firms practicing ethical leadership. In line with the quotation above, and summarizing positive-psychology research, McGonigle (2011) notes that having

---

7. http://www.upworthy.com/starbucks-ceo-serves-a-grande-cup-of-shut-the-hell-up-to-anti-gay-marriage-activ, media clip attributed to *Puget Sound Business Journal*. Accessed March 29, 2013.
8. http://en.wikipedia.org/wiki/Benefit_corporation. Accessed March 30, 2013.
9. http://socialfinance.ca/blog/post/doing-well-by-doing-good-the-b-corporation-way. Accessed March 30, 2013.

a guiding and meaningful purpose, the chance of success, satisfying work, and social connection is intrinsically motivating and leads to happiness. A significant contributor to the meaning employees experience comes from helping others.

A stream of work by Adam Grant and colleagues provides tangible evidence of this effect (c.f., Grant 2012; 2007; 2008). Grant studied employees at a call center whose purpose was to obtain funding for scholarships. A student who had benefited from a scholarship funded through the call center's efforts gave a 10 minute presentation to call center employees, talking about the difference the scholarship had made in his life. As reported by the *New York Times Magazine*, a month later, "workers were spending 142 percent more time on the phone and bringing in 171 percent more revenue, even though they were using the same script. In a subsequent study, the revenues soared by more than 400 percent" (Dominus 2013). This contact with beneficiaries made employees realize the prosocial nature of their work, which helped them see the meaning associated with their jobs (Grant 2007; Grant, Campbell, Chen, Cottone, Lapedis and Lee 2007). Their perceived prosocial impact was associated with more effort, more persistence, and better job performance (Grant et al. 2007; Grant 2008). In another study, Grant and colleagues found that employees at Borders who contributed to a fund for the support of other employees in need showed higher increased commitment to their employer than the recipients of the fund. They stated: "when employees act on the opportunity to give, they are able to see themselves and the organization as more caring, which is likely to strengthen their commitment to the organization that manages the program" (Grant, Dutton, and Russo 2008, 913).

This work highlights that employees are motivated by relational aspects of their jobs and they gain psychic benefits from helping others. A recurring theme in work on improving ethical decision making in companies is that adopting an ethic of care (Gilligan 1982), with its inherently relational focus, would improve ethical decision making (Maver and West 2012). A care ethic approach to business conceptualizes mutual interdependency and cooperative relationships as givens, and "challenges the assumption that an individualistic, competitive or aggressive marketplace is inevitable" (Sander-Staudt and Hamington 2011, x). The virtues of attention, respect, response, completion, compassion, empathy, and concern for others comprise the care ethic (ibid.).

The care ethic is inherently sympathetic with sustainable companies that exhibit more inclusive capitalism, as described by Hart (2011, 648):

> Third-generation corporations are developing fully contextualized solutions to real problems in ways that respect local culture and

natural diversity. This means engaging in 'deep dialogue' with local communities to cocreate businesses that are truly 'embedded' in the local context. Such companies will come to view the communities they serve as partners and colleagues, rather than merely as 'consumers.' (Hart 2011, 653)

In doing so, employees will have direct contact with stakeholders, understand their issues, and develop innovative solutions to interdependent problems.

Employees and managers working in companies that exhibit an ethic of care for their stakeholders are thus more likely to experience greater meaning in their work, which is associated with higher job performance, stronger organizational commitment (Grant 2012; Piccolo, Greenbaum, den Hartog, and Folger 2010), greater tendency to go above and beyond the call of duty, and reduced deviance (Mayer, Kuenzi, Greenbaum, Bardes, and Salvador 2009).

How Do We Ensure Ethics is Reflected Within the Firm?

An important cautionary note is in order, however. To maintain a consistent commitment to ethical leadership, ethical behavior must be exhibited and promoted by those at the top of the organization, but it must also trickle down through extensive modeling by immediate supervisors (Mayer et al. 2009). A clear ethical code of conduct is required, but it is insufficient. Consistent and repetitive communication of the code of conduct, along with cultural symbols and stories to make it real, will help embed ethical conduct into the culture. Accountability for ethics at all levels before accountability for profits is necessary—it must be understood that ethical conduct is nonnegotiable, and consideration of profits comes only once a firm can be assured that its actions fit its code.

Conclusion

I have argued that ethical leadership is increasingly being called for by members of society feeling disgusted by corporate scandals and abused by income inequality. I located the seeds of corporate misconduct in a focus on profit maximization and narrow self-interest seeking, and argued that Friedman's directive for businesses to maximize profits within the law is insufficient when the law can be subverted by powerful corporate interests. I have argued that there is increasingly room for ethical leadership, even within a highly competitive business environment, and that there are benefits for companies and their employees in pursuing ethical leadership, particularly as informed by an ethic of care. While the journey toward a more ethical corporation is unlikely to be an easy one, and the need is strong to maintain a consistent focus once a choice is made to pursue ethical leadership, the potential benefits to society, the firm, its employees, and its other stakeholders are substantial.

References

Allmendinger, J. and J. R. Hackman. 1996. "Organizations in changing environments: The case of East German symphony orchestras." *Administrative Science Quarterly* 41: 337–69.

Arndt, M. and B. Bigelow. 2000. "Presenting structural innovation in an institutional environment: Hospitals' use of impression management." *Administrative Science Quarterly* 45: 494–522.

Bakan, J. 2004. *The Corporation: The Pathological Pursuit of Profit and Power*. Toronto: Penguin Books.

Brief, A. P., J. M. Dukerich, P. R. Brown, and J. F. Brett. 1996. "What's wrong with the Treadway Commission Report?" *Journal of Business Ethics* 15: 183–98.

Brown, M. E., L. K. Trevino, and D. A. Harrison. 2005. "Ethical leadership: A social learning perspective for construct development and testing." *Organizational Behavior and Human Decision Processes* 97: 117–34.

Brumback, K. 2013. "3 dozen indicted in Atlanta cheating scandal." Associated Press, March 30, 2013. Accessed March 30, 2013. http://news.yahoo.com/3-dozen-indicted-atlanta-cheating-scandal-214241949.html.

Bauer, R. and J. Derwall. 2011. "Values-driven and profit-seeking dimensions of environmentally responsible investing." In *Oxford Handbook of Business and the Natural Environment*, edited by P. Bansal and A. J. Hoffman, 462–81. Oxford: Oxford University Press.

Devinney, T. M. 2011. "Using market segmentation approaches to understand the green consumer." In *Oxford Handbook of Business and the Natural Environment*, edited by P. Bansal and A. J. Hoffman, 384–403. Oxford: Oxford University Press.

Dominus, S. 2013. "Is giving the secret to getting ahead?" *New York Times Magazine*, March 31. Accessed March 29, 2013. http://www.nytimes.com/2013/03/31/magazine/is-giving-the-secret-to-getting-ahead.html.

Friedman, M. 1970. "The social responsibility of business is to increase its profits." *The New York Times Magazine*, September 13, 1970.

Gershooff, A. D. and J. R. Irwin. 2011. "Why not choose green? Consumer decision making for Environmentally friendly products." In *Oxford Handbook of Business and the Natural Environment*, edited by P. Bansal and A. J. Hoffman, 366–83. Oxford: Oxford University Press.

Gilligan, C. 1982. *In a different voice: Psychological theory and women's development*. Cambridge: Harvard.

Grant, A. M. 2007. "Relational job design and the motivation to make a prosocial difference." *Academy of Management Review* 32: 393–417.

———. 2008. "The significance of task significance: Job performance effects, relational mechanisms, and boundary conditions." *Journal of Applied Psychology* 93: 108–24.

———. 2012. "Leading with meaning: Beneficiary contact, prosocial impact, and the performance effects of transformational leadership." *Academy of Management Journal* 55: 458–76.

Grant, A. M., E. M. Campbell, G. Chen, K. Cottone, D. Lapedis, and K. Lee. 2007. "Impact and the art of motivation maintenance: The effects of contact with beneficiaries on persistence behavior." *Organizational Behavior and Human Decision Processes*, 103: 53–67.

Grant, A. M., J. E. Dutton, and B. D. Russo. 2008. "Giving Commitment: Employee Support Programs and the Prosocial Sensemaking Process." *Academy of Management Journal* 51: 898–918.

Hart, Stuart L. 2011. "The Third-Generation Corporation." In *Oxford Handbook of Business and the Natural Environment*, edited by P. Bansal and A. J. Hoffman, 647–56. Oxford: Oxford University Press.

Hawthorne, F. 2012. *Ethical Chic: The Inside Story of the Companies We Think We Love.* Boston, MA: Beacon Press.

Kidwell, R. E., III and N. Bennett. 1993. "Employee propensity to withhold effort: A conceptual model to intersect three avenues of research." *Academy of Management Review* 22: 730–57.

Mackey, J. 2009. "Creating a New Paradigm for Business." In *Be the Solution: How Entrepreneurs and Conscious Capitalists Can Solve All the World's Problems*, edited by M. Strong, Hoboken, NJ: John Wiley & Sons.

Maver, D. J. and H. S. West. 2012. "International Ethical Leadership: The Power of Diversity in Ethics." *International Journal of Ethical Leadership* 1: 96–114.

Mayer, D. M., M. Kuenzi, R. Greenbaum, M. Bardes, and R. Salvador. 2009. "How low does ethical leadership flow? Test of a trickle-down model." *Organizational Behavior and Human Decision Processes* 108: 1–13.

McCabe, D. L., and L. K. Treviño. 1993. "Academic dishonesty: Honor codes and other contextual influences." *Journal of Higher Education* 64: 522–38.

———. 1997. "Individual and contextual influences on academic dishonesty: A multicampus investigation." *Research in Higher Education* 38: 379–96.

McCabe, D. L., L. K. Treviño, and K. D. Butterfield. 2001. "Cheating in academic institutions: A decade of research." *Ethics and Behavior* 11: 219–32.

McCabe, D. L., K. D. Butterfield, and L. K. Treviño. 2006. "Academic dishonesty in graduate business programs: Prevalence, causes and proposed action." *Academy of Management Learning & Education* 5: 294–305.

McGonigal, J. 2011. *Reality Is Broken: Why Games Make Us Better And How They Can Change The World.* New York: Penguin Books.

Mendonca, M. and R. N. Kanungo. 2007. *Ethical Leadership.* Maidenhead, NY: Open University Press.

Morgenson, D. 2004. "Democracy's Dangers." *Ottawa Citizen*, May 9, 2004: A-12.

Piccolo, R. F., R. Greenbaum, D. N. Den Hartog, and R. Folger, 2010. "The relationship between ethical leadership and core job characteristics." *Journal of Organizational Behavior* 31: 259–78.

Reay T., and C. R. Hinings 2005. "The recomposition of an organizational field: Health care in Alberta." *Organization Studies* 26: 351–84.

Sander-Staudt, M. and M. Hamington. 2011. "Introduction: Care ethics and business ethics." In *Applying Care Ethics to Business* edited by M. Hamington and M. Sander-Staudt, vii–xxii. Dordrecht, NL: Springer.

Shell, E. R. 2009. *Cheap: The High Cost of Discount Culture*. New York: Penguin Books.

Winn, M., P. MacDonald, and C. Zietsma. 2008. "Managing Industry Reputation: The dynamic tension between collective and competitive reputation management strategies." *Corporate Reputation Review*, 11: 35–55.

Yankelovich, D. 2007. Unenlightened self-interest: the wrong response to market capitalism. *Leaders on Ethics: Real World Perspectives on Today's Ethical Challenges*, edited by J. C. Knapp, 12–18. Westport, CT: Praeger Publishing.

Leaders of Character? The Dangers of 'Integrity'

Martin L. Cook
Stockdale Chair of Professional Military Ethics,
US Naval War College

> It's commonly presumed that good character inoculates against shifting fortune…the person of good character will do well, even under substantial pressure to moral failure, while the person of bad character is someone on whom it would be foolish to rely. In this view, it's character, more than circumstance, that decided the moral texture of a life; as the old saw has it, character is destiny.
> —John M. Doris

Military Moral Vocabulary

All of the US military academies, and most postcommissioning professional military education, talk a great deal about the importance of the ethical foundation of the profession of arms. All of the academies have honor codes (or an honor concept, in the case of the Naval Academy). Those codes reflect an assumption that cadets and midshipmen who mature under them will acquire firm and abiding moral habits of honesty and rectitude they will carry forward throughout their careers. Each of the academies has a center devoted to character development and administration of the honor system. These centers conduct programs, conferences, and training events continuously. All this activity only makes sense if one believes that by repeated exposure, the cumulative effect will contribute to the formation of firm and unshakeable character.

Further, all the academies teach a core course in ethics, which is a mixture of basic philosophical concepts of ethics, just war theory, and usually some aspects of ethics unique to military service.

Postcommissioning, officers continue to talk and think about the importance of ethics in their careers and in the profession. The army in particular has made very impressive efforts to inculcate and develop these concepts through the creation of the Center of the Army Profession and Ethic (CAPE) and through the programs CAPE has developed. There too, the assumption is that by spreading the ideas and vocabulary of 'profession of arms' through the service, it will decisively improve character and the overall conduct of the service.

The philosophical concept of ethics at work in all of these efforts is manifest in the somewhat limited moral vocabulary of most military members. As one listens to ordinary discourse about morality in the military, it's impossible not to note that the words 'professional' and 'integrity' serve as all-purpose moral words throughout the service. Individuals are praised as 'having true integrity' and 'being true professionals,' terms of praise and approbation applied to a whole range of behaviors, from properly shined shoes to brave conduct under fire. Behaviors one wishes to express disapproval of, ranging from a messy desk to extreme moral failure, are similarly described as 'unprofessional' or failures of 'integrity.'

Broadly, efforts at moral education in the military consist of three kinds of activities. In the first, the emphasis on training, discipline, and rigid behavioral expectations are aimed at the formation of habits. Through the articulation of clear expectations for behavior, military bearing, and routinized procedures, military training aims at forming individuals into relatively predictable behaviors and relatively automatic responses to challenging circumstances that have been shown through time to be effective in stressful and combat situations. As we like to say, "the training took over," or "muscle memory" kicked in when circumstances didn't allow or require reflection.

The philosophical forefather of this aspect of military ethics training is, of course, Aristotle. He argued that we raise young people through the selective application of pleasure and pain to habituate them to desirable behaviors. If this process is successful, not only can they be expected to do the right thing when called on, but to do so nearly automatically, and to find pleasure in doing so. That combination of right action, grounded in formed habit, and accompanied by pleasure that has been shaped by training is a fair definition of 'character.' Aristotle completed this account with an element that usually drops out of the military instantiation of the concept: the role of the rational and reflective underpinning of those other aspects of character that he calls phronesis—practical wisdom.

The second general type of moral preparation for military service is aimed more at moral thinking. Here I mean the time spent on teaching ethics classes by the philosophy department. The core academic courses reflect the belief that the explicit study of traditions of moral philosophy, just war, and professional ethics will inform the cadet's mind and perhaps improve their moral reasoning. Lawrence Kohlberg's theory of moral development has historically provided a basis for the belief that exposure to moral dilemmas, reasoning about them with peers, and exploring one's reasons for holding a particular view of the correct course of action will advance students up the six-stage Kohlberg Scale. Kohlberg's framework, the Kohlberg Scale, is constructed around two major philosophical pillars. One is broadly Platonic, and assumes that if one reasons about moral questions correctly, moral conduct will follow (although since there's almost no empirical support for that assumption, Kohlbergians are careful not to overpromise in this regard). The other pillar is roughly Kantian. The postconventional stages of the Kohlberg scale culminate in something that looks like absolute Kantian principles of fairness, justice, and so forth. So the assumption underlying Kohlberg is that a particular philosophical tradition does, in fact, represent the pinnacle of moral reasoning.

The third major branch of moral preparation at the military academies is centered in various activities that cluster under the broad heading of 'character development.' Many of the character development center programs, at least in my experience of them at the Air Force Academy, are aimed as much at the heart and emotions as at the intellect. A combination of motivational movie clips, examples, motivational speakers, and cultural heroes are presented to cadets. The assumption here seems to be somewhat the same as in emotional preaching: that arousing emotion and presenting exemplars will inspire and motivate moral behavior. Since we all know the high from an emotional sermon or the glow after a week a church camp tends to fade fairly quickly, it is best to apply the treatment regularly in hopes that cumulative applications will move the baseline of each individual's character. Whether any of this is true is weakly supported by valiant attempts at assessment conducted by all the academies.

Underlying all these efforts are two very large philosophical assumptions: that there is such a thing as character, and that the activities I've described will in combination with each other form it properly. 'Character' is understood as a stable set of behavioral dispositions, formed by habit and education, which can be relied on to guide individuals' behavior and which others can use as a relatively reliable basis for predicting their behavior. That this assumption is true seems to most of us intuitively correct and perhaps even obvious.

However, in the past couple of decades the nascent branch of philosophy calling itself 'experimental philosophy' has raised fundamental challenges to these assumptions. Experimental philosophy in the area of ethics draws on a fairly large body of experimental work in moral psychology to draw out philosophical implications. The predominant result of this work, if taken seriously, forces us to fundamentally reassess our understanding of the whole idea of character. Further, if it is correct, is also provides some constructive suggestions about what besides character we would need to be thinking about if we wish to improve the odds that morally correct behavior will be present in a wide range of environments.

But before I turn to a review of the situationalist challenge to our taken-for-granted views of character, I thought it might be worth a brief digression into why I've gotten so interested in this question. As an ethicist working for the U.S. Navy, I've been drawn in to a discussion of one of the most troubling developments in recent navy history. The navy has been experiencing a dramatic increase in detachments for cause (that's navy-speak for firings) of relatively senior officers (mostly at the rank of O-5 and O-6, or Senior Enlisted). The vast majority of these detachments have been for personal misconduct, rather than operational failures—like running a ship around or navigational error. As you might imagining, removing an officer from his or her command, especially for misconduct, is extremely damaging to the navy and to individual units.

The inspector general of the navy commissioned quite a good study of this phenomenon. Among its findings were these: without exception, the officers in question report that they knew their conduct was wrong. They knew that, if caught, they'd lose their jobs (although they often report that they underestimated the gravity of the consequences). Almost without exception, they wrongly believed others around them were unaware of their conduct. But in fact, upon investigation, it almost always became apparent that their misconduct was fairly widely known and had already greatly damaged the morale, command climate, and trust relationships within their command. Further, it often takes years for units to fully recover from such events. So understandably, the navy is casting around for explanations and solutions to such a grave problem.

Just to give you a flavor of these firings, let me give you a couple of examples. Recently a commander (O-5), a forty-three-year-old married captain of a submarine, went online to a dating site, met, and impregnated a twenty-three-year-old woman. To escape the situation (and the consequences), he faked his death by email and impersonated someone else in the process. A senior enlisted chief of the boat, of the submarine *Nebraska*, began an affair with a female midshipman (mid) on summer cruise, and then continued it ashore, flying across the country to see her. His conduct caused another senior enlisted guy to begin an affair with another mid—so the person responsible for the conduct of the crew on the boat directly caused its deterioration. A navy captain (O-6), head of all logistics for 5th Fleet, was fired for swimming naked in the canals of Bahrain at the end of a drunken party, one that included junior officers and enlisted personnel—a pattern of partying that had gone on with his encouragement throughout his time in command.

This is just a sampler of such firings. In every case, the individual in question had twenty plus years of service under their belt. Of course, it's possible these were individuals who had been misbehaving all throughout their careers, and just finally got caught. If that's the case, it's not philosophically interesting, although it would be important for the navy to figure out how they got promoted that far through the system if they were doing such things all along.

But what if, as seems to be the case in at least in some cases, these are individuals who have reached high rank by being squared away 'officers of character' up until now, and some change in their environment, circumstance, power, or something else fundamentally disorients them morally? Could it be that changes in circumstance have far more bearing on actual behavior than we like to think—and certainly more than our preferred talk of fixed character and global virtues invite us to think about? And if that were true, ignoring situational factors and continuing to talk of global character and virtue is not only a philosophical and empirical mistake, but possibly downright pernicious insofar as we wish to do everything we can to insure good conduct in practice.

Since so many of these firings of officers seem to cluster at the rank of O-6, I have proposed and will be conducting a study, along with a research psychologist friend from the Air Force Academy, to better understand the nature of the transition to O-6 levels in the navy to see if we can identify any major changes in the environment at that level. Anecdotally, it does seem that this particular transition point in the navy brings responsibilities that are a quantum leap or two greater in complexity than the level below. In other words, in the navy at least, leadership challenges don't evolve in a linear fashion, but rather have sharp and dramatic spikes in a couple of places in the leader development continuum. If we are able to find any systemic features, it might be possible to better address those elements at the Major Command course these officers attend before taking their commands. But the general point is this: if the concept of character is less global and stable than our rhetoric suggests it is, we may be failing to prepare our people as effectively as possible for ethical challenges by inculcating a partial or false idea that they can rely on formed character alone to insure their proper conduct. Further, it might turn out that neglecting close attention to situational factors affecting behavior is preventing us from examining aspects of the environment and situation that do affect behavior and for which, if we understood them, we might better control. It is that situationalist challenge I wish to explore in the next section.

The Situationalist Challenge to Character

Philosophers have only recently begun to engage normative ethical thought with a fairly large body of empirical moral psychological studies. Most philosophers who do so are associated with experimental philosophy, a nascent and controversial movement in philosophy. Experimental philosophy takes the traditional armchair to represent the armchair approach to settling matters characteristic of Anglo-American philosophy of the past century. That approach not only avoided, but extolled the virtues of, avoiding of any taint of empirical information. Instead, philosophical ethics in the Anglo-American tradition of the past century has tended to focus on analysis of moral concepts and examination of ever more arcane (and increasingly embarrassing) thought experiments about trollies and the like.

In contrast to that approach, experimental philosophy takes as its symbol the flaming armchair. Experimental philosophy issues a call to engage directly in empirical examination of philosophically interesting questions, as well as to attempt to draw on good empirical research from beyond the scope of traditional philosophy.[1]

For the purposes of our question tonight, the single best book to deal with the topic is John M. Doris's *Lack of Character*. Doris critically and carefully reviews a large number of moral psychology experiments, many of which have become almost common knowledge in our culture, such as the Zimbardo Stanford Prison Experiment and Stanley Milgram's Peer Shock Experiment. He also includes lesser-known studies as well.

The studies he reviews are usefully summarized as follows:
According to Isen and Levin (1972), 87.5% of those participants who had just found a dime in the coin return slot of a public telephone helped a confederate (of the experimenter) who "accidentally" dropped a folder full of papers, while only 4% of those participants who had found no coin helped. According to Darley and Batson (1973) 63% of unhurried participants helped a coughing and groaning confederate who was sitting slumped in a doorway, while only

---

1. *See* Knobe and Nichols 2008 for the clearest statement of the fundamental aims and purposes of the movement.

10% of hurried participants helped. According to Milgram (1974), 65% of those participants who were prompted by an experimenter administered the maximum available (in fact fictitious) electric shock to a confederate, while only 2.5% of those participants who were allowed to choose the shock levels administered the maximum available shock. (Vranis 2004, 284–88)

The conclusion all these studies support, Doris argues, is that situational and environmental factors play a very large role in how people will actually behave. Indeed, in some cases the situational changes one would a priori think to be utterly trivial (my favorite is the finding a dime in a payphone coin return as such a powerful predictor of helping behavior!) have extremely significant and wholly counterintuitive effects on actual behavior.

Studies such as these force us to question whether the assumption that character and formed virtues are as globally relevant (i.e., they remain constant in a diverse range of environments) and are as reliable a guide to individuals' actual behavior as commonly thought.

Jonathan Haidt, a research psychologist, has done excellent empirical work showing how little rational reflection actually has to do with our fundamental moral beliefs, attitudes, and judgments. One of his essays is provocatively entitled, "The Emotional Dog and its Rational Tail: A Social Intuitionist Approach to Moral Judgment"—a title which well captures his fundamental claims. His recent book, *The Righteous Mind* is the best analysis I've seen yet about why the fundamental political and religious narratives we have are impervious to rational discussion. Haidt shows that such narratives are polarized to the point that people of opposite political and religious opinions often seem to literally live in different conceptual universes. Indeed, they are so polarized that what one group considers facts, the other considers completely false.

One of the most interesting and important of Haidt's contributions is to note that the modern West has an oddly narrow and limited palette with which to paint a moral canvas, compared to most other cultures now and in human history. As members of the post-Enlightenment West, we focus on individuals as bearers of rights, and on utilities to be maximized. In contrast, he argues that most cultures and most of human history have had a much richer set of important values and moral concerns. Indeed, he argues that one reason liberals and conservatives seem to talk as if they accepted different 'facts' and live in apparently different moral world is that they do! And, while a liberal himself (at least when he started his studies), he believes the conservatives' willingness and ability to paint with more of the palette (giving value to issues such as loyalty and tradition, for example) often accounts for their success in winning debates.

Most recently, Haidt has engaged in a spirited and fascinating discussion of the relative role of reason in moral deliberation with two other philosophers in the "The Stone" section of the *New York Times*—a section devoted to popular discussion of philosophical ideas. The philosophers, as one might expect, wrote two pieces doggedly defending the importance of reason in moral thinking and the relevance of moral thinking to moral behavior. Haidt's response is equally spirited, and is entitled "Reasons Matter (when Intuitions don't object)" (2012).

The current Inspector General of the Navy, Admiral Phil Wisecup, has been recommending a book throughout the navy called *You are Not so Smart* by David McRaney. This book captures in a fun and easily digestible form a very wide range of social science research. Each chapter is organized around two opening sentences. One he calls "the misconception," and it's what we all believe to be true about the issue in question. The second, which we don't believe and would fight to reject, he calls "the truth." The theme running through the book is that many important things we believe to be true about ourselves, our character, our autonomy, and even our memories are demonstrably false.

All of these perspectives converge to undermine some of the implicit assumptions embedded in military character development efforts. Doris causes us to have serious doubts about the idea of character and virtue as a reliable predictor of the behavior of individuals in a variety of contexts and situations. Haidt causes us to wonder whether appeals to our moral reasoning and efforts to improve it are nearly as effective as we think they are. To use another of his metaphors, reason is just the rider of the elephant of nonrational intuitions and impulses. As he summarizes his claims, "Intuitions come first, strategic reasoning second" (2012c, 52). Often, he demonstrates, reason comes in after the fact of moral intuition to try to find reasons to support those intuitions. Furthermore, even if reason is unsuccessful in doing so, we're unlikely to change our intuitions, and therefore our moral convictions unless (as he puts it) we find ways to "talk to the elephant."

McRaney's romp through our systematic cognitive errors, while breezy, captures a very wide range of empirical research, all of which goes to show we really aren't that smart, and a lot of what we quite sincerely believe to be true about ourselves, our memories, our motivations, and even our actions, is demonstrably false.

So, what are the implications for our thinking about officer development if we take the challenges posed by moral psychology more seriously than our traditional character development efforts have to date?

Situationalism's Implications for Military Ethics

To some degree, military leadership has long recognized the morally corrosive effects of some aspects of context and has stressed the need for leaders to take specific actions to prevent moral deterioration. For example, poor discipline, prolonged combat stress, and poor leadership are commonly recognized as strongly predictive of immoral and illegal conduct on the battlefield. Major General H. R. McMaster recommended a book to me that I commend to all of you: *Black Hearts* by Jim Frederick. In this book, Frederick chronicles in exquisite and painful detail the pattern of poor leadership, lack of discipline, and erosion of morale that culminated in four members of one platoon of the 101st Airborne plotting and executing a plan to rape and kill an Iraqi girl, murder her family, burn the bodies, and then attempt to cover up the whole affair. What's especially useful about Frederick's book is the dissection of the course of events and the climate that got that platoon there and the many points along the path to those events where effective leadership might have prevented them.

So at least at the level of the extreme, military culture and leadership recognizes the dangers of allowing situational factors to accumulate that may well culminate in atrocity. We certainly understand that sustained combat stress, poor unit morale, and poor leadership set conditions that may well end in catastrophic moral failure.

What's important about the situationalist contribution to the discussion is the emphasis on the often apparently small, even trivial, changes in the environment that may alter behavioral outcomes to a remarkable degree. In other words, while we already recognize the impact of obvious and large situational factors in either maintaining moral standards or eroding them, I think we've not begun to think seriously about the factors so small that intuitively we'd dismiss the possibility that they might significantly affect behavior. If the situationalist perspective is even partially correct, we do so at our peril. If we believe that integrity and character possess a global reliability and constancy that—if situationalism is taken seriously—they simply don't, we rely on such notions more completely and uncritically than we should. Further, if that's right, we might need to think more deeply about the apparently minor and negligible situational factors that might indeed have more influence than we like to think. Doing so would provide a foundation from which we can better educate, train, and lead military personnel to insure the highest levels of proper behavior we can attain.

John Doris provides a helpful and provocative nonmilitary example of how taking situationalism more seriously into account might guide behavior to protect against moral failure:

> Imagine that a colleague with whom you have had a long flirtation invites you for dinner, offering enticement of interesting food and elegant wine, with the excuse that you are temporarily orphaned while your spouse is out of town. Let's assume the obvious way to read this text is the right one, and assume further that you regard the infidelity that might result as an ethically undesirable outcome. If you are like one of Milgram's respondents, you might think there is little cause for concern; you are, after all, an upright person, and a spot of claret never did anyone any harm. On the other hand, if you take the lessons of situationalism to heart, you avoid the dinner like the plague, because you know that you are not able to confidently predict your behavior in a problematic situation on the basis of your antecedent values. You do not doubt that you sincerely value fidelity; you simply doubt your ability to act in conformity with this value once the candles are lit and the wine begins to flow. Relying on character once in the situation is a mistake, you agree; the way to achieve the ethically desirable result is to recognize the situational pressures may all too easily overwhelm character and avoid the dangerous situation. I don't think it wild speculation to claim that this is a better strategy than dropping by for a "harmless" evening, secure in the knowledge of your righteousness. (2002, 147)

The conclusion Doris draws from this is important, and has important implications for thinking clearly about how to minimize ethical failure in the military. We might more helpfully explain ethical failure less in terms of a single failure of moral will and look for "culpable naiveté or insufficiently careful attention to situations" (Doris 2002, 148).

Let me hasten to anticipate a likely objection to the argument I'm making. By no means am I suggesting that the importance of situational factors in influencing behavior can or should be used to eliminate the importance of moral responsibility and even of legal culpability. Confusion on this point is not just a theoretical possibility. My colleague and research psychologist Dr. George Mastrioanni skillfully dissected precisely such massive confusion in Zimbardo's testimony at the Abu Ghraib criminal trials, in which Zimbardo tied himself into conceptual knots trying to balance the personal responsibility of the individual agents with the situational factors that enabled their misconduct (2011, 2–16).

What the situationalist challenge invites us to do is not to reject moral and legal responsibility, but rather to more accurately and precisely locate where, as Doris puts it, 'culpable responsibility' lies. We may at the end of the day want or need to continue to criticize and punish individuals who—having gotten themselves into a highly dangerous situation they or their leaders should have anticipated—behave badly (as we might have anticipated to be highly likely on situational grounds). Taking situationalism seriously invites us to ask a wider range of questions and to anticipate and control for their negative influences on morally desirable behavior in a way that psychologically naïve reliance on individual character and virtue does not. I'm of course aware that I'm waterskiing at high velocity over some deep philosophical water here, and we'll have to think long and hard about the importance of situationalist considerations when we assess moral failure. Are we offering situationalist exculpations, extenuations, or just partial explanations?

But for our purposes here, let me stress the positive importance of insisting that we think deeply about situationalist considerations when we look at military organizations and questions of military leadership. Most importantly, it invites military leaders at every level to be more aware of the inherent limits of the moral vocabulary of integrity and character. Overreliance on character as a reliable bulwark against moral failure is, empirically speaking, a mistake and a very dangerous mistake if what we care about in the end is moral conduct. Situationalism leads military leaders at every level to think more clearly and explicitly about the situational factors at play in their unit and to recognize that even matters they might be inclined to dismiss as trivial might decisively affect their unit's ability to maintain high behavioral standards.

Lastly, if we want to do everything possible to prevent moral failure, situationalism suggests a productive line of empirical research of great importance. Studies and observations of the influence of situational factors are essential if we are to be better able to control and predict behavior in the real world. Insofar as excessive reliance on talk of character and integrity predisposes us culturally not to examine such questions, we run the risk of setting ourselves up for preventable failures of military ethics.

So my conclusions are necessarily a bit tentative. Experimental philosophy is a new and, in many philosophical circles, suspect field. But there's enough smoke coming from that flaming armchair to suggest to me there's probably some real fire there. And the fact that these questions lead directly to inherently intellectually interesting and potentially extremely practical important lines of research that might well pay off handsomely as we refine training and leader development programs. Military ethics that sees itself as the handmaid of the military profession (as opposed to merely philosophical military ethics) has to concern itself with the real world implications of its work. To that end, better dialogue and perhaps even joint research with situationalist moral psychology might do more for the ethical health of the profession than anything else we can do.

References

Athanassoulis, Nafsika. 2000. "A Response to Harmon: Virtue Ethics and Character Traits." *Proceedings of the Aristotelian Society, New Series* 100: 215–21. http://www.jstor.org/stable/4545326.

Doris, John M. 2002. *Lack of Character: Personality and Moral Behavior*. New York: Cambridge University Press.

Epstein, Seymour, and Edward J. O'Brien. 1985. "The Person-Situation Debate in Historical and Current Perspective." *Psychological Bulletin* 98 (3): 513–37.

Fleeson, William. 2004. "Moving Personality beyond the Person Situation Debate; The Challenge and the Opportunity of Within-Person Variability." *Current Directions in Psychological Science* 13 (2): 83–87.

Fleeson, William, and Erik E. Noftle. 2009. "In Favor of the Synthetic Resolution to the Person-Situation Debate." *Journal of Research in Personality* 43: 150–54.

Gutting, Gary. "Haidt's Problem with Plato." *New York Times*. October 6, 2012. http://opinionator.blogs.nytimes.com/2012/10/04/jonathan-haidts-plato-problem/.

Haidt, Jonathan. 2001. "The Emotional Dog and Its Rational Tail: A Social Intuitionist Approach to Moral Judgment." *Psychological Review* 108 (4): 814–34.

Haidt, Jonathan. 2007. "Moral Psychology and the Misunderstanding of Religion." *Edge*. September 21. http://www.edge.org/conversation/moral-psychology-and-the-misunderstanding-of-religion.

Haidt, Jonathan. 2007. "The New Synthesis in Moral Psychology." *Science* 316: 998–1002. http://www.sciencemag.org/cgi/content/full/316/5827/998/dc1.

Haidt, Jonathan. 2012a. "Out-Take from The Righteous Mind: Virtue Ethics." http://righteousmind.com/wp-content/uploads/2012/08/Righteous-Mind-outtake.virtue-ethics.pdf.

Haidt, Jonathan. 2012b. "Reasons Matter (When Intuitions Don't Object)." *New York Times*. October 8. http://opinionator.blogs.nytimes.com/2012/10/07/reasons-matter-when-intuitions-dont-object/.

Haidt, Jonathan. 2012c. *The Righteous Mind: Why Good People Are Divided by Politics and Religion*. New York: Pantheon Books.

Haidt, Jonathan, and Selin Kesebir. 2010. "Morality." In *Handbook of Social Psychology*. Edited by Gilbert D. Fiske and G. Lindzey, 797–832. Hobeken, NJ: Wiley.

Harman, Gilbert. 1999. "Moral Psychology Meets Social Psychology: Virtue Ethics and the Fundamental Attribution Error." *Proceeding of the Aristotelian Society* 99: 315–31. http://www.jstor.org/stable/4545312

Harman, Gilbert. 2000. "The Nonexistence of Character Traits." *Proceeding of the Aristotelian Society* 100: 223–26. http://www.jstor.org/stable/4545327.

Johnson, Robert N. 2000. "Virtue and Right." *Ethics* 113 (4): 810–34. http://www.jstor.org/stable/10.1086/373952.

Knobe, Joshua and Shaun Nichols. 2008. "An Experimental Philosophy Manifesto." In *Experimental Philosophy*. Oxford: Oxford University Press.

Kristjánsson, Kristján. 2008. "An Aristotelian Critique of Situationism." *Philosophy* 83 (1): 55–76.

Lynch, Michael. 2012. "A Vote for Reason." *New York Times*. October 6. http://opinionator.blogs.nytimes.com/2012/09/30/hope-for-reason/.

Mastroianni, George R. 2011. "The Pearson-Situation Debate: Implications for Military Leadership and Civilian-Military Relations." *Journal of Military Ethics* 10 (1): 2–16.

Maxwell, Bruce. 2010. "Does Ethical Theory Have a Place in Post-Kohlbergian Moral Psychology?" *Educational Theory* 60 (2): 167–88.

Presley, Sharon. 2010. "Not Everyone Obeys: Personal Factors Correlated with Resistance to Unjust Authority." *Resources for Independent Thinking*. http://www.rit.org/authority/resistance.php.

Prinz, Jesse. 2009. "The Normativity Challenge: Cultural Psychology Provides the Real Threat to Virtue Ethics." *The Journal of Ethics* 13 (2–3): 117–44.

Upton, Candace L. 2000. "Virtue Ethic and Moral Psychology: The Situationism." *The Journal of Ethics* 3 (4): 103–15.

Van Velsor, Ellen, and Jean Brittain Leslie. 1995. "Why Executives Derail: Perspectives Across Time and Cultures." *Academy of Management Executive* 9 (4): 62–72.

Vranas, Peter M. 2004. "Lack of Character: Personality and Moral Behavior by John M. Doris." *The Philosophical Review* 113 (2). http://www.jstor.org/stable/4147968.

Habits of the Heart: Poetry and Democracy

David Hassler
Director, Wick Poetry Center,
Kent State University

I have been facilitating poetry discussion groups and leading writing workshops in communities throughout Ohio for nearly twenty years. Whether the discussion occurs within a K–12 classroom, a senior center, a veterans' support group, a palliative care team of caregivers, or an outpatient therapy group, I have witnessed, time and again, how a single poem read aloud is refracted through the lens of each of our lives and becomes a trigger to provoke our own writing and deep listening. Indeed, poetry and the quality of conversation it inspires can break our hearts open to a deeper tenderness and connection with each other.

In his new book, *Healing the Heart of Democracy*, Parker J. Palmer identifies five "habits of the heart" crucial to the health of our democracy, habits that I believe are reinforced through the practice of reading, writing, and discussing poetry. He borrows this phrase from the nineteenth-century French political theorist Alexis de Tocqueville, who visited the United States in 1831–32 and wrote the classic, *Democracy in America*. Palmer writes, "Early on, Tocqueville saw that American democracy would fail if generation after generation of citizens did not develop what he called the 'habits of the heart' that democracy requires. By that phrase he meant deeply ingrained patterns of receiving, interpreting, and responding to experiences that involve our intellects, emotions, self-images, and concepts of meaning and purpose—habits that form the *inward and invisible infrastructure of democracy*" (Palmer 2011, 24). Palmer identifies these five habits as imperatives: "1. We must understand that we are all in this together; 2. We must develop an appreciation of the value of 'otherness'; 3. We must cultivate the ability to hold tension in life-giving ways; 4. We must generate a sense of personal voice and agency; 5. We must strengthen our capacity to create community" (Ibid., 44–45). In my experience, the use of poetry in community workshops and discussion groups calls forth these "habits of heart"—indeed, all five of them.

At Kent State University's Wick Poetry Center, our core mission is to encourage new voices by bringing poetry to people's everyday lives. Our

Traveling Stanzas™ community arts project is doing just that in innovative ways by engaging our community and traveling far around the world. A collaboration between Kent State's Wick Poetry Center and Kent State student designers, Traveling Stanzas™ places original poetry from our community writing workshops on posters in Northeast Ohio mass-transit systems, businesses, libraries, and classrooms. These poetry designs have also traveled around the world as free, animated e-greetings with original audio recordings of the poets reading their poems.

The seed bed of these poems is the quality of the conversation that takes place in our community workshops—which is often a deep and authentic heart-talk. Democracy thrives on this ability and opportunity to come together with our differences, to engage in an authentic dialogue, and to use that energy creatively.

What many call the "politics of rage," Palmer renames the "politics of the brokenhearted." It is in the heart, he points out, where we integrate all our different ways of knowing—"intellectual, emotional, sensory, intuitive, imaginative, experiential, relational, and bodily, among others" (6). Indeed, 'heart' is derived from the Latin *cor*, which points to the core sense of ourselves and is the root of the word *courage*. It is from the heart that we gather up the courage to act on our knowledge and beliefs. By connecting us to the emotional truths in our lives and each other's lives, poetry can literally *encourage* us, a word which derives from Old French meaning to "make strong, hearten." Poetry can give us heart, give us back our hearts, and connect us to the hearts of others—what the German poet Rainier Maria Rilke called "heart-work." In his poem, *Wendung* ("Turning Point"), translated by Stephen Mitchell (1982, 133), Rilke writes: "Work of the eyes is done, now / go and do heart-work / on all the images imprisoned within you…"

Ultimately, how we connect with each other, Palmer points out, how we are opened up to each other's lives, is in realizing that we have experienced "similar forms of grief." It is more often through our wounds that we are softened and sensitized to each other. Palmer makes clear that the heartache we feel in our society can be experienced as either a debilitating and destructive force that breaks our hearts "apart," or as a source of creative energy and connection that breaks our hearts "open." He reminds us that "the broken-open heart is a source of power as well as compassion" (Palmer 2011, 23). He points out that the heart is, in fact, "pre-political," the place from which we form our beliefs and find the courage to act.

What poetry does best is to encourage us to be feisty and engaged, to be participants and not passive observers, to wake us up to our own imperatives and the necessary task of making meaning out of our lives. Poetry helps us 'think the world together,' not apart. This is the real heart-work of poetry and where we can strengthen all five habits of the heart that Palmer elucidates: where we feel that we are 'in this together;' where we connect with 'the other;' where we hold the tensions in our lives creatively; where we discover the power and agency of our own voices; and finally, through the quality of this conversation, strengthen our communities.

References
Mitchell, Stephen. 1982. *The Selected Poetry of Rainer Maria Rilke*. New York, NY: Random House.
Palmer, Parker J. 2011. *Healing the Heart of Democracy: The Courage to Create a Politics Worthy of the Human Spirit*. San Francisco, CA: Jossey-Bass.

The three Traveling Stanzas that follow this article—"Flags Are Flying," "Soldier's Heart," and "Ode to my Body"— are reprinted with permission from the Wick Poetry Center, Kent State University, © 2010, 2011.

Flags are Flying

Today, flags are flying
outside my window, Fourth of July,
and I am back in my parents' home,
Boston, 1944.

Flags were flying then –
not all red, white and blue,
but white ones, too,
with gold stars
to signify broken hearts.

I remember when the telegram arrived,
just a piece of paper carrying tears
for a wife, a fatherless child,
parents in shock.

Now, more than sixty years
later, no telegram arrives,
yet feelings remain
for wasted lives
untimely end.
While, once again,
flags are flying.

—*Jo Steinhurst, Age 86*
Judson Manor

Soldier's Heart
—for The Warrior's Journey Home Veterans' Healing Circle

We sing the old wounds,
word by word, stitch by stitch,

many hands, many voices.
The needle hurts as the thread

is drawn through, the mouth
of the wound drawn shut.

Our work is to listen hard,
to look the wounded in the eye,

to stitch and pull
press through pain,

until every knot is tied,
every last wound closed,

every broken heart
healed and whole.

— Maj Ragain
Design by David Steckel

"All nurturing begins with inclusion" — Roshi Robert Aitken

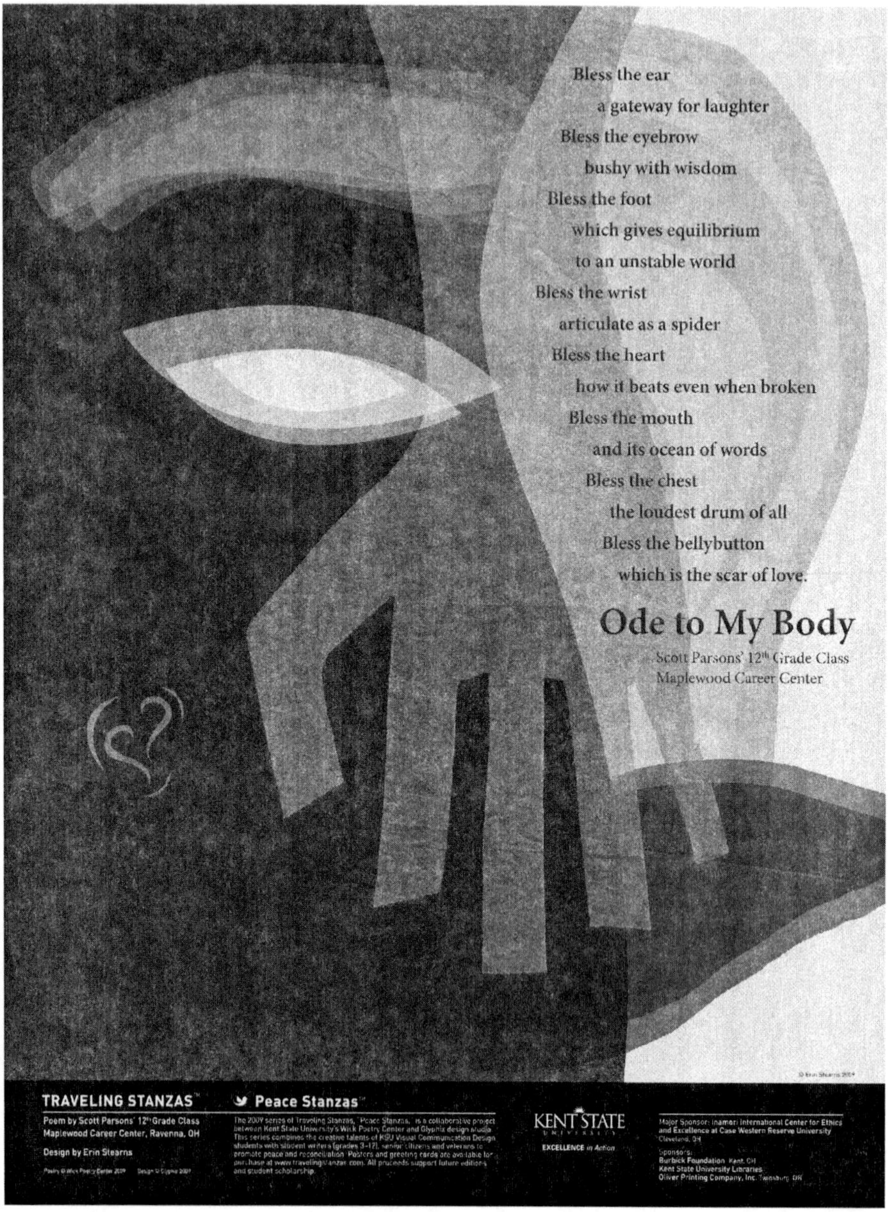
Bless the ear
a gateway for laughter
Bless the eyebrow
bushy with wisdom
Bless the foot
which gives equilibrium
to an unstable world
Bless the wrist
articulate as a spider
Bless the heart
how it beats even when broken
Bless the mouth
and its ocean of words
Bless the chest
the loudest drum of all
Bless the bellybutton
which is the scar of love.
Ode to My Body
Scott Parsons' 12th Grade Class
Maplewood Career Center
TRAVELING STANZAS™
Poem by Scott Parsons' 12th Grade Class
Maplewood Career Center, Ravenna, OH
Design by Erin Stearns
Peace Stanzas™
The 2009 series of Traveling Stanzas, "Peace Stanzas," is a collaborative project between Kent State University's Wick Poetry Center and Glyphix design studio. This series combines the creative talents of KSU Visual Communication Design students with student writers (grades 3–12), senior citizens and veterans to promote peace and reconciliation. Posters and greeting cards are available for purchase at www.travelingstanzas.com. All proceeds support future editions and student scholarship.
KENT STATE
UNIVERSITY
EXCELLENCE in Action
Major Sponsor: Inamori International Center for Ethics and Excellence at Case Western Reserve University
Cleveland, OH
Sponsors:
Burbick Foundation Kent, OH
Kent State University Libraries
Oliver Printing Company, Inc. Twinsburg, OH

Moral Choices and Leadership

Gregory L. Eastwood
Professor of Bioethics and Humanities and
Professor of Medicine
State University of New York Upstate Medical University

> We want to be famous and successful, we think our colleagues are cutting corners, we'll be damned if we lose out to them, and some day, when we've made it, we'll be role models. But until then, give us a pass.
> —Harvard professor Howard Gardner, quoted in the *New York Times*
>
> Don't even argue that all cheating is the same because it's not. Cheating on a national boards exam is a huge offense, cheating on a final exam is a big offense. 'Cheating' on weekly online ten question quizzes that have no bearing on how to be a doctor isn't cheating, its called getting your grunt work done fast so you can spend more time learning some real medicine and help REAL people.
> —News blog comment in response to a report of cheating at SUNY Upstate Medical University
>
> Leadership…is an essentially moral act.
> —A. Bartlett Giamatti

I have come to appreciate that for some college students, even among those who view themselves as moral creatures, college is not the time to be fussy about making moral choices. "Honesty is for after I graduate. Right now I need to get through school." This concerns me because I perceive that college is where most of our future business, political, academic, scientific, religious, athletic, and other leaders are right now and I believe that current behavior is a dependable predictor of future behavior. The connection between the present and the future, however, is not one of particulars of context, but rather one of moral character and associated behaviors.

We expect a great deal from our leaders, including right moral conduct, but we frequently are disappointed. Consult a preferred source of news and one learns quickly of the latest example of moral failure of leadership in business, politics, academia, science, religion, athletics, and so on. No discipline seems untouched.

What to do? I believe that the world needs leaders who have a broad understanding of human knowledge and experience, and who operate within a set of moral principles (Eastwood 2010b). The time to cultivate, or jump-start if necessary, this trajectory to moral leadership is during the college experience.

In the following, I will consider these questions: Do the moral choices I make now matter? What makes a good leader? Are you ready to run the world? Finally, despite my lack of ecclesiastical standing, I will deliver a benediction.[1]

Do the Moral Choices I Make Now Matter?

Popular wisdom holds that the best predictor of future behavior is current or past behavior. This observation is supported by both news media and research reports of cheating in high school, college, graduate and professional school, and later during certifying examinations; past cheating behavior seems perpetuated (Perez-Pena 2012; Baldwin 1996; Zamost, Griffen, and Ansari 2012; Roberts and Wasieleski 2012). These accounts also suggest that cheating now is easier, more prevalent, and tolerated. Internet access and other technologies appear to enable cheating (Anonymous 2011; Roberts and Wasieleski 2012). Cheating seems to be regarded by some students as an acceptable and ordinary method of getting through school.

What do we know about the relation between dishonest behavior in school and performance at work? Not much. Engineering students who also had engineering jobs reported a strong relationship between involvement in academic dishonesty during high school and involvement in present dishonest behavior, both in college and in the workplace (Harding 2004). Further, attitudes among engineering and preengineering students about cheating varied. Copying from another student during a test or quiz was regarded as cheating by 96.4 percent of 643 respondents, 2.3 percent thought this to be unethical but not cheating, and for 1.1 percent it was neither cheating nor unethical (Carpenter 2006). Although one might be reassured that over 96 percent thought copying was cheating, frankly, I am disappointed that it was not 100 percent. Perhaps of more concern, only 26.7 percent of students regarded asking another student about questions on an exam they have not yet taken as cheating. 45.6 percent thought it was unethical and, to my astonishment, 26.6 percent felt it was neither cheating nor unethical.

---

1. This essay was adapted from the keynote address for Integrity Week, Case Western Reserve University, Cleveland, Ohio, February 1, 2013.

A study of physicians in practice gets closer to the question of behavior in school as a predictor of later professional behavior (Papadakis 2005). Two hundred and thirty-five graduates of three medical schools, who had been disciplined by their state medical boards, were compared to 469 control physicians, who had not been disciplined and were matched to the case physicians according to medical school and year of graduation. Disciplinary action by a state medical board was found to be strongly associated with prior unprofessional behavior in medical school. Unprofessional behaviors that were most highly correlated with subsequent disciplinary action were severe irresponsibility and severely diminished capacity for self-improvement.

Of course, these reports and articles do not finger individuals. We cannot claim that a particular individual who cheats in high school will cheat in college and then be dishonest later. And although the physician study strongly correlates unprofessional behavior in medical school with the chance of running afoul of one's state medical board, we cannot say that an individual's unprofessional behavior in medical school is unerringly predictive of later unprofessional behavior. But these observations provide good evidence to expect that cheating, dishonesty, and unprofessional behavior during the educational experience increase the risk, the probability, for later misbehavior.

If cheating and dishonesty are acceptable and ordinary for some students, they are not so for all students. Many students do not cheat. Yet, some situations seem so provocative and unusual that students who ordinarily might not have cheated may feel they have no choice but to cheat. Such were the situations in the recent cheating scandal at Harvard College and several years ago at the State University of New York Upstate Medical University (Perez-Pena 2013; Mulder 2011). At Harvard, students 'collaborated' on a take-home examination; at SUNY Upstate students 'collaborated' on online quizzes. In both situations, students indicated they were confused about when it was acceptable to collaborate and when it was not, and both administrations were criticized for acting too slowly to address concerns. In the SUNY Upstate situation, fear of failure of the course added to a sense of despair and anxiety, leading many students to say they had no choice but to cheat.

These cases and ones like them raise the question whether there are alternatives to cheating. There are always alternatives, of course, but sometimes the alternatives seem unacceptable. Not to cheat and risk failure may not be acceptable. Yet some students do not cheat and accept the risk. Do we expect to encounter situations only in school in which the sole option seems to be to cheat or does that also occur later in life? Clearly, life beyond school presents many opportunities to cheat or engage in dishonest behavior. Some of them seem to leave few options, unless one examines them thoughtfully according to one's moral code and with an eye to both short- and long-term consequences. It is easier to cut corners if one has been in the habit of doing so and, conversely, it is easier to be honest if one practices the habit of honesty.

Does it make a practical difference what moral choices we make? We already reflected on the presumed relation between moral behavior in high school, college, and later. The notion that making the choice to cheat becomes perpetuated rests partly on anecdote and partly on empirical studies. But the habit of dishonesty has implications beyond test taking. In medicine, the field with which I am most familiar, the responses to seemingly innocuous questions may have unpredictable harmful consequences with regard to the welfare of patients. For example, senior physicians commonly ask medical students and doctors in training about facts and observations related to their patients. What was the serum potassium this morning? Did the cardiogram show any ectopic beats? Does the patient have double vision? If the student does not know and makes up an answer, that could lead to harm for the patient. A patient may ask her physician if they heard a heart murmur. Responding no when the physician did not listen is risky and immoral behavior on the part of the physician. An assistant in a physician's office may ask a physician how to code a procedure (for insurance purposes), implying that there may be some flexibility to enhance payment that may not be justified by the clinical situation. Outside of medicine, a senior lawyer may advise a junior lawyer to add a few hours to the billing of a client. In business, what would be your response if your boss tells you to substitute a product that is inferior to what was agreed in the contract?

What Makes a Good Leader?

Books, articles, and courses on leadership abound. My purpose here is not to present a primer on leadership, but rather to focus on several of the concepts and characteristics of leadership that I think are at the core of leadership and of being a good leader.

Who can be a leader? "Leaders come in a large variety of sizes, shapes, colors, and ages; from different career stages, geographic origins, social standings; and with varying personal styles" (Eastwood 1998). I start with the premise that nearly everyone, under the right conditions, can be a leader. Experience tells us that there is no single formula for leadership. Leaders combine a complex mix of personal attributes and abilities, which, in the successful ones, seems right for them. Circumstance, inclination, and natural and developed abilities all operate to determine whether someone exerts leadership. That is one reason why the education process, particularly the argument for a broad education as articulated later under "Are You Ready to Run the World?," is so important in preparation for leadership.

So what does it mean that anyone can be a leader? We commonly associate leadership with titles or positions. CEO, president, department head, principal, dean, director, chair, mayor, governor, and captain all connote a leadership position and thus the presumption that the incumbent is a leader. What about mother, father, associate director, teacher, journalist, lawyer, doctor, professor, pilot? Or student, employee, worker, soldier, player, secretary, clerk?

We expect leadership from people with titles and positions of respect, but the skills, attributes, and obligations associated with leaders are not the exclusive domain of those with titles. Nearly anyone can be called under appropriate circumstances to exert leadership. Also, for leaders who have the titles to be most effective requires synergy of leadership among the rank and file of all groups and organizations.

Leadership may not so much reside with individuals but is created during the interactions of two or more people. Further, I believe the old saw about a good leader being a good follower. An effective follower requires the leadership skills to move in that mutable space between leading and following.

Can you think of an example in which a person without title or position has exerted leadership? What were the circumstances and what were the characteristics of that person? I expect their characteristics are similar to those I discuss here.

What distinguishes a good leader? Certainly a strong moral compass is important. But that seems prerequisite. Good leaders help others realize their dreams. I borrow that idea from Professor Richard Boyatzis of the Weatherhead School of Management at Case Western Reserve University. He said that in my hearing several years ago and it stuck. Ordinary leaders usually do a good job of setting goals, identifying in the people they lead what they do well and what they do not do well, and working with them to improve. Good leaders somehow understand the people with whom they are associated and are able to tap into their aspirations and dreams and help facilitate them. Good leaders take pleasure in the attainment of the dreams of others—this is a remarkable ability of leadership. One of the joys of leadership is to take vicarious pleasure in the accomplishments of others. We see this ability to facilitate the dreams of others also in people who are not necessarily regarded as leaders, but who have affected our lives profoundly. Who has helped you realize your dreams? A parent? A teacher? A coach? A friend? What has it been about that person and about your relationship with that person that has been so meaningful? Perhaps the characteristics of the people who have helped you realize your dreams are the character traits, skills, and behaviors of good leaders.

What are the character traits, skills, and behaviors of good leaders? When I have asked that question of undergraduate, graduate, and professional students, and of others at later stages of life, a list similar to the one below emerges. I arbitrarily divide them into character traits and skills (or abilities), although there is much merging and connection between them. I take character traits to reflect a person's innate character and skills to be things we acquire. This clearly is a tenuous dichotomy. I believe that it is possible to improve most of the character traits listed, including courage, sense of humor, self-understanding, empathy, and even integrity. Also, people have great innate variability with regard to skills—for example, some simply are better listeners or organizers than others—but everyone, regardless of innate abilities, can improve. Undoubtedly, you have your own candidates for attributes of leadership that do not appear on this list.

Character traits
- moral principles
- integrity, honesty
- energy
- empathy
- self understanding
- respect for others
- humility
- sense of humor
- perseverance
- courage

Skills
- to communicate
- to listen
- to organize
- to conceptualize and plan
- to select good people
- to manage uncertainty
- to use power constructively
- to make difficult decisions
- to act and take planned risk
- to be unperturbed by praise and criticism

Here is something to think about. Are the leadership attributes indicated here different for different positions? When you look at this list, is there any character trait or skill that is unnecessary for, say, a corporate CEO, a school principal, a college department head, a leader of a student organization, or a leader of a neighborhood organization? I believe that all are important for leaders of any scope of responsibility, although some leaders may need to develop and use some traits and skills more than others.

Higher principles, integrity, and courage. *To Kill a Mockingbird*, by Harper Lee, tells the story of Atticus Finch, a lawyer in a small southern town in the 1950s, who agrees to defend a black man who has been wrongly accused of raping a white woman. Atticus has two children, Scout, age 8, and Jem, age 12. Scout takes some heat from her schoolmates for her father's action. Here is an exchange between Atticus and Scout.

> Atticus: "[T]here's some high talk around town to the effect that I shouldn't do much about defending this man."
> Scout: "If you shouldn't be defendin' him, why are you doin' it?"
> Atticus: "For a number of reasons. The main one is, if I didn't I couldn't hold up my head in town, I couldn't represent this county in the legislature, I couldn't even tell you or Jem not to do something again.... *Simply because we were licked a hundred years before we started is no reason for us not to try to win."* (Lee 1960; my italics)

In the play by Edmond Rostand (1950), my favorite old-time romantic Cyrano de Bergerac spoke to this when he said, "A [person] does not fight merely to win." Merely to win! As if there were something more important than winning, and winning was very important to Cyrano. But I realized, after thinking about Atticus's statement and former President Gerald R. Ford's (2001) claim, "In the age-old contest between popularity and principle, only those willing to lose for their convictions are deserving of posterity's approval," on receiving the Profile in Courage Award, that sometimes we are motivated by a principle so strong and meaningful that we risk losing, even may expect to lose, because acting on the principle is of utmost moral importance. Few of us are tested on this and if we are tested it is not often, but I believe that it is important for our moral integrity and development to know what those principles are that for us are beyond the consideration of winning and losing.

Self-understanding. "O wad some Power the giftie gie us/To see oursels as ithers see us!" begged the poet Robert Burns (1786). If you are in the business of leading others, it is helpful to know something about yourself—what motivates you, how you think, why you behave in certain ways (Eastwood 2010a). Part of knowing yourself is having some understanding of how others regard you. You can learn this by paying attention to what others say to you and about you and how they react to you, although what they say and do often is conveyed in a sort of code that more or less conforms to social rules and requires interpretation. We all vary in our ability to detect the cues that others send and to decipher this code. I believe that effective leaders understand how they come across to others and make modifications to correct ineffective behavior and strengthen what is effective.

Decision making and respect for others. Many decisions a leader makes involve balancing the interests of individuals and the collective interests of the organization to which the leader is responsible. How will this decision affect the person? How will it affect others? How will it affect the organization? What are the short and long term consequences?

When people are confronted with few options, they sometimes become angry and act in unproductive and unpredictable ways, ways that may be damaging to themselves and to others. This is especially evident in association with difficult personnel decisions, such as dismissal or reassignment. I have found the advice of Sun Tzu (1988), the third century B.C.E. Chinese general, to be helpful in these matters. "Surround them on three sides, leaving one side open, to show them a way to life." "When people are desperate, they will fight to the death." A comment in the context of contemporary politics also is relevant: "You never know what a cornered animal is willing to do" (Cross 2009).

The leader should decide what about the decision is important and nonnegotiable and what can be determined by the other person. For example, when the decision has been made to dismiss or reassign a person, that generally is nonnegotiable. But the manner, timing, and other conditions associated with that decision, depending on circumstances, often can be left to the person who is being dismissed. This is respectful but also may have practical consequences by diminishing the risk of unintended actions and preserving some loyalty and self-esteem.

Calmness and imperturbability. People want their leaders to appear unrattled and in control (Eastwood 2010a). This is a big order because all leaders experience anger, slipping of control, or nervousness at times. William Osler (1904), a respected physician of the late 1800s and early 1900s, when he addressed the graduates of the University of Pennsylvania School of Medicine in 1889, said: "Imperturbability means coolness and presence of mind under all circumstances, calmness amid storm, clearness of judgment in moments of grave peril…the physician [leader] who has the misfortune to be without it, who betrays indecision and worry, and who shows that he is flustered…loses rapidly the confidence of his patients [constituents]." Some of us are innately calmer than others, but all of us can work on this.

Like other characteristics of leadership, perhaps if we practice calmness, we can become calmer.

Listening. Good leaders often are regarded as good communicators. This usually means they can speak effectively in various contexts, to individuals and to small and large groups, to explain and persuade. It also sometimes means they can write effectively in articles, notices, e-mails, and so on. But communication is not simply a one-way vector from the leader to others. Listening is an essential part of communication. It informs and strengthens other forms of communication.

We usually think of listening as something we do—or not do—when someone else is talking (Eastwood 2010a). That is the commonly understood form of listening and one in which good leaders become adept. Although this form of listening may seem, at first, to be a passive experience, listening can be an active, energy-requiring process, sometimes even an intense one. A good listener commands our attention, makes us appreciative of the listener, and may even encourage us to communicate better.

The roles of listener and speaker change in any conversation, but leaders often find themselves in situations in which they are expected to listen. Good listening requires the ability to focus and pay attention. Some leaders are naturally interested in what other people have to say; others need to work on that skill. Listening is of value to both the sender and the receiver. People want to know that their point of view is heard by someone who is in authority and who cares. They may want something to be done or to contribute to the decision-making process. The listener also benefits. This is how one learns a great deal of information.

Listening includes paying attention to nonverbal cues, such as body language, habits, punctuality, demeanor, mood, dress, and the like, all of which may be helpful in understanding and working with another person and in learning useful information.

As I have thought about listening, I have discovered other dimensions of listening that augment the mode of listening just described. One is to listen to my own reactions. Why am I pleased, grateful, frustrated, angry? Also, what do I have stored in my brain from experience or knowledge that I can 'listen' to and is relevant to this conversation?

Finally, the broadest form of listening is to be attentive to all inputs of information. Louis Pasteur, the French microbiologist (1822–95), said, "Chance favors the prepared mind." Many important discoveries have been made because someone has been 'listening' with a prepared mind (e.g., the discoveries of penicillin and radiation) and countless enlightenments have been experienced by leaders whose receptors for new information were ready for it.

Style. Because many leadership styles are effective and depend on endless variables of personality, experience, and context, it would be foolish to prescribe any particular style (Eastwood 1998). However, I believe that leaders are well-served to adopt the following accompaniments of style.

Try to be approachable. Being approachable does not necessarily mean that you always have your door open or are available at all times. It has to do with a sense that people develop about you from implicit and explicit cues that are related to your interest in and respect for them and not so much about what your schedule or calendar allows.

Be on time. This applies both to when you are in charge of an event and when you are a participant. It shows respect and contributes to your reliability and authenticity.

Use and enjoy your sense of humor. Some of us are innately funny; some are not. Some can tell jokes well; others not so well. Some are what I call situationally funny; they see the humor or irony in context, as it is unfolding. I encourage you to practice and develop your sense of humor for your own sake, as well as the sake of others.

Treat everyone with respect regardless of the other person's point of view or capabilities. This may be the hardest order because it sometimes challenges our own beliefs and uncertainties. When we think ill of another person, that may be well-founded, but it also may tell us more about ourselves than the other person. As Ralph Waldo Emerson (1841) said, "To be yourself in a world that is constantly trying to make you something else is the greatest accomplishment."

Are You Ready To Run the World?

> The world will not be run by those who possess mere information alone....The world henceforth will be run by synthesizers, people able to put together the right information at the right time, think critically about it, and make important choices wisely. (Wilson 1998)

I said at the outset that I believe we need leaders who have a broad understanding of human knowledge, experience, and motivation and who operate within a set of moral principles (Eastwood 2010b). How can one become such a leader? Here are some suggestions.

Pay attention to examples of good and bad leadership. Every day each of us witnesses leadership, in our immediate environment and elsewhere in politics, business, and so on. Good leadership and bad leadership are modeled constantly, sometimes by the same person. Pay attention to what you think makes someone a good leader or a bad one. What can you try to incorporate and use; what should you avoid or try to remove from your own repertoire?

Listen to Aristotle. Aristotle believed in the power of habit and that we become what we do repeatedly. Thus, if we practice being virtuous, we will become more virtuous. He said, "Moral virtue comes about as a result of habit" and "It is by doing just acts that the just person is produced" (Aristotle 1998). If we were able to ask Aristotle how to become a moral leader, he might say, "If you behave like a good leader, you will become a good leader."

This makes a lot of sense when we consider some of the skills I list above. For example, practicing listening is likely to make us a better listener. I believe it also applies to character traits. Perhaps you have heard someone say, with regard to empathy, "You either have it or you do not. There is nothing we can do to teach empathy." I disagree. Assuming one is not a sociopath, I believe that one can learn to be more empathetic, both by intending to do so and by practicing being empathetic.

Learn from your peers. One of the obligations of those who have influence over others' lives, which clearly includes leaders, is to pay attention to the circumstances under which we learn from others and, in turn, influence others' lives by providing a source of learning for them. Heroes and role models play a big part in the growing up process, even well into adulthood. Parents, teachers, coaches, and others often do not fully appreciate the profound ways they emotionally and intellectually touch and influence the lives of children and young adults.

Somewhere along our educational and early career path we commonly encounter mentors. "Mentor was an old friend of Odysseus, to whom the King had entrusted his whole household when he sailed, with orders to…keep everything intact." (Homer 1958). Odysseus told Mentor to take responsibility for the education and upbringing of his son, Telemachus. Thus, the origin of the term mentor. Mentors typically have qualities that we admire and want to emulate. They usually guide us in practical, operational matters, helping us to find our direction and learn what to do and how to do it. They also often help us understand what is important and develop our values and sense of purpose.

After heroes and mentors, what then? The majority of one's years remain, the horizon of life is distant, and, we hope, the main learning of life has just begun. The unequal relationships with heroes, mentors, teachers, and the like recede and what persists is the routine of day-to-day interaction with many people, professionally and socially, who more or less are our peers in that they are people with whom we do not have an unequal relationship. I came to understand the power of peer relationships in influencing our thoughts and behaviors when I learned more about the remarkable friendship of the Nobel Prize-winning writer John Steinbeck and the marine biologist Ed Ricketts (Eastwood 2004). Steinbeck, Ricketts, and others, including the mythologist Joseph Campbell, met frequently at Ricketts' laboratory-home in Monterey, California, and exchanged ideas. The discussions, which lasted hours, sometimes days, aided by quantities of beer, produced several theories that found expression in Steinbeck's novels and ensured a place for "Doc" Ricketts in several of Steinbeck's novels. In remembering his friend, Steinbeck (1951) said, "Everyone near him was influenced by him, deeply and permanently. Some he taught how to think, others how to see or hear." We do not need to have such an intense relationship with our peers to benefit from them. I believe that relationships and friendships with peers, by the exchange of ideas or observation, are among the richest sources of our education as mature adults.

You are what you read…and see, and hear, and think and talk about. Steven Sample (2002), the former president of the University of Southern California, argues that leaders are influenced heavily by what they read. He also advises that leaders would be better served to spend their time reading the masterpieces of literature than the contemporary news. Perhaps. Although reading is an enjoyable and fertile source of information and perspective for many, I believe that we also can be enriched by television, movies, social media, solitary thinking, and conversation with peers to achieve a broad understanding of human knowledge, experience, and motivation (Eastwood 2010b).

The world needs leaders who use both analytical and intuitive thinking, who can fuse their left brain and their right brain; who appreciate the value of history, the social sciences, literature, biology, genetics, philosophy, mathematics, physics, engineering, nanotechnology, and so on, and who understand why all of these disciplines are important and how they are related, because everything is related; who can recruit from a broad knowledge and experience and, "put together the right information at the right time, think critically about it, and make important choices wisely" (Eastwood 2010b; Wilson 1998). "Science and technology teach us what we *can* do. Humanistic thinking can help us understand what we *should* do" (Brinkley 2009).

Develop your code. The columnist David Brooks (2001), in an essay titled "The Limits of Empathy," said, "People who actually perform pro-social action don't only feel [i.e., have empathy] for those who are suffering, they feel compelled to act by a sense of duty. Their lives are structured by sacred codes.... [Empathy] is overshadowed by their sense of obligation to some religious, military, social or philosophic code. They would feel a sense of shame or guilt if they didn't live up to the code. The code tells them when they deserve public admiration or dishonor. The code helps them evaluate other people's feelings, not just share them.... The code isn't just a set of rules. It's a source of identity. It's pursued with joy. It arouses the strongest emotions and attachments. Empathy is a sideshow."

What is your code?

A Benediction

May you never forget the ideals that drive you now. The hardening process of life and experience will work at you. But if you lose your passion and ideals, you will die inside before you are forty and you will be an unhappy person. I urge you to nurture whatever ideals you now have, because that is what will sustain you and keep your spirit alive for as long as you live, and you will find it remarkably fulfilling.

May you look for ways to change the world. You will have many opportunities for personal growth and satisfaction, but you also will have opportunities to benefit humankind and change the world. Usually those opportunities, which arrive everyday, seem small and insignificant by themselves. But each is important and together, and as they accumulate, can be magnificent and remarkably effective.

May you look for opportunities to be a leader. You are ideally suited for leadership. You are so gifted with wonderful intellectual and humanistic abilities, and you are strongly motivated and you have a great deal of energy. These all are important characteristics of good leaders. The world needs leaders like you, who can access diverse, complex information and synthesize it, put it together in a coherent way, and explain it so people can understand. Leaders who can think big and can think small. Leaders who use both analytical and intuitive thinking. I urge you to answer the call to leadership. The need is great for the leadership that you are so capable of giving.

May you be truthful and trustworthy. People often will forgive you if you make a mistake in good faith and your reputation is one of honesty and forthrightness. They will not forgive you easily and will cease to respond to your leadership if you are deceptive and untrustworthy.

May you be wildly successful. If success for you means social prominence, influence, money, and achievements that society values, I hope you *are* successful in those areas, without harm to others. If success means a feeling of commitment, fulfillment, and self worth, I hope you are successful, without qualification.

Finally, may you be a credit to this university, to those who love you, and to yourself.

References

Anonymous. 2011. Comment on Syracuse, NY, *Post-Standard* blog in response to report of cheating at SUNY Upstate Medical University. March 24.

Aristotle. 1998. *The Nicomachean Ethics*. Oxford: Oxford University Press.

Baldwin, DeWitt C, Jr., et al. 1996. "Cheating in Medical School: A Survey of Second-year Students at 31 Schools." *Academic Medicine* 71 (3): 267–73.

Brinkley, Alan. 2009. "Half a Mind is a Terrible Thing to Waste." *Newsweek*, November 23, 48.

Brooks, David. 2011. "The Limits of Empathy." *New York Times*. Sept 29.

Burns, Robert. 1786. "To a Louse."

Carpenter, Donald D, et al. 2006. "Engineering Students' Perceptions of and Attitudes Towards Cheating." *Journal of Engineering Education* 95 (3):181–204.

Cross, Al. 2009. "*Louisville Courier-Journal* regarding comments by Sen. Jim Bunning." *New York Times*, March 6.

Eastwood, Gregory L. 2004. "Commentary: About Ed Ricketts." *Academic Medicine* 79: 680–81.

Eastwood, Gregory L. 2010a. "How Literature Informs Notions of Leadership." *Journal of Leadership Education* 9:173–89.

Eastwood, Gregory L. 1998. "Leadership Amid Change." In *Mission Management*. Washington, DC: Association of Academic Health Centers.

Eastwood, Gregory L. 2010b. "Leadership to run the world: A Mandate for Higher Education." *Journal of Academic Leadership* 8 (3).

Emerson, Ralph Waldo. 1841. *Self Reliance*.

Ford, Gerald R. 2001. "Acceptance speech, Profile in Courage Award Ceremony." John F. Kennedy Presidential Library, Boston, Massachusetts, May 21.

Giamatti, A. Bartlett. 1988. *A Free and Ordered Space. The Real World of the University*. New York: Norton and Co.

Harding, Trevor S., et al. 2004. "Does academic dishonesty relate to unethical behavior in professional practice?" *Science and Engineering Ethics* 10 (2):311–24.

Homer. 1958. *The Odyssey*. Translated by E. V. Rieu. Baltimore: Penguin Books.

Lee, Harper. 1960. *To Kill A Mockingbird*. Philadelphia: J. B. Lippincott Company.

Mulder, James T. 2011. "Upstate Medical Students May Be Disciplined if Investigation Shows They Cheated on Quizzes." *Syracuse Post-Standard*, March 10.

Osler, William. 1904. *Aequanimitas*. Philadelphia: P. Blakiston's Son, & Co.

Papadakis, Maxine A., et al. 2005. "Disciplinary Action by Medical Boards and Prior Behavior in Medical School." *New England Journal of Medicine* 353: 2673–82.

Perez-Pena, Richard. 2013. "Students Disciplined in Harvard Scandal." *New York Times*, February 1.

Perez-Pena, Richard. 2012. "Studies Find More Students Cheating, With High Achievers No Exception." *New York Times*, September 7.

Roberts, Jeffrey A. and David M. Wasieleski. 2012. "Moral Reasoning in Computer-Based Task Environments: Exploring the Interplay between Cognitive and Technological Factors on Individuals' Propensity to Break Rules." *Journal of Business Ethics* 110 (3): 355–76.

Rostand, Edmond. 1950. *Cyrano de Bergerac*. Translated by Brian Hooker. New York: Bantam Books.

Sample, Steven B. 2002. *The Contrarian's Guide to Leadership*. San Francisco: Jossey-Bass.

Steinbeck, John. 1951. "About Ed Rickets." In *The Log From the Sea of Cortez*. New York: Viking Press.

Tzu, Sun. 1988. *The Art of War*. Translated by Thomas Cleary. Boston: Shambala.

Wilson, Edward O. 1998. *Consilience: The Unity of Knowledge*. New York: Alfred A. Knopf.

Zamost, Scott, Drew Griffen, and Azadeh Ansari. 2012. "Doctors Cheated on Exams." *CNN*, January 13. http://www.cnn.com/2012/01/13/health/prescription-for-cheating.

The Definition of Terrorism

Duncan Gaswaga
Distinguished Jurist in Residence,
Case Western Reserve University

Introduction

Terrorism, just like the crime of aggression, is a recognized crime which the international community has been very slow to formulate or assign a single, all-encompassing or universally agreed upon and legally binding criminal law definition. In some quarters, the difficulty in defining terrorism is in agreeing on the basis for determining when the use of violence (directed at whom, by whom, for what ends) is legitimate. Thus, the difficulty lies in the fundamental values at stake in the acceptance or rejection of terror-inspiring violence as means of accomplishing a given goal (Bassiouni 1988, xv–xvi). Interestingly, terrorism is a global phenomenon which is easy to recognize, but yet difficult to define (Prabha 2013). At the World Summit on terrorism in New York on September 14, 2005, terrorism, "in all its forms and manifestations, committed by whomever, wherever and for whatever purpose," was condemned. Historically, the dispute over the meaning of terrorism arose when the laws of war were first codified in 1899 (Pustogarov 1996, 300–314). As such, different legal systems, scholars, international organizations, and government agencies use different definitions of terrorism, sometimes based on their socioeconomic and political conditions (Hoffman 1998, 32). No wonder then, that there are over 130 definitions of terrorism that have been coined or formulated by various scholars and entities.

The situation is also complicated by the failure to draw a line between actual terrorists and those persons that try to justify their actions by claiming to be freedom fighters. Technically, freedom fighters struggling for the right to self-determination would not be categorized as terrorists, although, in many cases the groups have carried out atrocities akin to those committed by terrorists. Moreover, it has long been stated that one man's terrorist is another man's freedom fighter. In some instances there is also a religious aspect to it as well. In the Arab and Islamic world, some have considered and praised certain factions of extremists as martyrs and not as terrorists for the atrocities carried out by their militant wings. It is worth noting that terrorism is a pejorative term. It is an ambiguous word with intrinsically negative connotations that is generally applied to one's enemies and opponents or to those with whom one disagrees and would otherwise prefer to ignore. Defining terrorism has emerged as a central focus of power politics and propaganda (Acharya 2009, 653). Hence the decision to label someone or an organization 'terrorist' becomes almost unavoidably subjective, depending largely on whether one sympathizes with or opposes the person/group/cause concerned.

The violence that uses terrorism as a tactic includes not only state-sponsored regimes of fear, but also a religious ideology-based terrorism, which calls for securing and protecting sacred lands and sacred religious and cultural practices (Maan 1998, 13). The fatwa declared by the 1998 World Islamic Council, of which Bin Laden was a co-author, can be considered an ideology-based statement of terrorism translated into action on September 11, 2001 (Bodansky 2001, 226–27). This fatwa calls for "kill[ing] Americans and their allies—civilians and military...in order to liberate the Al-Aqsa [Jerusalem] Mosque and the Holy Mosque [Mecca] from their grip, and in order for their armies to move out all of the lands of Islam...and plunder their money wherever and whenever...and launch the raid in Satan's U.S. troops and Devil's supporters allying with them...." (Bodanksy 2001, 226–27; see also Freamon 2003). The 9/11 event, a recent example of ideology-based terrorism, established state and nonstate terrorist activities and forced the world to ponder once again the nature, meaning, and understanding of terrorism. With 9/11 came fluctuations in the political agenda of powerful nations and oppressed groups,[1] artificially manufactured, ideologically motivated or naturally evolving to address internal or external political situations (Acharya 2009, 654–55).

This article critically analyzes some definitions of terrorism with a view to pointing out the weaknesses and pertinent missing components. A comparison of some of the definitions formulated by scholars, governments, or agencies will be done to assist in creating what the author believes to be a list of the crucial ingredients or elements of the offense of terrorism. In particular, the paper will also discuss the question of whether pirates on the high seas could be considered terrorists, since they use firearms in their attacks, which at times results in severe injuries and death, as well as political actions taken against them by the affected governments.

---

1. Suppressed groups have been identified with devaluation and ideology, poverty, relative deprivation, sense of injustice, difficult life conditions, repressive societies, and us-them differentiation. These suppressed groups are a potential root cause of nonstate terrorism. *See* Staub 2002, 207, 209–12.

The Need for a Definition of Terrorism

I shall start by posing a question: Why should further scholarly effort be engaged towards coming up with another definition which may create more uncertainty or confusion to an already unclear situation?

It is imperative to first underscore the importance of having a definite and concise definition of terrorism. The constitutions (supreme law) of many countries[2] provide, and indeed it is a universal cardinal rule, that no person should be charged and punished with an offense that is not clearly defined in a given piece of legislation and the corresponding punishment thereof clearly prescribed. Acts tantamount to criminal conduct should be spelled out and codified well before the fact, since criminal law does not operate retroactively. It therefore follows that without a good definition encompassing all the elements of the offense, the perpetrators will fall through the loopholes and escape punishment. The authorities would only be able to stand firm on a good piece of legislation to initiate prosecutions and enforce law and order to contain terrorism.

Under international law, defining terrorism is important for the ability to condemn violations of human rights, to protect the state and deliberative politics, to differentiate public and private violence, and to ensure international peace and security (Saul 2008, 1). It would also help to protect community values and interests. Generally, criminal law has three purposes: to declare that a conduct is forbidden, to prevent it, and to express society's condemnation for the wrongful acts. The symbolic, normative role of criminalization is of particular importance in the case of terrorism. The criminalization of terrorist acts expresses society's repugnance at them, invokes social censure and shame, and stigmatizes those who commit them. Moreover, by creating and reaffirming value, criminalization may serve, in the long run, as a deterrent to terrorism, as those values are internalized (Diaz-Paniagua 2008, 41). Thus, as Diaz-Paniagua (2008, 41) observes, international criminal law treaties that seek to prevent, condemn, and punish terrorist activities, require precise definitions.[3] As a result of the world's failure to reach agreement on

---

2. For instance, Art. 19 (4) of the Seychelles Constitution.
3. Ibid., 46–47, "The definition of the offence in criminal law treaty plays several roles. First and foremost, it has the symbolic, normative role of expressing society's condemnation of the forbidden acts. Second, it facilitates agreement. Since states tend to be reluctant to undertake stringent obligations in matters related to the exercise of their domestic jurisdiction, a precise definition of the crime, which restricts the scope of those obligations, makes agreement less costly. Third, it provides an inter-subjective basis for the homogeneous application of the treaty's obligations on judicial and police cooperation. This function is of particular importance in extradition treaties because, to grant an extradition, most legal

the definition, countries cannot fully cooperate against terrorism without knowing the scope of the phenomenon against which they would be required to impose legal sanctions.

Definition of Terrorism in Some Domestic Jurisdictions

Many countries have come up with Suppression of Terrorism Acts (SOTA) to fight against terrorism. Some definitions of terrorism by domestic jurisdictions are briefly examined below. In this regard, countries such as India, United States of America, United Kingdom, and Uganda will serve as examples, each with a definition that will suit their respective socioeconomic and political situations.

India

In the context of India, Kshitij Prabha (2013) defined terrorism as:

[A]n act or threat of an act of tactical violence by a group of trained individuals, having international linkage, to achieve political objective. This group could be sponsored by non-state or state agencies.

According to Prabha, this definition precisely covers all the aspects of terrorism. Before arriving at this definition, he analyzed and critiqued a few definitions of terrorism, each of which he felt were missing some vital components. Adopting David Easton's system theory, Prabha stated that he adopted the theory not merely because the phenomenon of terrorism has a direct effect on the socioeconomic and political system, but also because it (terrorism) emanates from within the same system. Therefore, a definition devoid of the socioeconomic and political issues involved in terrorism holds only for academic purposes, not for practical implications. In order to arrive at a functional definition of terrorism, a pragmatic approach to the problem would be more relevant, in which context terrorism could be broadly defined from two perspectives: the political perspective (group action and international linkage),[4] and the means perspective (violence and training).[5]

---

systems require that the crime be punishable both in the requesting state and the requested state. Fourth, it helps states to enact domestic legislation to criminalize and punish the wrongful acts defined in the treaty in conformity with their human rights' obligations. The principle of *nullum crimen sine lege* requires, in particular, that states define precisely which acts are prohibited before anyone can be prosecuted or punished for committing those same acts."

4. From the political perspective point of view, terrorism is defined as a political rather than a criminal or psychological phenomenon in the light of the fact that terrorists do not believe in personal gain or accumulation of wealth. Their sole objective is to acquire political power be it in the form of autonomy or creation of an independent state.

5. In the means perspective, terrorism is defined as a means in pursuit of realization of a political mission. While explaining the means, the model emphasizes the necessity of violence in terrorism. Violence employed by terrorists is of specific type i.e. tactical by nature.

However, this definition also excludes some vital components of the definition of terrorism—for example, an 'intentional' act or threat, which is very crucial in terrorism. Terrorist acts are not accidental but well-planned, directed, and therefore, intended. The definition also does not take note of the fact that these acts or attacks target civilians. Civilians are vulnerable and usually defenseless and therefore easy to attack. This, in turn, attracts the attention of the authorities (government). Terror tactics have always been used as means to an end (Crenshaw 1987, 13) and have been fairly effective in helping the terrorists to achieve their political objective. This definition does not explore other forms of terrorism like 'state terrorism' or 'cyber terrorism' being propagated by other authors. It works on the assumption that terrorism can only be perpetrated by nonstate entities. However, the Supreme Court of India adopted Alex P. Schmid's definition of terrorism in a 2003 ruling (*Madan Singh v. State of Bihar*),[6] "defining acts of terrorism veritably as 'peacetime equivalents of war crimes.'"

United States of America

The U.S. has several definitions of terrorism but the one that attempts to encompass all the components of terrorism is their definition of international terrorism, as codified in Title 22 of the United States Code. It contains a definition of terrorism and requires that annual reports on terrorism be submitted by the secretary of state to Congress. It reads:

> Definition ... the term 'terrorism' means premeditated, politically motivated violence perpetrated against noncombatant targets by subnational groups or clandestine agents;[7]

Title 18 of the United States Code (regarding criminal acts and criminal procedure) defines international terrorism as follows:

> [T]he term 'international terrorism' means activities that...involve violent acts or acts dangerous to human life that are a violation of the criminal laws of the United States or of any State, or that would be a criminal violation if committed within the jurisdiction of the United States or of any State; [and] appear to be intended...to intimidate or coerce a civilian population;...to influence the policy of a government by intimidation or coercion; or...to affect the conduct of a

---

Violence conveying a message to government is terrorism. Killing and arson devoid of publicity do not fit into the definition of terrorism. Furthermore, the tools of violence terrorists use demands professional training. A layman cannot operate sophisticated weapons and missiles used by terrorists. This aspect also needs attention while defining terrorism.
6. *Madan Singh v. State of Bihar*. 2003. Crl. Appeal No. 1297. Court of Appeal, India.
7. 22 U.S.C. § 2656f.

government by mass destruction, assassination, or kidnapping; and [which] occur primarily outside the territorial jurisdiction of the United States, or transcend national boundaries in terms of the means by which they are accomplished, the persons they appear intended to intimidate or coerce, or the locale in which their perpetrators operate or seek asylum.[8]

This definition appears to be all encompassing, but does not actually consider the aspect of state terrorism.

The United Kingdom

The United Kingdom[9] defines terrorism to include an act "designed seriously to interfere with or seriously to disrupt an electronic system." The drafters of this provision had in mind several crimes, including cybercrimes. But short as the definition may be, it seems to cover quite extensive ground. However, the definition fails to capture the crucial elements already listed above, like the purpose, the target group, other forms of terrorism, etc. For this definition, an act of violence is not even necessary.

Uganda

The definition in the Uganda anti-terrorism legislation is worth looking at in detail. Article 7(2) states:

A person commits an act of terrorism who, for purposes of influencing the Government or intimidating the public or a section of the public and for a political, religious, social or economic aim, indiscriminately without due regard to the safety of others or property, carries out all or any of the following acts—

(a) intentional and unlawful manufacture, delivery, placement, discharge or detonation of an explosive or other lethal device, whether attempted or actual, in, into or against a place of public use, a State or Government facility, a public transportation system or an infrastructure facility, with the intent to cause death or serious bodily injury, or extensive destruction likely to or actually resulting in major economic loss

(b) direct involvement or complicity in the murder, kidnapping, maiming or attack, whether actual, attempted or threatened, on a person or groups of persons, in public or private institutions;

(c) direct involvement or complicity in the murder, kidnapping,

---

8. 18 U.S.C. § 2331(1) (http://www.law.cornell.edu/uscode/18/usc_sec_18_00002331.000-html).
9. Terrorism Act, 2000.

abducting, maiming or attack, whether actual, attempted or threatened on the person, official premises, private accommodation, or means of transport or diplomatic agents or other internationally protected persons;

(d) intentional and unlawful provision or collection of funds, whether attempted or actual, with the intention or knowledge that any part of the funds may be used to carry out any of the terrorist activities under this Act;

(e) direct involvement or complicity in the seizure or detention of~ and threat to kill, injure or continue to detain a hostage, whether actual or attempted in order to compel a State, an international intergovernmental organization, a person or group of persons, to do or abstain from doing any act as an explicit or implicit condition for the release of the hostage;

(f) unlawful seizure of an aircraft or public transport or the hijacking of passengers or group of persons for ransom;

(g) serious interference with or disruption of an electronic system;

(h) unlawful importation, sale, making, manufacture or distribution of any firearms, explosive, ammunition or bomb;

(i) intentional development or production or use of, or complicity in the development or production or use of a biological weapon;

(j) unlawful possession of explosives, ammunition, bomb or any materials for making of any of the foregoing.[10]

This is a catchall definition (catering to not only the perpetrators, but also different aiders and abettors), which was drafted immediately after the 9/11 attacks, and given its imprecision, many human rights groups, NGOs, and political groups have criticized it. The criticism stems from the appearance that the government's intention was also to deal with its political opponents and stop them from demonstrating. It addresses the act of terrorism itself, against whom this act is directed, and the actions that will facilitate the act. It also makes provisions for more aggressive investigation techniques. Although the definition appears comprehensive in response to domestic terrorism, it may be wanting in response to international terrorism.

Ghana

The Ghana anti-terrorism Act No. 762 came into force on the October 13, 2008. According to Estelle Appiah (2013, 3–4), it was enacted in furtherance of the United Nations Security Council Resolution (SCR) 1373,

---

10. Anti-Terrorism Act, No. 14 of 2002, Uganda.

the Commonwealth Plan of Action on Terrorism, and the Organization for African Unity Convention. The act addresses terrorism, terrorist financing, and the issues contained in SCR 1373. It prohibits terrorist acts. In the act, an act is a terrorist act if it is "in furtherance of a political, ideological, religious, racial or ethnic cause, if it causes serious bodily harm, causes serious damage to property, endangers a person's life, creates a serious risk to the health or safety of the public or involves the use of firearms." Just like the definition in the Uganda terrorism law, this act does not include aspects of international terrorism.

Definition of Terrorism by Regional and International Organizations

European Union

The European Union defines terrorism for legal/official purposes as follows: [T]errorist offences are certain criminal offences set out in a list comprised largely of serious offences against persons and property which: given their nature or context, may seriously damage a country or an international organization where committed with the aim of: seriously intimidating a population; or unduly compelling a Government or international organization to perform or abstain from performing any act; or seriously destabilizing or destroying the fundamental political, constitutional, economic or social structures of a country or an international organization.[11]

Although this definition is more detailed compared to all those above, it does not also have the aspect of state terrorism.

United Nations

For over forty years, the United Nations (UN) has been struggling with acts of terrorism. Since the member states have no agreed upon definition of terrorism, this continues to be a major obstacle to meaningful international countermeasures. Of course, a terminology consensus would be necessary for a single comprehensive convention on terrorism, which some countries favor, in place of the present twelve piecemeal conventions and protocols. It is worth noting that the UN General Assembly Report of the Ad Hoc Committee on International Terrorism was an important document in the history of terrorism[12] as it triggered a lot of debate in this direction.

---

11. In Art. 1 of the Framework Decision on Combating Terrorism (2002).
12. UN General Assembly Report of the Ad Hoc Committee on International Terrorism, twenty-eighth session, A/9028, 1973; Prabha 2013, stating that after recalling the 1972

So, in order to create an effective legal regime to prevent and punish international terrorism, rather than only working on a single, all-encompassing, comprehensive definition of terrorism, the international community has also adopted a 'sectoral' approach, aimed at identifying offenses seen as belonging to the activities of terrorists and working out treaties in order to deal with specific categories thereof (Gioia 2006, 4). The UN approach has therefore been that the treaties focus on the wrongful nature of terrorist activities, rather than on their intent, where specific offenses are considered *in themselves* as offenses of international concern, irrespective of any 'terrorist' intent or purpose (ibid.). The advocates of this approach contend that it helps in avoiding problems of defining 'terrorism' or 'terrorist acts.' The conventions so far adopted include:[13]

- The 1963 Convention on Offenses and Certain Other Acts Committed On Board Aircraft
- The 1970 Convention for the Suppression of Unlawful Seizure of Aircraft
- The 1971 Convention for the Suppression of Unlawful Acts Against the Safety of Civil Aviation
- The 1979 Convention on the Physical Protection of Nuclear Material

---

resolution entitled "Measures to prevent international terrorism which endangers or takes innocent human lives or jeopardizes fundamental freedoms, and study of the underlying causes of those forms of terrorism and acts of violence which lie in misery, frustration, grievance and despair, and which cause some people to sacrifice human lives, including their own, in an attempt to effect radical changes," the Ad Hoc Committee established three subcommittees to examine definition, causes, and prevention of terrorism. Seven draft proposals were submitted by different nations to the subcommittee on the definition of terrorism. Apparently the house was divided. Therefore no resolution on the definition of terrorism could be adopted. The matter remained suspended until 1987 when the Secretary General convened an international conference to define terrorism and differentiate it from freedom fighting. This conference was successful in the sense that members agreed to identify terrorism with crime and accordingly a future plan of action was proposed. Taking note of the Secretary Generals` report of the conference, the UN General Assembly condemned all acts of terrorism except those fighting for the right to self-determination against foreign and racist regimes as `criminal` (Resolution adopted on the reports of the Sixth Committee, General Assembly, 94th Meeting, Dated December 7, 1987, Report: A/42/832). An overwhelming majority adopted this resolution. However, remarkably the U.S. and Israel voted against the resolution while Honduras abstained. Thus after fifteen years of deliberations and counter-deliberations, finally the UN came to the conclusion that all acts of terrorism are criminal.

13. Following this approach, the international community has adopted these sectoral counter-terrorism conventions, which are open to the ratification of all states.

- The 1988 Protocol for the Suppression of Unlawful Acts of Violence at Airports Serving International Civil Aviation
- The 1988 Convention for the Suppression of Unlawful Acts Against the Safety of Maritime Navigation
- The 1988 Protocol for the Suppression of Unlawful Acts Against the Safety of Fixed Platforms Located on the Continental Shelf
- The 1991 Convention on the Marking of Plastic Explosives for the Purpose of Identification
- The 1997 International Convention for the Suppression of Terrorist Bombings
- The 1999 International Convention for the Suppression of the Financing of Terrorism
- The 2005 International Convention for the Suppression of Acts of Nuclear Terrorism

Certain aspects are inescapable when one looks at these treaties. They all adopted an 'operational definition' of a specific type of terrorist act; one that was defined without reference to the underlying political or ideological purpose[14] or motivation of the perpetrator of the act. This reflected a consensus that there were some acts that were such a serious threat to the interests of all that they could not be justified by reference to such motives. They all focused on actions by nonstate individuals and organizations and the state was seen as an active ally in the struggle against terrorism. The question of the state itself as terrorist actor was left largely to one side; and finally, they all adopted a criminal law enforcement model to address the problem, under which states would cooperate in the apprehension and prosecution of those alleged to have committed these crimes.

Again here, depending on the individual state interests, one cannot be sure whether fugitives in foreign countries could be prosecuted or extradited for terrorism charges if there is an unwillingness or lack of commitment on the part of the relevant state. Before going too far, it should be pointed out that it is problematic for the UN to rely entirely on states as allies in their definition of terrorism and totally ignore state terrorism or state-sponsored terrorism, which involves acts of terrorism conducted by governments or terrorism carried out directly by, or encouraged and funded by, an established government of a state (country) or terrorism practiced by a government against its own people or in support of international terrorism.

---

14. http://en.wikipedia.org/wiki/Motive_(law)

Be that as it may, the UN still feels the need for having a comprehensive, agreed upon, and workable general definition, and since 2000, a comprehensive convention on international terrorism is ongoing. The definition of terrorism therein, which has been on the negotiating table since 2002 reads thus:

1. Any person commits an offence within the meaning of this Convention if that person, by any means, unlawfully and intentionally, causes:

(a) Death or serious bodily injury to any person; or

(b) Serious damage to public or private property, including a place of public use, a State or government facility, a public transportation system, an infrastructure facility or the environment; or

(c) Damage to property, places, facilities, or systems referred to in paragraph 1 (b) of this article, resulting or likely to result in major economic loss, when the purpose of the conduct, by its nature or context, is to intimidate a population, or to compel a Government or an international organization to do or abstain from doing any act.[15]

This definition, too, has attracted some controversy and opposition, as Deen (2005) states "what distinguishes a 'terrorist organization' from a 'liberation movement'? And do you exclude activities of national armed forces, even if they are perceived to commit acts of terrorism? If not, how much of this constitutes 'state terrorism'?" The debate continues. Various resolutions on and definitions of terrorism have been formulated and adopted or used by different UN instruments and agencies such as: the UN General Assembly Resolution 49/60,[16] the UN Security Council Resolution 1566 (2004),[17] and a UN panel, on March 17, 2005.[18]

---

15. United Nations General Assembly, Report of the Ad Hoc Committee, sixth session, (January 28–February 1, 2002), Annex II, art. 2.1.

16. Adopted on December 9, 1994, titled "Measures to Eliminate International Terrorism," contains a provision describing terrorism: Criminal acts intended or calculated to provoke a state of terror in the general public, a group of persons or particular persons for political purposes are in any circumstance unjustifiable, whatever the considerations of a political, philosophical, ideological, racial, ethnic, religious or any other nature that may be invoked to justify them.

17. Gives a definition: criminal acts, including against civilians, committed with the intent to cause death or serious bodily injury, or taking of hostages, with the purpose to provoke a state of terror in the general public or in a group of persons or particular persons, intimidate a population or compel a government or an international organization to do or to abstain from doing any act.

18. Described terrorism as any act "intended to cause death or serious bodily harm to civilians or non-combatants with the purpose of intimidating a population or compelling a government or an international organization to do or abstain from doing any act."

Some of the treaties define their offenses by including special intent requirements, but those fall short of requiring a political or other motive. For instance, the 1999 Terrorist Financing Convention prohibits the financing of certain acts where the purpose "is to intimidate a population or to compel a government...to do or abstain from doing any act."[19] While this definition partly signals a focus on repressing public-oriented violence—by targeting acts directed at the community or a government—it still does not accurately capture terrorism.[20] For it is still possible to intimidate a population or compel a government for a host of private, nonpolitical reasons, including simple extortion.

As a result of their failure to include motive elements, many of the existing anti-terrorism treaties reach considerably beyond the common understanding of terrorism, since violence for public and private motives alike is equally criminalized. Thus hostage taking or hijacking for profit or to obtain custody of a child in a family dispute is treated no differently than identical acts committed in pursuit of a political cause. The lack of differentiation arguably fails to distinguish between other violent acts and terrorism, which is not inherent in a physical act of violence alone (Lambert 1990, 49). As Levitt writes:

> Not all hijackings, sabotages, attacks on diplomats, or even hostage-takings are 'terrorist;' such acts may be done for personal or pecuniary reasons or simply out of insanity. The international instruments that address these acts are thus 'overbroad'...(Levitt 1986, 115; *see also* Saul 2008)

Can Pirates Be Categorized as Terrorists?

It is well beyond dispute that pirates use violence to capture ships, merchandise, and crew, which they hold for ransom. On the other hand, terrorists are not necessarily criminals.[21] Criminals have no political aim, yet politics is the main consideration for terrorism. In the case of *Rep. v. Mohamed Dahir and Others*,[22] it was argued by the attorney general that the pirates had used firearms to shoot at the coast guard, who were executing lawful orders by policing the Seychelles territory. Further, that by firing at them, the pirates

---

19. 1999 Terrorist Financing Convention, art 2(1) (b).
20. Human Rights and Equal Opportunity Commission (Australia), Supplementary Submission to the Security Legislation Review Committee (2006), 8.
21. The link between crime and terrorism could be established, but to identify the two as one would be misleading. Criminals do not have political purpose unless they are converted to terrorism. Normally their aim is to acquire wealth. They are more concerned about the economy of the state and the individuals rather than the political situation; whereas politics is the main consideration of terrorists.
22. Supreme Court of Seychelles, Cr. No. 51 of 2009.

intended to interfere with the surveillance and sabotage the economy of the government of Seychelles, knowing very well that the main activities of fishing and tourism could not continue in such circumstances. The Supreme Court held that not every firing of a rifle is terrorism; for it to be terrorism, it was crucial to establish that the perpetrators had a political aim.[23] Perhaps if the attorney general's position was argued in the European Union, following the above definition, it could have succeeded, since the Seychelles government was unduly compelled by the pirates to abstain from continuing with the patrolling of its territorial waters. The Uganda definition (above) is the only one that directly includes piracy, as it appears that the drafters were looking to categorize all types of violence as terrorism.

Definition of Terrorism by the International Criminal Tribunals/Courts: The United Nations Special Tribunal for Lebanon (STL)

This is a special tribunal[24] that was set up specifically to deal with the crime of terrorism which arose as a result of the bombing that killed former

---

23. Ibid, pp. 19–20, paras 40, 41 and 43, per Judge Gaswaga: [40] "Whereas it is true that by firing at the *"Topaz"* there was a possibility of it getting damaged and preventing the crew or the Government of Seychelles from patrolling its EEZ, I am unable to agree with the prosecution that this was the objective of the accused." [42] "Like I have already stated intention can be inferred from the facts and surrounding circumstances. However, I see no pertinent concrete facts to base such requisite logical and irresistible inference here. This decision is fortified by the evidence on record. Both parties accept that pirates hijack ships for a financial ransom. On the fateful day they were on the high seas waiting to chance on any ship that came by and not in particular the *"Topaz"*. No evidence on record tends to suggest that *"Topaz"* or the government of Seychelles was being targeted. *"Topaz"* was not even expected in that area at the time of the incident, it had been called upon and directed there by the maritime aircraft. The Captain of *"Topaz"*, Major Simon Laurencin's testimony is pertinent in strengthening this position. He stated that unless one is close and well informed about ships, it's difficult to tell at night whether *"Topaz"* is a war ship or passenger ship especially when the lights are on. According to him, had the accused known that *"Topaz"* was a war ship they would not have attacked it." [43] "It cannot therefore be strongly argued that the intention of the whole attack was to compel the Government of Seychelles to limit or to stop patrolling and monitoring its EEZ. Although one could attempt to say that the presence of the accused in a piracy infested area combined with their subsequent attacks on *"Topaz"* in a way impacted on the business of the Seychelles Government in its EEZ, it should be noted that this is too remote to hold the offenders criminally liable for. And even if it were so, it does not tantamount to terrorism. Not every use or firing of riffles is taken as terrorism. It is true that the Government of Seychelles may have suffered as a result in many aspects i.e. security, transport, fishing, tourism, and maritime business generally, but all this cannot be stretched and heaped on the accused in criminal charges of terrorism as it was never their intention."
24. Having been established by an agreement between the United Nations and the Lebanese Republic pursuant to Security Council resolution 1664 (2006) of March 29, 2006, which responded to the request of the government of Lebanon to establish a tribunal of an international character to try all those who are found responsible for the terrorist crime which killed the former Lebanese Prime Minister Rafiq Hariri and others.

Prime Minister Rafiq Hariri, as well as other related offenses. The failure by the international community to agree on a legal definition for such a long time was somehow brought to an end[25] by Judge Cassese's definition of a customary international crime of transnational terrorism in 2011.[26] In spite of all the criticism that followed, it is imperative to acknowledge that these were indeed steps taken in the right direction, towards establishing a definition of terrorism in international law, one which mainly consisted of the three elements listed below:

(i) the perpetration of a criminal act (such as murder, kidnapping, hostage-taking, arson, and so on), or threatening such an act;

(ii) the intent to spread fear among the population (which would generally entail the creation of public danger) or directly or indirectly coerce a national or international authority to take some action, or to refrain from taking it;

(iii) when the act involves a transnational element.[27]

Ben Saul has observed that the requirement of a transnational element[28] rules out purely domestic terrorism. That while the tribunal recognized only peace-time terrorism as a crime, it indicated that "a broader norm that would outlaw terrorist acts *during times of armed conflict* may also be emerging."[29] Further, that state practice does not, however, support the conclusion reached by the tribunal. Instead, a close analysis of relevant treaties, United Nations resolutions, national laws, and national judicial decisions[30] confirms the near-universal scholarly consensus that there does not yet exist a customary law dealing with terrorism as defined by the tribunal (Saul 2012).

Potential Areas for Consideration

The definition of terrorism should be forward-looking as well, considering areas which are new and unclear, yet very vital in the arena of terrorism.

---

25. By recognizing a definition of terrorism in customary law, the Special Tribunal neatly sidestepped almost a century of legal deadlocks in (ongoing) treaty negotiations and debates in bodies such as the UN General Assembly and Security Council.

26. UN Special Tribunal for Lebanon (Appeals Chamber), *Interlocutory Decision on the Applicable Law: Terrorism, Conspiracy, Homicide, Perpetration, Cumulative Charging*, STL-11-01/I, February 16, 2011.

27. Ibid., para. 85.

28. Ibid., para. 90.

29. Ibid., para. 107–9.

30. Including regional anti-terrorism treaties, General Assembly resolutions, UN Security Council resolution 1566 (2004), the UN Draft Comprehensive Anti-Terrorism Convention, the Terrorist Financing Convention 1999, thirty-seven national laws, and nine national judicial decisions.

Some of these situations pose potential terrorism issues, which are emerging with the rapid development in technology, and one cannot afford to ignore them. The above definitions have not considered these offenses, which are most likely to come up in the future, such as cyberterrorism, poisoning of water sources or other natural resources on which a given population of the pertinent territory depends for survival, threatening, instilling fear, or scaring people with anthrax in envelopes and parcels, etc.

There is also the aspect of 'nonpolitical violence,' which may require the critical eye of researchers or investigators when dealing with this subject, so as to be able to categorize them. This includes operations of piracy, mafia groups, hate crimes, bomb threats, and transborder terrorism by narcotics gangs, all of which have elements similar to or in one way or the other related to terrorism. The most visible link is the funding of terrorist groups which have a political agenda. Since it is said that a country will legislate based on its problems and aspirations, so it is imperative that a definition of such an evolving crime looks at other potential areas, giving rise to related crimes to avoid legislating for each and every eventuality in future.

General Discussion and Observations on the Definition of Terrorism

Generally, of the many definitions commonly cited by authors, the following usually appear in authoritative publications.[31] Yonah Alexander (1976, XIV) defines terrorism as: "the use of violence against random civilian targets in order to intimidate or to create generalized pervasive fear for the purpose of achieving political goals." After studying a number of definitions by various authors, Alex P. Schmid compiled the following elements which he contends adequately define terrorism:

> Terrorism is an anxiety-inspiring method of repeated violent action, employed by clandestine individual groups or state actors, for idiosyncratic, criminal or political reasons, whereby—in contrast to assassination—the direct targets of violence are not the main targets. The immediate human targets of violence are generally chosen randomly or selectively from a target population, and serve as message generators. Threat and violence based communication processes between terrorists' victims, and main targets are used to manipulate the main target, turning it into a targeting of terror, a target of demands, or

---

31. Authors such as Prabha 2013.

a target of attention, depending on whether intimidation, coercion or propaganda is primarily sought. (Schmid and Jongman 1988, 28)

An examination of Alexander's definition would reveal that it is precise and is often quoted by scholars, but lacks an important aspect of terrorism, i.e., international linkage. Terrorists cannot inflict terror without the funding and infrastructure facilities that they receive from international connections. For instance, the Kashmiri militants received military and financial assistance from mujahideens from Pakistan and Afghanistan, while the U.K. based IRA had operational units in the U.S. (Corrado 1979, 198). They also received funds from Libyan mercenaries. (Carlton and Shaerif 1974, 38). The international connections also help with training, especially in operating the sophisticated gadgets used in terrorism. Besides, eighty years ago, the League of Nations had already considered terrorism as a transnational legal problem (Saul 2006, 78). As for Alex Schmid, his definition goes into detail of the phenomenon of terrorism, but remains more focused on targets and objectives than its basic nature.

Another author, Brian Jenkins (1978, 115–23), writes that the threat of violence, individual acts of violence, or a campaign of violence designed primarily to instill fear is terrorism. This definition of terrorism is close to the concept of terrorism, but ignores two significant aspects, e.g., training and international support. The definitions offered by Christopher Dobson and Martha Crenshaw tend to stress the aspects of training and international support. Dobson stated that "[to] use explosive devices of any but the simplest kind needs a good deal of training" (Dobson and Payne 1979, 67), while Martha Crenshaw (1987, 13) stressed the need for international assistance in her definition of terrorism, opining that terrorism is a means to accomplish certain political objectives with international support. As for Michael Walzer (1980, 201–3), who defines terrorism in historical perspective, he believes that "random terror for political achievement emerged as strategy of revolutionary struggle after the World War II."

Perhaps I should mention at this point that state terrorism, which is not mentioned as much by scholars in most of the definitions, is as controversial a concept as that of terrorism itself. Terrorism is often, though not always, defined in terms of four characteristics: (1) the threat or use of violence; (2) a political objective; the desire to change the status quo; (3) the intention to spread fear by committing spectacular public acts; and (4) the intentional targeting of civilians. This last element—targeting innocent civilians—is problematic when one tries to distinguish state terrorism from other forms of state violence. Moreover, it is not uncommon to hear that democratic regimes may foster state terrorism of populations outside their borders; but they do not terrorize their own populations because a regime that is truly based on the violent suppression of most citizens (not simply some) would cease to be democratic. Dictatorships terrorize their own populations; democracies do not, but they can engage in state-sponsored terrorism in other countries. Likewise, some scholars define terrorism in the light of violence and coercion by state agencies. Walter Laquer (1987), for instance, defines acts of violence and repression carried out by the government against their own people as terrorism. In the same vein, Neil Livingston (1982, 11) says that the state is the main perpetrator of terrorism today.

This scenario has given rise to a number of questions: whether terrorism should be defined as the peacetime equivalent of war crimes;[32] whether, in a situation where illegal or unlawful orders have been obeyed, terrorism could be used as a legitimate defense; whether purely terrorist acts committed by extremists 'in the name of God' could be permissible and excused on religious grounds, with the perpetrators categorized as martyrs; and whether there should be an exception for fighting against a repressive regime.

But a distinction must be quickly made here to avoid confusion—declaring war and sending the military to fight other militaries is not terrorism, nor is the use of violence to punish criminals who have been convicted of violent crimes. However, many would still argue that democracies are also capable of terrorism, for example, Israel has for many years been characterized by critics (especially in the Arab world), by United Nations Resolutions, and by human rights organizations as perpetrating terrorism against the population of the territories it has occupied since 1967. Further criticism also accuses the United States of terrorism for backing not only the Israeli occupation, but other repressive regimes willing to terrorize their own citizens to maintain power. Palestinian militants call Israel terrorist, Kurdish militants call Turkey terrorist, Tamil militants call Indonesia terrorist; and, of course, the nation-states call the militants who oppose their regimes terrorists. As already pointed out herein above, like beauty, terrorism is in the eye of the beholder—one man's freedom fighter is another man's terrorist. Hence, the difficulty in coming up with a definition for terrorism which would be acceptable to all.

Therefore, the focus should be on the acts of terror and not on the actors, when defining terrorism. And if terrorism is thought to seriously violate human

---

32. Scholars like Jay Mallin, 1977, "Terrorism as a Military Weapon," *Air University Review* 28 (2): 54–64, define terrorism as a substitute for overt warfare.

rights, then this must be reflected in the definition, to prohibit serious violence that causes serious bodily injury to a person. The prohibition should also extend to attacks on public or private property where intended or likely to physically endanger people, including acts against essential utilities and public transport. The serious violence could remain as an open-ended catchall category to ensure that offenders do not evade liability by perpetrating violence by new or unanticipated methods (Saul 2008, 12). This open-ended clause could, however, be challenged for a lack of specificity. The definition should also aim to protect both the state and the broader population by requiring that the purpose of an act, "by its nature or context," must be "to intimidate a population, or to compel a government or an international organization to do or to abstain from doing any act," just like the European Union definition.[33] Ben Saul (2008, 13–14) proposes a definition consisting of the following elements: (a) any serious, violent, criminal act intended to cause death or serious bodily injury, or to endanger life, including by acts against property; (b) committed for a political, ideological, religious or ethnic purpose; and (c) where intended to: (i) create extreme fear in [or seriously intimidate] a person, group, or the general public; or (ii) unduly compel a government or an international organization to do or to abstain from doing any act.

Conclusion

One must note that generally, the difficulty in defining terrorism hinges on the fact that for some people, terrorism is an offense (Lazare 2002, 13), for others, it is an activity assigned by God. For some, it is a distinctive act of maintaining power, and for others, it is a justified action against oppression; for some, it is an attack on peace and security, and for others, it is a quest for identity. It is worth noting that the Organization for African Unity (OAU) convention excludes a legitimate struggle for national liberation from colonialism, aggression, and other forms of foreign domination from the meaning of terrorism.[34]

Whatever the case, this discourse, which examines a number of definitions of terrorism, is clear—coming up with a universally acceptable definition is not easy. That is why this article did not attempt to formulate a new definition

---

33. 1999 Terrorist Financing Convention, art 2(1) (b); see also UNSC resolution 1566(2004); UN High-Level Panel on Threats, Challenges and Change, A More Secure World: Our Shared Responsibility (2004); UN Secretary-General, In larger freedom: towards development, security and human rights for all, UNGA (59th Sess), 21 March 2005, UN Doc A/59/2005; UN Draft Comprehensive Convention, art 2(1).
34. Section 4 of the Convention.

of terrorism, but lists those elements which are proposed as crucial ingredients for the definition of terrorism. States operate in different circumstances, so their views on who should be considered a terrorist and who should be considered a freedom fighter or a martyr are poles apart. Moreover, their political and economic agendas may also be dissimilar or, if not, may be pursued in different ways. For each situation, the following considerations and elements are crucial when formulating a definition.

A group of people with organizational structure akin to that of a political party, rather than a criminal gang. They intentionally use violence, threats, and intimidation with political implications because both the nature and purpose of terrorism is political. Socioeconomic or psychological aspects are causal factors for the growth of terrorism, and not the basic nature of the phenomenon. The whole subject should also be discussed in light of the political and means perspective. Maintenance of uniformity of some sort of the terrorism laws, especially with regard to elements, standard of proof, and sentences, would be a good idea, so that the suspects don't run to other jurisdictions with lighter punishments or where they can easily escape trial. International linkages, mostly for financial and logistical support, like training and purchase of equipment is necessary. This support or sponsorship is usually by a state or nonstate entity. Also, terrorism is a phenomenon that very often affects multiple states, which are all compelled to cooperate to repress it. Publicity of their agenda to achieve a political aim or power is an important element; the target group is usually civilians. It is worth noting that the language of the conventions speaks of protected persons, which excludes other persons, say professors, business people, etc., yet everybody needs protection, and most importantly, the excluded persons could turn out to be the target group.

References
Acharya, Upendra D. 2009. "War on Terror or Terror Wars: The Problem in Defining Terrorism." *Denver Journal of International Law and Policy* 37 (4).
Alexander, Yonah. 1976. "International Terrorism: National, Regional and Global Perspectives." *Journal of International Affairs*.
Appiah, Estelle Matilda. 2013. "Legislative Sovereignty and the Globalisation of Law, Experience From Ghana." Paper presented at the Commonwealth Association of Legislative Counsel Conference, Cape Town, South Africa, April.
Bassiouni, M. Cherif. 1988. "A Policy-oriented Inquiry of 'International Terrorism'." In *Legal Responses to International Terrorism: U.S. Procedural Aspects*, edited by M. Cherif Bassiouni. Dordrecht, Boston, and London: Martinus Nijhoff Publishers.

Bodansky, Yossef. 2001. *Bin Laden: The Man Who Declared War On America.* New York, NY: Forum.
Carlton, David, and Carlo Shaerif. 1974. *International Terrorism and World Security.* London: Croom Helm.
Corrado, Raymond R. 1979. "Ethnic and Student Terrorism in Western Europe." In *The Politics of Terrorism*, edited by Michael Stohl. New York: Marcel Dekker.
Crenshaw, Martha. 1987. "Theories of Terrorism: Instrumental and Organizational Approaches." *Journal of Strategic Studies* 10 (4).
Deen, Thalif. 2005. "Politics: UN Member States Struggle to Define Terrorism." IPS, July 25.
Diaz-Paniagua, C. F. 2008. "Negotiating Terrorism: The Negotiation Dynamics of Four UN Counter-Terrorism Treaties, 1997–2005." PhD diss., City University of New York. http://ssrn.com/abstract=1968150.
Dobson, Christopher and Ronald Payne. 1979. *The Weapons of Terror.* London: MacMillan Press.
Freamon, Bernard K. 2003. "Martyrdom, Suicide, and the Islamic Law of War: A Short Legal History." *Fordham International Law Journal* 27 (299).
Gioia, Andrea. 2006. "The UN Conventions on the Prevention and Suppression of International Terrorism." In *International Cooperation in Counter-terrorism: The United Nations and Regional Organizations in the Fight against Terrorism*, edited by Giuseppe Nesi. Burlington, VT: Ashgate Publishing.
Hoffman, Bruce. 1998. *Inside Terrorism.* New York: Columbia University Press.
Jenkins, Brian. 1978. "International Terrorism: Trends and Potentialities." *Journal of International Affairs* 32 (1).
Lacquer, Walter. 1987. *The Age of Terror.* London: Wiedenfield and Nilcolson.
Lambert, J. 1990. *Terrorism and Hostages in International Law: A Commentary on the Hostages Convention 1979.* Cambridge: Grotius.
Lazare, Daniel. 2012. "We are all Terrorists." *Radical Society* 29.
Levitt, G. 1986. "Is 'Terrorism.' Worth Defining?" *Ohio Northern University Law Review* 13 (97) at 115.
Livingston, Neil. 1982. *The War against Terrorism.* Massachusetts: D.C. Health and Co.
Maan, Bashir. 1998. "Missiles Will Only Make Matters Worse." *The Glasgow Herald*, Aug. 24. Quoted in Stephanie R. Nicolas. "Negotiating In The Shadow Of Outlaws: A Problem-Solving Paradigm For Unconventional Opponents." *Journal of Transnational Law and Policy* (2000): 385, 400.
Prabha, Kshitij. 2013. "Defining Terrorism." Accessed July 25. http://www.idsa-india.org/an-apr-08.html.
Pustogarov, Vladimir. 1996. "Fyodor Fyodorovich Martens (1845–1909)—A Humanist of Modern Times." *International Review of the Red Cross* May–June (312).
Saul, Ben. 2012. "Civilizing the Exception: Universally Defining Terrorism." Sydney Law School, Legal Studies Research Paper No. 12/68. http://ssrn.com/abstract=2145097.
Saul, Ben. 2008. "Defining 'Terrorism' to Protect Human Rights." Sydney Law School, Legal Studies Research Paper, No. 08-125. http://ssrn.com/abstract=1292059 .

Saul, Ben. 2006. "The Legal Response of the League of Nations to Terrorism." *Journal of International Criminal Justice* 4.
Schmid, Alex, and J. Albert Jongman. 1988. *Political Terrorism*. New Brunswick: Transaction Books.
Staub, Ervin. 2002. "Notes on Terrorism: Origin and Prevention." *Peace and Conflict: Journal of Peace Psychology* 8.
Walzer, Michael. 1980. *Political Principles*. New York: Basic Books.

Self and Other in Northern Ireland: The Challenge of Ethical Leadership in an Ethnic Conflict

Duncan Morrow
Lecturer in Politics,
University of Ulster

Roots

Northern Ireland is possibly one of the longest running territorial disputes in the Western world. Modern politics has been defined for generations by the struggle between those seeking a united all-Ireland republic, independent from and distinct to Great Britain, and those seeking to defend and deepen the British 'Union.' This drew on deep historic roots in imperialism in Ireland, in which a militantly Protestant British Empire expanded its reach over an island where the majority population was and remained stubbornly loyal to Roman Catholicism. The association of religion, politics, and economics with imperialism and resistance combined to embed a deep sense of suspicion, antagonism, and hostility, which was especially difficult to resolve where people living on both sides of the hostility lived in close proximity and made simultaneous claims to legitimate power. Critically, it bred a political rationale for violence, which came to mark Ireland out from the rest of the British Isles. Whereas by 1920, the rise of democracy as the source of legitimacy created decisive majorities for Irish nationalism in much of Ireland, but it merely deepened the sense of division and resentment in the North.

Ireland's position on the western periphery of Europe and the absence of significant mineral resources acted to limit the extent to which Irish territory could be entangled with wider international relations. While Catholic advocates and Irish nationalists persistently sought support from France and Spain, the sheer logistics of establishing a successful military bridgehead against British interests in Ireland largely prevented serious effort. Irish history is instead characterised by episodes of local uprising, deep intercommunal antagonism, and sporadic attempts to engage French or Spanish military interest.

At the same time, Ireland was, in historical terms, an early participant in the expansion of parliamentary democracy, especially after discriminatory restrictions on Catholic participation in political life were abolished in 1829. Thereafter, until 1920, Ireland participated in the expansion of the franchise at the same pace as those in the rest of the United Kingdom. As elsewhere, the ethical thrust of liberal democracy was on the political equality of individual citizenship. Daniel O'Connell, the first great Irish democratic leader, took a leading role in the Chartist movement, which rallied huge crowds in favour of the universal franchise throughout Victorian Britain. During the nineteenth century, the emphasis was on establishing the principle of equal citizenship against the traditional privileges of inheritance. By the turn of the century, attention had turned to the inclusion of women in the electorate, a principle finally conceded in 1918.

The Ethics of Ethnicity

The political and ethical framework within which modern Ireland emerged therefore rested on two fundamental pillars: the principle of democratic participation in general, and the assertion of the right of Irish people to self-determine their destiny as a distinct and defined nation and territory, free from external domination. Self-determination was directly connected to specifically ethical claims for freedom and justice, and it was both personal and national. By implication, Irish nationalists understood their project as an ethical, as well as a power-political, enterprise. By the end of the nineteenth century, discomfort with the implication that imperialism was incompatible with the principle of human equality convinced the Liberal Prime Minister of the United Kingdom to champion the cause of Irish Home Rule, an issue that was to bitterly divide British politics for thirty years.

But whereas in much of Ireland democracy resulted in large majorities for Irish parliamentary nationalism, imperialism in the richest and most industrial part of Ireland—the North—left a very different settlement pattern and a very different democratic legacy. Local protestant majorities, extending across all classes, organised to resist what they saw as the extension of Roman Catholic authoritarianism and the potential for revenge against Protestant domination, which an Irish national framework would create. In 1912, hundreds of thousands signed a petition with profoundly religious overtones, known as the Ulster Covenant, which rejected Home Rule as "disastrous to the material well-being of Ulster as well as of the whole of Ireland, subversive of our civil and religious freedom, destructive of our citizenship, and perilous to the unity of the Empire," and asserted their willingness to use "all means which may be found necessary" to resist its application.[1]

Both sides to the dispute over Home Rule now defined their cause in moral terms. Central ethical principles—like freedom, justice, and democracy—were deployed by all parties to appeal to external allies. Unionists spoke directly to principles of loyalty to comrades and to the British conservative conceit that British imperialism was, in practice, the primary vehicle for international liberty, through the spread of free trade and democracy. This sentiment is most clearly reflected by Rudyard Kipling in his bitter anti-Home Rule poem, "Ulster 1912":

> Rebellion, rapine hate
> Oppression, wrong and greed
> Are loosed to rule our fate,
> By England's act and deed.
>
> The Faith in which we stand,
> The laws we made and guard,
> Our honour, lives, and land
> Are given for reward
> To Murder done by night,
> To Treason taught by day,
> To folly, sloth, and spite,
> And we are thrust away. (Kipling 1919, 9–11)

Irish nationalism found its most enthusiastic support among the radical diaspora in North America, who nurtured bitter memories of starvation, forced emigration, and landlessness in rural Ireland. Already in 1867, Fenian supporters in the US framed the rebellion in moral terms:

> We appeal to force as a last resort ... unable to endure any longer the curse of a monarchical government, we aim at founding a Republic based on universal suffrage, which shall secure to all the intrinsic value of their labour. The soil of Ireland, at present in possession of an oligarchy, belongs to us, the Irish people and to us it must be restored. (Lee 2008, 56)

Both Unionists and Nationalists therefore pursued projects which they understood not merely as 'ethical' in a general sense, but as moral imperatives whose realisation necessitated the use of violence. Both understood them-

---

1. Available at http://www.historylearningsite.co.uk/ulster_covenant.htm.

selves as victims in an ontological and not merely circumstantial sense: the morality of specific actions was to be measured against the scale of historic injustice—either in the past, in the form of political oppression or in the future in the threat of imminent catastrophe—which was the alternative. In a powerful echo of Dostoevsky's dictum that: "The more I love humanity in general, the less I love man in particular" (Dostoevsky 2004, 60), the sacrifice of lives was a regrettable element in the liberation of life. The most incorruptible, and by implication the most noble, like Robespierre, were the most ruthless. Under pressure from violence and threats, violence became imperative rather than detestable, and the notion of the universal human subject was submerged under the clear distinction between friend and foe.

Antagonism and Its Consequences

As Frank Wright commented, the definition of antagonism is a relationship in which the other is perceived as part of a conspiracy, and against which eternal vigilance is required (Wright 1987, 122). People caught up in an antagonistic relationship cannot dismiss the possibility that the other is part of a hostile conspiracy. Anxiety is lessened, but not eliminated, by the calming rhetoric of moderates and personal relationships if the other is perceived to belong to a hostile group. But by treating the conspiracy as real, we are driven to conspire ourselves.

Once antagonism to another becomes embedded as a political imperative, its most profound consequence is to invert the ethical logic which sees all human beings as worthy of fundamental respect and replace it with a struggle in which the freedom of one depends on the destruction of the other. The language of ethnic cleansing which emerged in the Balkans in the 1990s reflects a view that the destruction and expulsion of the other is an act of purification.

The result is a pervasive but fundamental distinction between friend and foe, a distinction which is treated as 'fact' and 'common sense.' Antagonism creates a self-replicating engine of vigilance in which each act of violence promises to end violence, but actually generates more violence, in a pattern of reciprocity and escalation. What persists is the structure of 'them and us,' where responsibility lies with 'the other,' and can only be solved by 'them' or by victory over them. Antagonism hides the mechanism through which we are also contributory within the reciprocal cycle, raising resisting the enemy to heroism and declaring compromise as appeasement. The heart of antagonistic conflict is this self-perpetuating dynamic of conspiracy, discrimination, and terror in which everyone participates and nobody feels responsible, and in which violence and ethics align in a kind of logical death spiral.

This in itself has further ethical consequences. In a conspiratorial world, it is simply irrational to promote equality. Antagonism turns everything into a conflict to get and hold the maximum amount of resources before rivals can claim them. If inequality creates conflict, it is equally true that conflict rationalises inequality.

The coming into existence of Northern Ireland in 1920 had the effect of embedding intergroup hostility at the core of political life. Furthermore, it implicated democratic procedure in this by promoting leaders who reflected the antagonistic relationship and offered to act to protect the group against its enemies, rather than to transcend the relationship. Unsurprisingly, the higher ethical claims of democracy—including the core principle that every person counts, in relation both to fundamental individual rights and to the principle of equal political value—were qualified in this prism. For as long as the existence of Northern Ireland itself remained contested, voting in elections was essentially reduced to a head-counting exercise on that apparently existential question.

Paradoxically, the fact that neither Britain nor Ireland had any immediate interest in resolving this dilemma allowed it to remain in a state of unstable equilibrium for fifty years. Unionist Prime Ministers in Northern Ireland were first and foremost leaders of their Protestant tribe against Nationalist ambition, rather than uniting symbols of shared citizenship. Within the formal apparatus of a democracy, informal political culture reflected the fundamental antagonism between groups of citizens. Without a formal trace, the friend and foe dynamic was embedded in the routine of the state.

This in its turn provides and provided a new breeding group for polarisation and resentment. Once systematic inequality is rationalised as necessary for self-defence, the antagonistic pattern of citizenship becomes embedded in discrimination and resentment, institutionalising a de facto experience of first- and second-class citizenship based on group divisions. Inevitably, Unionists explained the root of this crisis by the malevolent intentions of Nationalism, whereas Nationalists condemned the system of larger and smaller exclusions institutionalised in the fabric of the state.

The erosion of universal ethics under ethnic antagonism is profound. Freedom can no longer be treated as a universal human ethical principle, but is a finite good dependent on political or military triumph over specific others. By equating victory with justice, violence is raised to the highest ethic. In the face of existential threat, war is necessarily just. The only justice is victory. By equating peace with treachery, cooperation is anathema.

Internal participants present a narrative of provocation (by others) and reaction (by us) in which differences in moral responsibility are absolute. Outside observers without stake in the antagonistic relationship see a pattern of reciprocity and similarity, where heroes and villains perform essentially the same acts observed from different sides of an antagonistic relationship. The gap between justice and revenge reduces to an almost indistinguishable level. Unsurprisingly, it is this insight of the equivalence of heroism and crime and the ambivalence of our categories of victim and perpetrator which provoke the greatest resistance of all (Girard 1987).

Identity is defined against the other and it becomes almost impossible to distinguish the extent to which identity is in the solidarity of being 'anti-them' or in being 'pro-us.' Peace will thus not only demand a change in relationship with the other, it will radically alter our understanding of self. Politicians discover that any compromise or refusal to represent the fear underlying antagonism will lead to their replacement by more radical elements. Unless some mechanism is found to break this, politics is reduced to a Clausewitzian extension of war, with the inherent potential to 'escalate to the extremes' (von Clausewitz 1984, 77).

The Exhaustion of War

Northern Ireland is unusual in international relations, in that it did not draw in the surrounding states to the logic of its internal antagonism. Instead, the violence of divisions in Ireland acted to repel outsiders. After 1920, both Britain and Ireland sought to protect themselves against the potentially destabilising impact of its hostilities rather than be drawn into them. On the other hand, not only were they unable or unprepared to act to resolve the antagonism, they increasingly lost any sense of direct responsibility for it; Northern Ireland was to be managed. Even once violence broke out in earnest between 1969 and 1972, the primary political goal of the British government was to restore the 'acceptable level of violence.'

The consequences of this were unusual. On the one hand, as part of a Western European welfare state, Northern Ireland continued to draw on considerable financial and economic subsidy, in spite of the collapse of any substantial private economy. This combination of active security policy, conflict management, and economic support simultaneously created a curious and unusual hybrid of ethnic and nationalist polarisation, alongside a functioning administration and civic society. Most of the violence took place either between paramilitary organisations or between paramilitary organisations and the state. There was no interstate war, but the antagonism between the Nationalist population and the British state was exacerbated at times through the often-violent interface between the British army and the local population. Intergroup violence on a wider scale was prevented through public engineering, such as the erection of permanent security barriers between exclusively Catholic and Protestant neighbourhoods (interfaces) and the subsidy of parallel systems of community development. Meanwhile, the civil service was expanded to create new jobs and the hardest edges of discrimination were removed.

Eventually, a new unstable equilibrium emerged, in which violence was endemic but increasingly strategically counterproductive. When, almost by accident and against her instincts, Margaret Thatcher was persuaded to sign a new strategic alliance with the Irish republic in 1985 (the Anglo-Irish Agreement), the unexpected result was the reemergence of a new universal ethic for peace-building in Northern Ireland which refused the 'ethnic' implications of Northern Irish antagonism and promoted instead a new doctrine of universal and inclusive 'reconciliation.'

While some of this was already visible to the leaders of moderate nationalism, such as John Hume and (particularly) Garret Fitzgerald, and the more conciliatory parts of the British Conservative party (Sir Geoffrey Howe) who were its architects, the emergence of a settlement rooted in universal ethical framework can more plausibly be traced to a combination of near-despair at the failure to contain the endless spiral of violence and a vaguely articulated sense that the ethics which had shaped Western European politics since Auschwitz were at stake. In a general sense, this was welfare state leadership: a combination of pragmatism and principles, interests and instincts and of committees and diplomacy, rather than grand gesture. Reconciliation was understood in principle rather than in practice. Nonetheless, and in a real sense it changed the game in Northern Ireland, from one of ethnic one-upmanship to a search for a universal framework.

The Ethical and the Ethnic in Transition

The power of the Northern Ireland peace process rested on an ethical framework rooted in universalist values which were both consciously taken for granted and often only intermittently observed in Western capitals. While ethical inconsistency and hypocrisy were hardly new in international affairs, it became clear, however, that if the argument for an inclusive peace was stronger, the more it could be championed as an ethical alternative to violence and ethnic separatism. Reconciliation proved to be a powerfully attractive proposition for all those who were repelled by the violence of Northern Ireland, rather than drawn to it.

Thus although the Anglo-Irish reconciliation project initially set the governments of the UK and Ireland and their international allies in the US and Europe at extreme odds with their ethnic clients in Northern Ireland—and Unionists mobilised in hundreds of thousands to reject any involvement of the Republic of Ireland in internal Northern Irish affairs, while Republicans vocally rejected the new initiative—it had the effect of limiting this rejection largely to Northern Ireland and to militant partisans outside. Elsewhere, the ethical appeal of an inclusive peace was utterly persuasive, especially as direct material interests in Northern Ireland were so limited. As a result, the ethnic antagonists of Northern Ireland now faced the utter indifference of the international community to their causes and an ethical rejection of both their methods and their arguments. In strategic terms, the opportunity costs of violence increased exponentially. Gradually, and against their initial will, all parties were drawn into the negotiating framework which it created.

What is remarkable is the extent to which the process was articulated by the system rather than by individuals. The custodians of the process were the governments of Britain and Ireland, supported by US diplomacy and finance, and even more finance from the European Union. They were of course also interested parties, at least to the extent that they had profound historic allegiances and political, security, and civic responsibilities. But they shared a common view that the crisis in Northern Ireland had to be brought to an end for both in the national and ethical interest. For a combination of domestic and international reasons, the US leadership, especially under the Clinton Presidency, gave Northern Ireland a prominence which its size and importance did not deserve, while Jacques Delors saw in Northern Ireland an opportunity to realise both the historic peace-mission of the European Union and an opportunity for direct intervention.

This combination of political, security, and financial muscle was then deployed through diplomacy, legislation, and an unusual and noteworthy strategy of social and economic intervention. Reconciliation was promoted through targeted interventions in the labor market (equality), through support for integrated education, through economic and community regeneration, and through support for dialogue and mediation at the local level (community relations). Intercommunity peace initiatives, whether by heroic individuals ,such as Gordon Wilson, or longstanding champions of reconciliation, such as the Corrymeela Community, were given both publicity and encouragement. Although the initial steps in all of these areas were tentative, relying often on experimentation and coalitions of willing volunteers and pioneers, over twenty-five years they became embedded aspects in the landscape of social and economic development in Northern Ireland. Leadership was distributed across civic society and through legislative interventions to promote independent institutions guided by principles of equality and, after 1998, of human rights.

The holy grail, and most difficult challenge lay with change in politics. Without local political leadership and partnership, the project continued to rely on external supporters. Furthermore, while the governments were convinced of the centrality of an ethical peace process, their primary interest was to divest themselves of direct entanglement in Northern Ireland. In the absence of the emergence of a new leadership, the implicit narrative of the peace process was therefore one of creating the conditions under which the old leadership would find room to change. In this, all parties shared a dilemma: local political leadership continued to reflect the underlying antagonism and suspicion of Northern Irish voters, yet at the same time were now expected to explore opportunities for ending violence and establishing a better future. Furthermore, it was abundantly clear that further violence was tactically useless and increasingly nihilistic. The story of the Northern Ireland peace process is a story of the engagement of these hostile parties within a common framework while attempting to find linguistic and political formulations which allowed politicians to make significant changes without appearing to betray established causes and positions.

The result was a contorted, complex, and difficult process of accommodations, compromises, and trade-offs which came together as the Belfast or Good Friday Agreement in 1998.[2] Problematically, even this gigantic achievement was insufficient to completely eliminate the suspicions underpinning antagonism. Within four years, the political institutions and the intercommunity coalition underpinning the agreement collapsed and the governments were faced with further endless decades of external administration or further compromises with Northern Ireland antagonists to devolve responsibility and power. In the event, after five years of living with the former, they succeeded in renegotiating elements of the 1998 agreement to the satisfaction of the outer wings of

---

2. Belfast Agreement, April 10, 1998. Available at http://cain.ulst.ac.uk/events/peace/docs /agreement.htm.

Unionism and Republicanism. In 2007, an exhausted intergovernmental and international coalition closed the book on Northern Ireland and declared peace achieved, guaranteed by previously unthinkable images of enemies sitting together as joint patrons of the new intercommunity system of government.

Afterword

The Missing Link: Ethical Leadership for an Ethical Society

The Northern Ireland peace process is an almost paradigm case of systemic action for peace in the Western world. Reconciliation emerged as clear ethical alternative to ethnic and national conflagration after 1985 and it engaged the political systems of two western states and their allies for two decades in an almost unique effort to transform a deeply polarised society. In doing so, it deployed all of the weapons of western democracy: the cajoling leadership of political figures such as Garret Fitzgerald and John Hume, John Major and Albert Reynolds, Tony Blair and Bertie Ahern; the military logic of containment; the economics of incentives for peace, diplomatic, and international attention; platform and flattery in Washington, Brussels, and the Nobel Committee in Oslo; and the heroic efforts of small scale community-led initiatives to promote a shared future against the odds of ethnic hatred at community, religious, and educational levels. This coalition introduced frameworks for equality and human rights, established a consensus against the use of violence, and was flexible and open in its treatment of prisoners and former combatants. Within their own movements, prisoners, combatants, and victims often themselves became important persuaders for the new process.

All of this activity created a space for political leadership to shape and to own, a process which was completed in 2007. Problematically, however, no visible political leader emerged in Northern Ireland for whom the new reconciliation was in itself a vision to champion. Instead, all parties continued to see the agreement process not as a miraculous escape from antagonism, but as a necessary, if difficult, compromise with the unpalatable. Instead of an agreement which replaced the unethical with the possibility of ethics, political leadership was unable to eliminate the suspicion that the agreement and the peace process were an unethical compromise with an evil enemy. As a consequence, neither part was willing to institute any process of reviewing their past relationship which might highlight the unethical nature of the violence deployed to prosecute their cause. As time went on, it became increasingly clear that this unwillingness to risk ethical equality in relation to violence in the past was preventing any progress towards real trust in the future.

Northern Ireland therefore still stands at its crossroads, evidence that peace is a decision in human affairs, requiring people who make decisions, at least as much as a process or a mechanism or an event. Northern Ireland does not lack for a sophisticated political, administrative, and legislative model for peace. But it lacks a champion, a vision, and a model of a shared vision of the future, still paralysed and lacking someone or some mechanism to plausibly move towards a different future. Pending leadership, peace will remain fragile and tantalising.

References

Dostoevsky, Fyodor. 2004. *The Brothers Karamazov*. Translated by Constance Garnett. New York: Barnes and Noble.

Girard, Rene. 1987. *Things Hidden from the Foundation of the World*. London: Athlone Press.

Kipling, Rudyard. 1919. *The Years Between*. London: Methuen.

Lee, Joseph. 2008. *The Modernisation of Irish Society 1848–1918*. Dublin: Gill and Macmillan.

von Clausewitz, Carl. 1984. *On War*. Princeton: Princeton University Press.

Wright, Frank. 1987. *Northern Ireland: A Comparative Analysis*. Dublin and London: Gill and MacMillan.

Talking Foreign Policy Transcripts

Broadcast quarterly, *Talking Foreign Policy* is a one-hour radio program hosted by Case Western Reserve University Law Professor Michael Scharf, in which experts discuss the salient foreign policy issues of the day. The premier broadcast (airdate: March 1, 2012) covered the controversial use of predator drones, humanitarian intervention in Syria, and responded to Iran's acquisition of nuclear weapons. The second broadcast (airdate: May 24, 2012) covered the issues of using drones to kill Americans abroad, the challenges of bringing indicted tyrants to justice, and America's Afghanistan exit strategy. The third broadcast (airdate: September 27, 2012) focused on the issue of presidential power in a war without end. The fourth broadcast (airdate: February 4, 2013) examined President Obama's second term foreign policy team (Kerry, Hagel, and Brennon).[1]

In a recent interview, Scharf said: "We want to cover the most salient and interesting foreign policy topics in each program."[2] Because international policy issues are so prominent in a day-to-day news cycle but often can be difficult to grasp, Scharf pitched the idea for *Talking Foreign Policy* to WCPN 90.3 ideastream, Cleveland's NPR affiliate, late last year. He then lined up a few colleagues known for their ability to discuss complex foreign policy topics in an easy-to-digest manner. Sort of a radio version of the McLaughlin Group, each episode features a regular cast of participants, with Scharf serving as host:

- The ethicist: Shannon French, director of Case Western Reserve's Inamori Center for Ethics and Excellence;
- The military expert: Mike Newton, professor of law at Vanderbilt University;
- The international law professor: Milena Sterio, law professor at Cleveland State University; and

---

1. Transcript edited and footnotes added by Cox Center Fellows JoAnna Gavigan, Heather Lee, Elizabeth Krupar, Michael Kind, Laura Smolley, and Meghan Kane. In order to improve readability of the transcript, minor editorial changes have been made. Extraneous words have been taken out and replaced with ellipses; none of the content has been changed.
2. "School of Law Professor's Radio Show Gets Green Light: Set to Air March 1," *The Daily*, February 17, 2012, http://thedaily.case.edu/news/?p=5769.

- The negotiator: Paul Williams, president of the Public International Law and Policy Group.

The commentators offer listeners a broad expanse of views, as their political beliefs range across the entire spectrum, Scharf said. In addition, the participants strive to make the show casual and sometimes humorous, even when discussing serious topics. Additional experts may join the Group depending on the topic.

Archived broadcasts (both in audio and video format) of *Talking Foreign Policy* are available at: law.ecae.edu/TalkingForeignPolicy. The transcripts of the first four broadcasts appear below.

Talking Foreign Policy, March 1, 2012 broadcast

Participants:
Michael Scharf
Paul Williams
Shannon French
Mike Newton
Milena Sterio

SCHARF: U.S. drone strikes are coming under criticism around the world. Israel is hinting that an attack on Iran's nuclear power plant may be imminent.[3] And with respect to Syria, [quote from Michael Newton later in the broadcast] "the real challenge is to transcend the political paralysis and debate into concrete action that actually does something." When you hear about international events like these in the news, do you ever wish you had access to a group of experts who could break the issues down for you and provide their unvarnished opinions? Well, that is what we are providing. This program brings you expert debate on today's pressing issues of international relations. I am your host, Michael Scharf. Our expert panel today will be discussing predator drones, humanitarian intervention, Syria, and the threat of nuclear weapons in Iran. First the news.

SCHARF: Welcome back to the Foreign Policy Roundtable. I am Michael Scharf, Director of the Cox International Law Center at Case Western Reserve

---

3. "Attacking Iran: Up in the Air," *Economist*, February 25, 2012, http://www.economist.com/node/21548228. In the early months of 2012, Iran continued to fortify its nuclear facilities, decreasing its vulnerability to a physical attack by Israel. However, the civil uprising against the Assad regime in Syria (Iran's only significant Arab ally), combined with the Israeli military's increasing capacity for in-air refueling, led many Israeli and American officials to suspect that Israel would launch an air strike on one or more of Iran's nuclear facilities.

University in Cleveland, Ohio. Today, our experts will be discussing the controversial use of predator drones, military intervention against the Syrian regime, and the threat of Iranian nuclear weapons. Our panel consists of an international negotiator, Dr. Paul Williams; a military expert, Colonel Mike Newton; an ethicist, Dr. Shannon French; and an international law professor, Milena Sterio.

SCHARF: We will begin by having each guest tell us a little bit about his or her background. First, our studio affiliate in Washington, DC, Paul Williams. Welcome to the program, Paul.

WILLIAMS: Thank you Michael, it is a pleasure to be here.

SCHARF: Tell us a little bit about yourself for the audience.

WILLIAMS: I am a professor of law at American University here in Washington, DC. I am also the president of the Public International Law and Policy Group, a global pro-bono law firm which advises countries involved in peace negotiations.

SCHARF: How many of those peace negotiations have you done to date, Paul?

WILLIAMS: I have done about twenty-four peace negotiations for PILPG, some successful, some not so much.

SCHARF: So that is our negotiator. In our Cleveland studio with me, we have Michael Newton, who flew in from Nashville to be with us today. Thanks for joining us, Mike.

NEWTON: Thanks Michael, it is great to be here.

SCHARF: And your background?

NEWTON: As a West Point graduate, I served more than twenty-one years in uniform, both in special operations and as a military prosecutor, and I served at the highest levels of the State Department during both the Clinton and Bush administrations. Most recently and relevantly perhaps, I am a professor of the practice of law at Vanderbilt University School of Law in Nashville, Tennessee; a great place to go to school.

SCHARF: Mike is joined in the studio by Shannon French. Welcome, Shannon.

FRENCH: Thanks, Michael. I am currently the Director of the Inamori International Center for Ethics and Excellence at Case Western Reserve University. My research field is military ethics, and before I came here to the lovely city of Cleveland, I taught for eleven years at the U.S. Naval Academy in Annapolis. I am also a member of a research consortium that that is called

CETMONS, which is a consortium on military technologies, military operations, and national security.

SCHARF: Our final expert is Milena Sterio, who recently appeared with me on WCPN's *Sound of Ideas* to discuss piracy. It is good to see you again, Milena.

STERIO: It is good to see you too, Michael.

SCHARF: And your background?

STERIO: I am currently an associate professor of law at Cleveland State University here in Cleveland, Ohio. I specialize in international law, international human rights law, and international criminal law. Before that, I worked as a lawyer at an international law firm in New York City for a number of years.

SCHARF: So we have the right group of experts with us today. Let's kick off this part of the program by talking about the controversial issue of predator drones. For some, these high-tech weapons might conjure images of the Terminator movies in which menacing robots battled against humans. Mike, why don't you start by telling us what a predator drone really is?

NEWTON: Well, I think the first part of your setup is correct. These are war-making machines that are designed to fly over very long distances. They do not rest. They serve two basic functions, the first being surveillance. You can have on-site surveillance for extended periods of time over a precise target. The second function is the one that has been in the news, the targeted dimension.[4] Not all drones target, but many do, and they bring a capability that is hard to match in other ways.

SCHARF: How many drones would you say that the U.S. possesses at this time?

NEWTON: The absolute number is classified. There are public reports of about five thousand in the inventory that are split between a variety of different purposes and a variety of different authorities.

SCHARF: Who controls them? Is it the Air Force, the CIA, or the military?

NEWTON: The Air Force has a whole branch of people who train in what I call 'the care and feeding.' This includes maintenance issues, uplinks of intelligence and those kinds of things. Regarding the recent strikes, there have been indications in the press of CIA involvement with a heavy CIA fleet as well, which mostly does targeting and some surveillance.

---

4. *See e.g.* Charlie Savage, "Pentagon Says U.S Citizens With Terrorism Ties Can Be Targeted in Strikes," *New York Times*, February 22, 2012, http://atwar.blogs.nytimes.com/2012/02/22/pentagon-says-u-s-citizens-with-terrorism-ties-can-be-targeted-in-strikes/. (Discussing the legality of using drones to target U.S. citizens who join Al-Qaeda.)

SCHARF: You mention the press reports. Where is it reported that we have been using these drones?

NEWTON: Primarily, there have been lots of reports recently in Pakistan, the most visible perhaps from the Iranian influence was a surveillance drone that the Iranians were proudly displaying on worldwide television.[5] Yemen has been in some press reports. I think it is fair to say that there is any number of other classified locations that we do not have public press reports about.

SCHARF: I assume if it is classified, we are not getting the host country's permission to fly over and use the drones. Is that correct?

NEWTON: Many times not, but I think it is fair to say that we may in some cases have either back-channel express or implicit understanding from the host government.

SCHARF: You mention that the drones never sleep. What are the advantages to using the drones over other means of fighting?

NEWTON: The fact is that you have long-term sustained ability over a precise place, such as when you are trying to target the movements and the locations of someone like Osama Bin Laden. It is great to have that on-station presence. Back in the old, old, old days, we had to wait for the earth to turn to have a satellite view and it was cumbersome and problematic. We have solved that problem with drones, provided that you have forward bases where you can refuel and provide maintenance and uplinks, etc. So that is the primary thing. The other thing is that you can reach out. You do not require kinetic force on the ground. You can reach out with lethal force in places that would be extremely difficult, if not impossible, to get in even a very small special operations ground force team. So you can do that with drones and extend your reach.

SCHARF: Let's bring Shannon into the conversation. Your particular expertise, as you just described, is the ethics of high-tech weaponry. Why do some people find that these drones, which seem so effective as Mike just described them, are actually so troubling?

FRENCH: There are a number of issues, but I think the general one has to do with the fact that it feels more like a videogame, and the sense is that the

---

5. John Walcott, "Iran Shows Downed Spy Drone as U.S. Assesses Technology Loss," *Bloomberg Business Week*, December 12, 2011, http://www.businessweek.com/news/2011-12-12/iran-shows-downed-spy-drone-as-u-s-assesses-technology-loss.html#p2. In December 2011, Iran recovered a RQ-170 surveillance drone operated by the United States after it came down in Iranian territory. A video showing the drone appeared on Iran's state-owned Press TV channel.

more it is like a video game, the more we are dehumanizing our enemies. There is a concern that if you do not put skin in the game, that if you are not putting your own troops at risk, then you lose the sense of the moral weight of what you are doing. It makes war too easy. There are many things that people may choose among as a response and it makes that choice a little too fast, so that concerns me.

SCHARF: What about on the other side? If you're a Pakistani or an Afghan and you are used to the nobility of facing your enemy face to face, does the drone somehow make the United States less noble?

FRENCH: Of course it does. If you can imagine being on the ground as either someone who is a combatant or someone who is a civilian and having these lethal robots essentially fly overhead and rain down death, the experience of that is going to make you feel that maybe these folks are somehow supernatural; not literally, but they have that sense of "How do I fight this?," and that just raises the anger level another degree. You also have the sense of "Is there cowardice here? You are not letting me fight back at you, you're just dropping your bombs from this incredibly safe distance." I want to add something here, Michael. I don't know if it gets enough attention, but there is the fact that we do not yet fully know the effect of having troops back here in the U.S. using things like predators and having to switch back and forth from their normal civilian type lives to this kind of killing. Someone could be killing someone in Pakistan and then running out the door jumping in their car and driving to their kid's soccer game. We don't know yet what that does to our own troops. As you mentioned, we do know it affects our heart and mind strategy[6] at the other end.

SCHARF: I assume it is not just our own troops but the other regular pilots who are looking at their colleagues who are just drone disc jockeys or drone jockeys, and who are safe behind enemy lines. How do they feel about the use of drones?

FRENCH: There is a sense that it interferes with an entire culture, the culture of the pilot. When I was at the naval academy, I used to be able to tell which of my students wanted to be pilots. There was a certain attitude and a certain swagger. That is not necessarily the same type of person as someone who is

---

6. Eli Berman et al., "Can Hearts and Minds Be Bought? The Economics of Counterinsurgency in Iraq," National Bureau of Economic Research, Working Paper No. 14606, 2009, p. 4. http://www.nber.org/papers/w14606. The "hearts and minds" counterinsurgency strategy purports to reduce the demand for rebellion. According to the strategy, when a government keeps a population safe and addresses popular grievances, the population will reward the government with its support.

manning the equipment for these drones; the joystick, basically, of these drones. So you have a clash of cultures that are not always going to respect one another.

NEWTON: Let me interject on that because I think it is critically important to understand that the way you bridge that gap, the idea surfaces a lot that all these are just video games. No, these are trained professional pilots that in many other ways are the absolute epitome of Air Force professionalism. I think that the fighter or jock mentality that you refer to is very resident there and it is just an odd, almost incongruent, idea of a guy wearing this flight suit with his combat patch and picking his kids up from soccer. That does happen. So what is the check in that system? I think it is critically important to understand the absolute professional ethos of the war fighter mentality that says 'I am a professional and as a professional, I have particularized, very rigid rules of conduct and rules of expectation and both legal and ethical dimensions as to how I do it and it is not a video game.' I think in some ways, some of the people that I have talked to who do this have erred on the side of being so conscientious of that line that in some cases they have hesitated. The nice thing about drones is that they are kind of a one shot deal, no pun intended. You cannot take a particular target and then take your time to go back to the legal/ethical framework, to go back to the target methodology and take that same target at another time and another place when it is perhaps more appropriate or more lawful.

SCHARF: What you are saying, Mike, might well be true but a lot of this is about perceptions. I note that you can actually watch a real video of drone-targeted killings on YouTube now.[7] Let me bring Paul into this discussion. Paul, you have negotiated peace agreements with a dozen countries. From your perspective as a peace negotiator, do you think that the expanded use of drones may make it harder for Americans to win hearts and minds in places like Afghanistan, Pakistan, and Iraq?

WILLIAMS: Well, look Michael, I think we have to be honest with ourselves here. The approach and the strategy of hearts and minds did not work in Iraq. It is failing in Afghanistan and it is certainly not going to work in Pakistan. Quite frankly, I think we have shifted our methodology from hearts and minds to scare and kill the bad guys. The drones are just a symptom of this fundamental shift. They allow it to happen and they allow us to be very effective at the scare and kill approach.

---

7. *See* "Hunter Killer Drone Strike," YouTube video, posted by "noahmax6000," February 28, 2007, http://www.youtube.com/ watch?v=3PjR8v1njsg.

SCHARF: Okay, so we heard Mike mention earlier that the drones are sometimes controlled by the CIA and not by the regular armed services. I understand that the critics of the CIA are saying that having the CIA operate the drones creates an accountability void. Is that something that we should be concerned about?

WILLIAMS: No, I do not think we should be concerned about that. The same law applies to the CIA as it does to the other armed forces. There is this notion that you pick up from the movies of the *rogue agency*. No, we should not have to worry about the CIA. We should worry about the American people. The reality is that the American people now, for whatever reason, are more likely to accept more civilian causalities, more collateral damage, in order to kill the bad guys. Now, on the one hand, this actually makes it easier to kill the bad guys, as there is a lot less to worry about in terms of moral outrage. On the other hand, it erodes our moral core, both as Americans and as human beings, and that is kind of worrying.

SCHARF: Well, Paul, you said that the CIA plays by the same rules. I do not know how we would know that definitively. We do know that when it came to Guantanamo Bay, there was concern that the CIA had created a law-free zone and that they were not playing by the same rules. What is your take on that, Milena?

STERIO: First of all, let me respond to something Paul and Mike have raised. Clearly it is sort of in our interest to go after the bad guys to scare them, to kill them if we feel like they are threatening our national security. But, from my perspective as a professor of international law, I do think that there are serious concerns regarding the use of drones under international law. To justify our current policy of using drones, and the way that we are using them, you have to make a certain number of assumptions and believe that every single one of those assumptions is true. So you have to believe that 9/11 was an act of war and that we are in a global war of terror. All these targets are enemy combatants and the battlefield moves with them, so wherever you are, you can target them. Every single one of those assumptions is questionable, so I do worry about our use of our aggressive policy and compliance with international law.

SCHARF: Well, I think this debate is going to continue on the national scene since the Obama administration is committed to rapidly increasing the number of drones. It is time for us, however, to take a short break. When we return we are going to be discussing the issue of intervention to halt atrocities in Syria. Stay with us.

SCHARF: Welcome back to Foreign Policy Roundtable on WCPN 90.3. I am Michael Scharf, and I am joined by Mike Newton of Vanderbilt, Shannon French of the Inamori Center, Milena Sterio of Cleveland State University and in DC we have Paul Williams of the Public International Law and Policy Group. We have been discussing the pros and cons of predator drones. In our second segment today, we will debate humanitarian intervention to stop the killing in Syria. In March, the Arab Spring protest spread to Syria. Just as Muammar Gaddafi did in Libya, the Assad regime has used deadly military force against the Syrian protest movement, resulting in over five thousand deaths so far, and that figure seems to be rising every day. Shannon, let's start with you. What is the situation on the ground in Syria right now?

FRENCH: Well, the broad answer is violent and unstable. The kind of language that we hear coming out of Syria is chaotic. It has to do with these clashes between these government troops and the rebels which happen in the capital city, the suburbs, and some of the southern villages. We get more and more reports of death. There is an ebb and flow to it and sometimes it seems to dial back a little. But it doesn't seem like it is going to go away any time soon.

SCHARF: And who are the protesters?

FRENCH: It is interesting because, on the one hand, there has not been an attempt to organize a political opposition. There is something called the Syrian National Council[8], and that includes representatives from the Damascus Declaration group, which is a prodemocracy network. There is also the Syrian Muslim Brotherhood, which is an Islamic political party, various Kurdish factions and local coordination committees. But the majority of people protesting in the streets appear to be unemployed youths.

SCHARF: Why should we care about what Assad is doing to unemployed youths in Syria?

FRENCH: I am an ethicist, so I think we ought to care simply because the protesters are fellow human beings whose rights are being violated, so that is enough right there, and they are demanding freedom and democracy, which we claim to share. But if a more pragmatic reason is required, recent and current governments of Syria have been obstacles to peace in the region.

---

8. "SNC Objectives," *Syrian National Council*, last modified November 29, 2011, http://www.syriancouncil.org/en/objectives.html. The Syrian National Council is a revolutionary proto-government that aims to provide an interim government and a roadmap for democratic change in post-Assad Syria. The SNC also mobilizes support for and represents the Syrian Revolution in the international community.

Now, do we know if a new government would be any better? We do not know that. It is a roll of the dice and I certainly would not support an Iraq-type intervention, but I do not know, maybe something like what we did in Libya. Perhaps I would need to hear more about the options.

SCHARF: And the death toll there is actually greater than Libya's, is that correct?

FRENCH: That is correct. Unfortunately, it is continuing to climb.

SCHARF: Paul, what are the options that are currently being considered for responding to this crisis?

WILLIAMS: Well, Michael, there is a whole array of options. If you are the Russians, you are considering selling them more weapons so that Assad could do this even quicker and carry out more atrocities against his own people. If you are the Arab League, fortunately they have become very aggressive lately. They are seeking regime transition. They would like to see Assad set aside and have one of his deputies take his position and transform the regime. Turkey, more aggressive, is calling for humanitarian zones and there are even a few countries like Qatar and Saudi Arabia directly calling for regime change. I think there is a lot on the table and it is very eclectic and it is very disorganized, but I think the international community is beginning to coalesce around some serious action and maybe even humanitarian intervention.

SCHARF: So the situation is very similar to the way it was this summer in Libya. Why does Russia say it will veto at the Security Council any proposal to authorize humanitarian intervention in Syria?

WILLIAMS: Well, Russia has Syria as a client state. We can talk about whether they were surprised by what happened in Libya and they can talk about international law. The reality is that the Russians have a relationship with Syria. They have a very lucrative arms trade with Syria and it suits their interest to have an element which is destabilizing the Middle East, which in large part is an American and European area of significant interest.

SCHARF: At the Security Council last summer, they passed a resolution[9] that authorized the NATO forces to bomb and to assist in the Libya situation. The Russians are now saying that they felt deceived. They said that they didn't think that the Security Council resolution went that far—that it was designed to protect Libyan civilians and it was morphed somehow by the West into a bombing campaign that led to regime change. So, Milena, what is the story behind that?

---

9. S.C. Res. 2009, U.N. Doc. S/RES/2009 (September 16, 2011).

STERIO: I do think that there is an element of the Russian sentiment that they were being deceived. That is true in the sense that the Security Council resolution regarding Libya, I think, was purposely vague. It was drafted to say that we are going there to protect civilians, and who knows where that could lead. On the other hand, Shannon mentioned this concern about fellow human beings being slaughtered or their human rights not being respected, and there are a number of other areas in the world like Syria where there are significant violations taking place, and nobody is really talking about it. For example, Uzbekistan is one of those areas.[10] For the United States, Uzbekistan tends to be a strategic area. We go through there to send our supplies to Afghanistan, and we kind of need Uzbekistan on our side. There is also Bahrain, where significant human right violations took place last summer or last spring,[11] and we have not really seen much involvement. That being said, I do think now there is a serious situation in Syria. I do think that I would support Shannon's proposal for some kind of a humanitarian-type intervention.

FRENCH: I would just like to say that I certainly agree with Milena, and even though our humanitarian intervention policy in the past has not been consistent and probably won't be consistent, that, in and of itself, should not be used as an argument against intervening. The fact that we do not intervene everywhere, where we perhaps should or could, often gets raised as an argument for not intervening here and that really troubles me. If you cannot do everything, you should still do something where you can.

SCHARF: So let's assume American policy makers agree with you and they would like to intervene, but the Russians are threatening a veto. Let me turn to Mike. Does international law allow humanitarian intervention if it is not approved by the Security Council?

NEWTON: Well, that is the $64,000 question. You should tell me. In fact, there are very few instances in history of what I call pure humanitarian interventions. They are always coming up with political circumstances regarding political refugees, economic ties, and a whole variety of other circumstances. So to ask

---

10. "World Report 2012: Uzbekistan," *Human Rights Watch*, http://www.hrw.org/world-report-2012/world-report-2012-uzbekistan. Human Rights Watch described Uzbekistan's human rights record as "appalling." According to the report, authorities severely restrict freedom of expression and target journalists, civil society activists, and opposition members.
11. Alex Delmar-Morgan, "Protests, Investigator Pressure Bahrain," *Wall Street Journal*, March 11, 2012, http://online.wsj.com/article/SB10001424052970204603004577271481007329636.html. In early 2011, thirty-five people were killed and nearly three thousand were arrested when the Sunni-led Bahraini government violently put down a mainly Shiite protest movement.

that simple question—in one way there is sort of a false assumption that there is a purely humanitarian basis. We are past that. I would say that we are in the age of YouTube and Twitter. So Saddam slaughters thousands of Kurds in the fall of 1988[12] and it is very possible for the world to say, well, we did not know in time.—we were not positioned to take action. We have seen that change, so we did take action in Kosovo[13] because of very clear, timely information from incredible reporters on the ground and, in this case, U.S. diplomats. I was there. So we took action in Kosovo, which was the first clear example where we had after-the-fact de facto recognition by the Security Council. So the short answer to your question is that it is an open issue against this entire backdrop of very strong, very clear human rights law and what we call crimes against humanity law that says these things are criminal. These are the most serious crimes, the most serious violations in the world. We have to do something about it.

SCHARF: Paul, Mike mentioned the 1999 NATO bombing campaign to halt the ethnic cleansing in Kosovo. You have written about this. I know that the 1999 intervention was not authorized by the Security Council. Russia was threatening to veto back then as well. Was that bombing campaign seen as lawful or legitimate?

WILLIAMS: I think there are a lot of similarities between what happened in Kosovo and what is happening in Syria at the moment. The first step was to find ways through the Security Council, through the General Assembly, to wrap it up in a legal bow. But in both cases the simple reality was and is that humanitarian intervention is inevitable. We all knew what Milosevic was going to do in Kosovo. He was going to do bad things. We know what Assad is going to do in Syria. We are trying to put it into legal context through the United Nations, but if that does not work, there are players out there—if it is humanitarian safe zones or arming the free Syrian army, there will be humanitarian intervention to stop this. As Mike says, in the context of YouTube and basically instantaneous information about these atrocities, fortunately the ethical core of the international community is still there and will not allow it to happen. The sooner they get in and stop it, the better.

---

12. "Anfal: Campaign Against the Kurds," *BBC*, June 24, 2007, http://news.bbc.co.uk/2/hi/middle_east/4877364.stm. In 1988, the central government in Baghdad executed nine military campaigns to exterminate the Kurdish population of northern Iraq. Thanks to the government's use of chemical weapons, such as mustard gas and sarin, up to a hundred thousand people perished in the genocide.
13. "Bombing Still Pain Serbs," *BBC*, March 24, 2009, http://news.bbc.co.uk/2/hi/europe/7960116.stm. After peace talks failed to stop Serbian military action against Albanian separatists in Kosovo, NATO launched an eleven-week bombing campaign on March 24, 1999.

SCHARF: Well, Milena, if we do see humanitarian intervention without the Security Council's authorization and there is condemnation by the international community, what is the effect?

STERIO: I agree with Paul that the effect is similar to the one in Kosovo. The difference being obviously that now Syria is farther from the NATO zone of influence, so it is very unlikely that NATO is now somehow going to get involved. I think one possible outcome from the perspective of international law is to say these kinds of things. Even though at the time they may be viewed as violations of international law, they actually serve to create new norms of international law. So we see the development of a customary norm of international law which is this paradigm of humanitarian intervention.

FRENCH: Now I sound like the cynic, but I want to say if it turns out well, then public opinion shifts and the law adapts. If it turns out poorly, then they say, see, we told you so.

SCHARF: Well, after the Kosovo intervention, the countries of the world got together and came up with some new doctrine that they called "responsibility to protect."[14] There is a bumper sticker, R2P, as they call it, and the Security Council and the General Assembly endorsed that doctrine. Would that doctrine apply to this situation? What are the requirements of that doctrine?

STERIO: I think that doctrine actually would apply to this kind of a situation. It basically says that in this kind of a situation where in a sense there is a sovereign, but that sovereign does not play by the rules the same way that maybe Milosevic did not play by the rules, or Assad does not play by the rules, then the other states have a responsibility to protect the citizens of that state. On the one hand, it goes against this very supreme norm of territorial integrity and the respect for sovereignty of other states and on the other

---

14. Office of the Special Adviser on the Prevention of Genocide, "The Responsibility to Protect," http://www.un.org/en/preventgenocide/adviser/responsibility.shtml. The responsibility to protect is a United Nations genocide prevention mechanism consisting of three pillars:

The state carries the primary responsibility for protecting populations from genocide, war crimes, crimes against humanity and ethnic cleansing, and their incitement;

The international community has a responsibility to encourage and assist states in fulfilling this responsibility;

The international community has a responsibility to use appropriate diplomatic, humanitarian and other means to protect populations from these crimes. If a state is manifestly failing to protect its populations, the international community must be prepared to take collective action to protect populations, in accordance with the charter of the United Nations.

hand, now that you have violated those sovereignty rules, you do not get to be a sovereign any longer.

NEWTON: Well, that is important, because I think what Milena points out is the changing priority of international norms. Sovereignty, really since World War II, has not been the dominant narrative of international law; it has been supplemented in so many other ways by human rights norms, by international criminal norms, and by this R2P doctrine. The real challenge, though, is to transcend just the political paralysis in the political debate into an effective action that actually does something.

FRENCH: Can I point out the connection to the last topic we went over about drones? In that case, the argument had to do with, well, yes, we can use drones even if they are violating the sovereignty of another country in order to achieve our aims. Here, where some folks might be trying to use sovereignty as an excuse to not do something that has ethical weight behind it, so I think we can call people on that and say you can't use sovereignty as a cover just because you do not want to do something, and yet dismiss it completely when you do want to do something.

SCHARF: Well, let's turn then from the legal question to the practical question, and I will ask Mike this: From a military standpoint, what would successful intervention into Syria and how is it different from our recent experience with Libya?

NEWTON: Well, there are at least two fundamental things that come to mind when you ask that. One is that there is a very, very long debate, not only in U.S. military circles, but in worldwide military circles about the balance between pure air power, between whether they be drones or stealth bombers, or any other approach. Pure air power and ground power: there were a long line of developments that say we can use overwhelming force and achieve this only through the air. As an army guy, I will tell you this is wrong. It has been proven wrong in every context, most recently Libya. Imagine Libya with just NATO air cover and no on-the-ground people. In Afghanistan, we conquered Northern Afghanistan with very small teams of international operators and a whole range of allies on the ground. So that is the first problem. You need to have an integrated in the air/ground campaign, which then raises the second real problem in that particular context, which is that you do not have any viable, at least conceivable right now, mechanisms for moving in large troops for supporting them—for really seizing control. As Paul said, even if you want to set up a safe haven or safe zone, that requires on-the-ground perimeters of troops to protect them. Even if they are not our troops, they are allies that we are supplying, we are equipping, we are rearming, and training in some cases. So that is a real fundamental problem. How do you have a viable effective ground presence that respects the role? And remember the whole point is that we have a concrete force that respects the rule of law. That implements the laws and customs more appropriately. That takes a big effort on the ground and we are just not in position to do that.

SCHARF: So as difficult as it is to do that, it might be possible that there is still going to be action on the ground. Let me go back to Paul and ask him: what do you think the likelihood is that the intervention might lead to all sorts of grim outcomes—a stale mate, regional conflicts, de facto partition, sectarian cleansing?

WILLIAMS: Well Michael, those of us who are arguing for or who are in favor of humanitarian intervention, we have to be candid. Any change in Syria is going to be destabilizing; that is simply a fact when you are going to topple an authoritarian dictatorial regime and replace it with democracy. That is going to be difficult; it is going to be complicated. We have seen that in Libya.[15] Here, in Syria, we have the fact that there are serious strategic interests for Iran and Syria. The Hezbollah has a very serious interest in Syria.[16] You have large minority communities—the alawites, the druze, the shi'a. They are going to fear for their security under changed circumstances. I do not think we can be naive about it if humanitarian intervention is going to lead to a flowering democracy, but the alternative is a totalitarian regime that continues to and could literally threaten and kill its own people.

SCHARF: Mike, do you want to add to that?

NEWTON: Well, I think that Paul raises an excellent set of points and this goes back to what I said about a pure humanitarian intervention and, in the context of Syria, I think it is fair to say it cannot be cauterized. You cannot

---

15. *See* Sean Lynch, "An Invitation to Meddle: The International Community's Intervention in Libya and the Doctrine of Intervention by Invitation," *Creighton International and Comparative Law Journal* 2 (2012): 173, for an evaluation of the international community's intervention in Libya.

16. *See e.g.* Babak Dehghanpisheh, "Hezbollah Increases Support for Syrian Regime, U.S. and Lebanese Officials Say," *Washington Post*, September 26, 2012, http://www.washingtonpost.com/world/hezbollah-increases-support-for-syrian-regime-us-and-lebanese-officials-say/2012/09/26/d1970396-0591-11e2-afff-d6c7f20a83bf_story.html; and Adam Entous and Farnaz Fassihi, "Hezbollah Helping Assad, U.S. Says," *Wall Street Journal*, August 10, 2012, http://online.wsj.com/article/SB10000872396390443404004577581073528920242.html.

contain it. Shannon pointed out there are implications for the larger regional peace process. There are implications for Hezbollah. There are implications for all kinds of Iranian influence. In fact, I can hear the cynics saying, well, this is all just a cover to go fight a proxy war with Iran. You have to be clear that there are a whole range of consequences and we can plan for them, and we can foresee them from to the extent possible, but this is not just a pure, simple, moral, ethical, legal issue that we can neatly categorize and neatly contain. It is incredibly complicated and, if we know nothing, we know that we are going to find a lot of consequences that we cannot plan for.

SCHARF: Shannon?

FRENCH: Well, the recent historical context, I think is so relevant because people are scarred from what happened in Iraq and the sense, fair or not, we did not do a good job of anticipating what was going to happen next and after that had so much harm follow on from having to scramble to figure out, well, how do we respond to what actually has occurred. So I think there is a real fear out there and frankly it reminds me of after Somalia: the Somalia intervention and the problems that occurred there. For a long time we were shy to do anything similar and some people even blame the inability of the international community to help in Rwanda[17] on that.

STERIO: So just to come back to Paul's original about being candid about what we can do in our humanitarian intervention, I do think though that it is relevant to have some kind of an end goal in mind. In other words, yes, in the short term we are going there to stop violence against civilians, but in the longer term and maybe not over twenty years, but maybe in the next two to three years, what are we trying to achieve? Shannon brings out an excellent point of all these other places, Afghanistan also being one of them, and now we are withdrawing from Afghanistan and who knows what is going to happen. Egypt, where Mumbarak was toppled, and now we have basically renewed violence and the revolution is ongoing.[18] Libya is basically a mess. So I do think we need to have some end goal—not necessarily end goal, but a longer-term goal in mind.

---

17. *See* Scott Baldauf, "Why the U.S. Didn't Intervene in the Rwanda Genocide," *Christian Science Monitor*, April 7, 2009, http://www.csmonitor.com/World/Africa/2009/0407/p06s14-woaf.html.
18. *See* "Egypt News—Revolution and Aftermath," *New York Times*, October 19, 2012, http://topics.nytimes.com/top/news/international/countriesandterritories/egypt/index.html (Providing a comprehensive description of the ongoing events in Egypt).

SCHARF: And while we are thinking about intervention in Syria, we have got this looming problem of a nuclearized Iran, which might also need a military approach. You are suggesting that our means are limited. So let's take this opportunity to take another break and when we come back we will be looking at the international threat from nuclear weapons in Iran.

SCHARF: We are back with foreign policy roundtable. We have been debating the use of predator drones and how to respond to the humanitarian crisis in Syria. In our final segment today, our expert panel will discuss the options for countering the threat of nuclear weapons in Iran. A recent headline of a major U.S. newspaper declared, "August Surprise? Iran could have fuel for the bomb before U.S. elections, study says."[19] Shannon, let's begin with you. Iran insists that its uranium enrichment program is aimed at producing civilian power only.[20] Why does the International Atomic Energy Agency in the United States believe that Iran is using the uranium to start to build nuclear bombs?

FRENCH: Okay this is for the Star Trek fans out there, "Damn it, Jim, I am a philosopher, not a physicist." I don't know—I am not an expert so I cannot explain it in technical terms, but I gather it has to do with the way they are enriching this particular uranium. There are different uses and they require different enrichment levels and I gather that Iran's uranium is being enriched to 20 percent purity and that is the quality or the level of quality required for nuclear weapons.[21]

SCHARF: So, it there any chance that this will be like Iraq was in 2003 where the U.S. intelligence and the UN mistakenly concluded that Iraq had obtained yellow cake and it was building nuclear bombs?[22]

FRENCH: Well again, I don't know but if it is, their reaction is going to be magnified by the comparisons to the past and I think that the fallout from that would be tremendous.

---

19. *See* Howard LaFranchi, "August Surprise? Iran Could Have Fuel for Bomb Before U.S. Election, Study Says," *Christian Science Monitor*, February 1, 2012, http://www.csmonitor.com/USA/Foreign-Policy/2012/0201/August-surprise-Iran-could-have-fuel-for-bomb-before-US-election-study-says.
20. Tanya Ogilvie-White, "International Responses to Iranian Nuclear Defiance: The Non-Aligned Movement and the Issue of Non-Compliance," *European Journal of International Law* 18 (2007): 453, 457.
21. *See* Jay Solomon, "Report Finds Iran Is Closer to Weapons-Grade Fuel," *Wall Street Journal*, October 9, 2012 http://online.wsj.com/article/SB10000872396390443294904578046721515565966.html.
22. *See* Michael Duffy and James Carney, "Iraq: A Question of Trust," *Time*, July 21, 2003, http://www.time.com/time/magazine/article/0,9171,1005234,00.html.

SCHARF: Paul, let's go to Washington and bring you into the conversation. What do you think the G.O. political effect in the Middle East would be if Iran got nuclear weapons?

WILLIAMS: Well I think it would be very, very destabilizing. I think it is important to understand how we got to this point. I think diplomatically, the Americans and our allies, essentially went out into the sand, dug a big hole, and stuck our heads into it. We have tried to convince ourselves that if we could just delay the acquisition of a nuclear weapon by Iran that there might some regime change. We fail to understand the fundamental drive for the Iranians for a nuclear weapon. It is not Ahmadinejad's bomb, it's the Iranian political entity that seeks to have an atomic weapon for political leverage, for sovereignty, and because they have seen what having a weapon does with the Koreans in Pakistan and they have seen what not having a weapon does, in terms of Libya.

SCHARF: Now Paul, the North Koreans claim they got the nuclear bomb because they wanted to protect themselves from a nuclear invasion—that if Iraq had had the nuclear bomb it would not have been invaded in 2003. That was their argument.

FRENCH: The nuclear umbrella, right?

SCHARF: Is that what Iran is looking at or is Iran trying to take its power and project it throughout the region by having this nuclear threat?

WILLIAMS: Think about the current situation of Iran, it sees itself as deserving of a seat at the international table. It does not have that seat. Saudi Arabia has that seat. Saudi Arabia is its long-term protagonist in the region. Essentially Iranians have been shunted aside. They are thinking that they need to protect their sovereignty, they want to be at the table making the important decisions and they want to replace Saudi Arabia as the major player in that region. It cannot do it with the Americans protecting the Saudis, so you need a weapon in order to basically protect their G.O. political interests.

SCHARF: Mike do you think that Israel or the United States should be afraid that if they had the bomb that they would use it?

NEWTON: Well let me back track ten seconds and agree with Paul, and this often gets overlooked is a Persian-Arab-schism. Not just the religious schisms or the regional schisms but…Secretary of State Clinton said this is a game changer precisely because the stated purpose is to take this weapon and use it against Israel.[23] Yes, it is a game changer. There is a clear denial of the right of Israel to exist as a nation state. So yeah, Paul is right, this is a huge regional source of instability and it is a game changer. Especially, and it is very difficult for us from this side of the water, these are intellectual issues to us. To the Israelis these are visceral and motive issues; this is truly an existential threat to them in a way that we have not experienced in our culture.

SCHARF: Well Mike, speaking of Israel, its defense minister, Ehud Barak, recently hinted that Israel is ready to attack Iran's nuclear reactors saying that Israel would rather have its diplomatic solution, [but] all options are on the table.[24] Would such an attack be lawful under international law?

NEWTON: The technical legal answer and I think the ethical answer is, it would depend on the immanency and the clear demonstration on a demonstrable threat that is imminent and the technical legal language is "proportionate response."[25] I think Shannon is exactly right to go back in the gestalt of the region. Where have we seen this play before, of denial and obfuscation, and regime that exercises deceit in order to obtain its own purposes of the entire western community with the continued engagement of the Security Council? This is Iraq all over again. We have seen this play and it did not turn out so well. But this is different in the sense that this is compounded in a way that you did not have in Iraq with bellicosity and express statements about using this weapon, developing this technology in a clear way that threatens the very survival of a neighboring nation in the region. I think that Paul is exactly right. A big part of all this is to aggrandize politically influence. So, if an attack is directed just to help balance out political influence that is a problem under international law. If an attack is focused on a clear imminent articulate demonstrable threat and that attack is proportionate in its response, international law clearly allows Israel or any other state to use the degree of force necessary to eliminate the threat. Shannon is exactly right—the key is demonstrating that threat.

---

23. *See e.g.* Ethan Bronner, "Just How Far Did They Go, Those Words Against Israel," *New York Times*, June 11, 2006, http://www.nytimes.com/2006/06/11/weekinreview/11bronner.html?_r=0, (discussing Iranian President, Mahmoud Ahmadinejad's statements to "wipe [Israel] off the map").
24. *See e.g.* Jodi Rudoren, "Israeli Defense Minister Keeps All Options Open on Iran," *New York Times*, April 30, 2012, http://www.nytimes.com/2012/05/01/world/middleeast/barak-says-all-israeli-options-remain-open-on-iran.html.
25. Thomas M. Franck, "On Proportionality of Countermeasures in International Law," *American Journal of International Law* 102 (2008): 715, 716.

SCHARF: Well Milena, we are not acting in a historic vacuum here. Iraq actually had a nuclear reactor called the Osiris Nuclear Plant that Israel bombed in 1981. What was the world's reaction to that?

STERIO: That is right, Michael. Back in 1981, Israel at the time, I am presuming through intelligence ports, decided that Iraq that had this nuclear reactor was a threat because they were obviously going to develop a nuclear weapon. Israel sent at the time a squad of planes that then bombed the nuclear reactor, destroyed it and in the attack eleven people were also killed.[26] I am hesitant to say civilians because some people would say they were not exactly civilians if they were engaged in the production of a nuclear weapon, but by all accounts they were scientist involved in that project. The international community at the time was swift in condemning Israel. There was a Security Council resolution condemning the attack asking Israel to pay reparations. There was a UN general assembly resolution asking for the same thing and even the International Atomic Energy Agency also condemned Israel. Now some people would say, that was back in '81, rules have evolved and changed, but I think Mike is correct in pointing out that it does hinge on the immediacy of the threat. How certain are we that Iran is building these nuclear weapons and they are going to use them?

FRENCH: I think that just war theory makes this distinction between preemption and prevention. We are all talking about that right here, and it is preemptive war when you can, as Mike was ably describing, when you can prove that they are about to attack. The original paradigm for that was that the troops are assembled on your border; can you fire at them right now? Well, yes you could, that was allowed. It is a very different thing when you skip on into this preventative war where you are not sure as clearly if the attack is imminent.[27]

SCHARF: But doesn't it change when the kind of attack is nuclear weapons with total obliteration?

FRENCH: Well this is the language right, we heard the first sign of attack may be the mushroom cloud, and maybe that was rhetoric that did not make as much sense in one case, and maybe it does make more sense in this case.

---

26. Anthony D'Amato, "Israel's Air Strike Against the Osiraq Reactor: A Retrospective," *Temple International and Comparative Law Journal* 10 (1996): 259.
27. Mark L. Rockefeller, "The 'Imminent Threat' Requirement for the Use of Preemptive Military Force: Is It Time for A Non-Temporal Standard?," *Denver Journal of International Law and Policy* 33 (2004): 131.

NEWTON: I think Milena is exactly right to describe the public political fallout, but do not forget, behind closed doors, there are high fives in the foreign ministries all around the world when the Israelis take out an imminent budding nuclear threat in those days. So this all operates against a very complex background of politics, and yes, the law, and yes, the human rights, and I know some ethicists who would argue, wait a minute, it is infinitely better to have a small amount of damage now, than waiting until we are dealing with a real omnipresent risk of mushroom clouds. That is a much more dangerous situation in, say in five years, or seven years, or however far into the future.

SCHARF: Shannon, would you be one of those ethicists?

FRENCH: I am not sure because we are also skipping toward the territory of assassination as well because these same sort of arguments come into play when you say, well, if you could just kill these very few specific people you could take care of the problem, and there are some practical arguments for that, but I worry about whether we are eroding key principles that we are going to wish we had later on.

SCHARF: Paul, what is your take on this?

WILLIAMS: I think one of those key principles that we have eroded is deterrence. We are all here talking about will there be an attack, is there any nuclear facilities, and in part because we got on this diplomatic path of negotiate-negotiate. We skipped over the path of serious deterrents. There was an opportunity early on, after the changed circumstances in Iraq, where the Iranians were anxious about what our military capabilities and intentions were, and even now we are talking about the use of force, but we are not putting ourselves in a strong deterrent position both with economic sanctions, but we have come to them both, but very timidly and very tardy. We have not positioned our Air Force assets in assertive positions around that make a credible deterrence and I am a little worried that we have been caught off guard, yet again.

FRENCH: Although we are using the dolphins,[28] I understand.

WILLIAMS: I don't think that scares the Iranians too much.

---

28. *See e.g.* John Hudson, "The Navy is Depending on Dolphins to Keep the Strait of Hormuz Open," *Atlantic Wire*, January 13, 2012, http://www.theatlanticwire.com /global/2012/01/militarys-weapon-against-iranian-mines-high-tech-dolphins/47384/#.

SCHARF: Isn't it true that we have put computer bugs[29] that have destroyed their—or set them back, also apparently there have been assassinations of their nuclear scientists.[30]

WILLIAMS: But that is the whole concern. It is this whole piecemeal. If we could just slow it down. There needs to be a strong—if we are going to avoid the actual use of force, there has to be a strong signal of deterrence. It is sort of a catch-22, but you have to position yourself to use serious force so you do not have to. We have not positioned ourselves that way. We have messed around with software bugs and then as you guys indicated, presumably targeted assassinations, which isn't necessarily a better alternative to serious deterrents.

STERIO: While I agree with Paul, the deterrents are necessary but I think deterrents are useful if we have decided ahead of time that the use of force would be lawful. I share Shannon's concerns about have we reached that point, Yes, Iran is a serious threat, but presumably there are other places in the world that are serious threats, and we do have to respect the rule of law and any time we engage in these preventive strikes, we may be crossing that line and it is a slippery slope. I do think that deterrents are important, but that determination that we are ready to use force if necessary and we think that it is legal, I think that is extremely important here.

SCHARF: Now Milena, before when you were describing the earlier Israeli attack on Iraqi nuclear reactor, you described it as being way out in the desert and eleven scientists were killed. It could have been done with a lot of precision and there were not many deaths. On the other hand, U.S. defense secretary Leon Panetta said that even the most sophisticated U.S. bunker buster bombs are not powerful enough to penetrate all of Iran's defenses.[31] Israel's Vice Premier, Moshe Ya'alon, very recently said that Iran's nuclear weapons installation are vulnerable to military strikes. Let's go to our military expert Mike. What is the correct analysis here?

NEWTON: Well, I tend to follow the military professionals, but by the time we get to the core questions about military experts and military capabili-

---

29. *See* David Sanger, "Obama Order Sped Up Wave of Cyberattacks Against Iran," *New York Times*, June 1, 2012, http://www.nytimes.com/2012/06/01/world/middleeast/obama-ordered-wave-of-cyberattacks-against-iran.html?pagewanted=all.
30. "Iran Car Explosion Kills Nuclear Scientist in Tehran," *BBC*, January 11, 2012, http://www.bbc.co.uk/news/world-middle-east-16501566.
31. Elisabeth Bumiller and Jodi Rudoren, "U.S. and Israel Intensify Talks on Iran Options," *New York Times*, August 1, 2012, http://www.nytimes.com/2012/08/02/world/middleeast/in-israel-panetta-warns-iran-on-nuclear-program.html?pagewanted=all.

ties you have to take a step back. What the military is going to want if in fact there is military action here, is a clear mission, a definitive playing state that they can plan against. What they don't want is a strategic naivety that we have displayed to say to the military: go do this and anything else that comes along after the fact and whatever we are also going to task to you because we are going to presume that you are capable. That is a recipe for the ultimate strategic disaster. I do think, to tack onto Milena's point, we did miss a critical strategic window back several years ago when their outcry, popular outcry from the Iranian people, might have achieved regime change in a nonmilitary way. In a completely legitimate way of people rising up and saying, I want human dignity. I want my human rights preserved from the regime. Oh by the way, regime change that might or might not have changed the situation—we sat silently by, so the military looks at that and says that is all ancient history. The military says, give us a clear-cut mission and we will do our very best to plan for it and in military parlance, we will not lose. If it does not work, we will try something else until we accomplish the mission. I think that is the mindset going in.

SCHARF: Apparently, while we sat silently by, Iranians were not so quiet. They were digging this new nuclear processing plant way underground and they were burying it under a major population center. So this does seem to be a different kind of military operation than the Israelis took twenty years ago. If they have to attack and kill a whole city or if they have to use nuclear weapons to penetrate that far underground, how is that going to change the equation?

STERIO: Well, now you are getting into the heart of international humanitarian law, the rules that apply to the way you can fight a war and I think that Mike already mentioned this proportionality analysis. You can do things if you think that the military objective you are trying to achieve will not be outweighed by the civilian casualties, nonmilitary casualties you are going to cause. So if for example, we are calculating and we are trying to figure out if destroying this Iranian nuclear reactor that is our primary military goal and that is going to cause three thousand civilians to die, you would have to say if we are going to destroy the reactor, does that outweigh the civilian death. That is a very complex calculus and I do think that policy makers in the United States and military commanders when they perform those kinds of calculations, I think they are extremely careful and extremely respectful of the rules that we have.

NEWTON: Let me just add the school lessons for the day for our listeners. All commanders, especially NATO commanders and western and especially U.S. commanders, have the legal obligation, and here is the language from the protocol, to do all means feasible to minimize or eliminate all proportionality analysis, the kind of civilian damage to civilian lives and civilian property. So the point is that there is a huge range of options and a whole variety of decisions and it is an incredible complex decision-making process both the targeting model ones and the alternative ones. What is feasible, what is practical, and then try to anticipate the collateral consequences both in terms of damage and destruction, but also to the larger mission. This is why it is very important to give the military an instate that they can plan against.

SCHARF: This balance that you are talking about where you can balance the collateral damage and you were talking about proportionality—it's always in terms of proportionality to a threat. So in this case the threat is nuclear Armageddon launched from Iran, doesn't that mean that this is the kind of case where the military planner, using your calculus, would likely accept broad casualties of the civilian population?

NEWTON: Well the international court of justice who is adjudicating exactly that issue, refuse to make a categorical bright line rule and this is why it is so hard? This is why we have radio shows to talk about this, right? Clear cut bright line rules you put on a 3 x 5 card. You are allowed to use an international law, the necessary amount of force to eliminate the threat. Once you are into a conflict, the same term 'proportionality' has a very, very different meaning. It simply means, as Milena was alluding to, the balance between the military value and the larger damage to civilian lives or civilian property. It is a very different concept. The point is that once you have begun conflict, the use of permissible force is not keyed to what you see in front of you. We are talking on the front end of that.

SCHARF: So I am picturing this Israeli attack may be coming in the summer. Many civilians dying, lots of destruction and maybe successfully getting rid of all the nukes, maybe just setting them back a little bit. What is the likely reaction of the international community? Now, Mike, you suggested that there would be people secretly clapping against Iran and capitals, but Shannon what do you think would be the public reaction?

FRENCH: Well it won't be uniform that's for certain, but I think the key here is last resort, and that is going to be whether or not people are persuaded that in fact that it was at that point of last resort. The burden is going to be on Israel to prove a counter factual. They are going to have to prove that if we had not done this, this worse result would have not occurred and that is incredibly hard thing to prove without having to show people, no this is what would have happened—I am skeptical. I think the results would not pass the reasonable person test with everyone internationally.

SCHARF: Well, everyone is going to have to make that decision for themselves and I think we are all going to have to hold our breath to see how this plays out in a couple of months. Unfortunately, we are just about out of time. We have been looking at some really scary issues today, but we hope that we have been able to shed some light before there was only heated debate. All of us will have a chance to weigh in during this election year. Thanks for joining us and thank you to our guests: Mike Newton of Vanderbilt Law School, Shannon French of the Inamori Center at Case Western Reserve University, Milena Sterio at Cleveland State University, and Paul Williams at the Public International Law and Policy Group from Washington, DC. This is Michael Scharf. Thank you for joining us.

Talking Foreign Policy, May 24, 2012 broadcast

Participants:
Michael Scharf
David Crane
Shannon French
Milena Sterio
Paul Williams

SCHARF: The U.S. Attorney General recently gave a controversial speech justifying assassination of Americans abroad. Meanwhile, despite the International Criminal Courts arrest warrants, indicted war criminals like al-Bashir of the Sudan remain on the loose. And just a few weeks ago, President Obama and Afghan President Karzai shook hands on a plan that critics are comparing to Vietnam. When you hear about international events like these do you ever wish you had access to a group of foreign policy experts who could break the issues down for you and provide their unvarnished opinions? Well, that is what we provide on *Talking Foreign Policy*. I am your host, Michael Scharf. Our expert panel today consists of an international prosecutor, a peace negotiator, a military ethicist and an international law professor. We will be discussing these topics after the news.

SCHARF: Welcome back to *Talking Foreign Policy*. I am Michael Scharf, the director of the Frederick K. Cox International Law Center at Case Western Reserve University. Today, our experts will be discussing the controversial policy of targeted killing of Americans abroad. We will also be talking about the failure of bringing to justice tyrants, who are on the loose. And finally, we will be assessing America's exit strategy from Afghanistan. We are very fortunate today to have with us, from Washington, DC, a famed international prosecutor, David Crane. Dave was appointed in 2002 by the secretary general of the United Nations to be the founding prosecutor of the Special Court for Sierra Leone. Just a few weeks ago Dave got to see his courts come to fruition when they convicted former president of Liberia, Charles Taylor.[32] Dave, thanks for being with us today.

---

32. "In a landmark ruling, an international tribunal found former Liberian President Charles Taylor guilty [April 26, 2012] of aiding and abetting war crimes in neighboring Sierra Leone's notoriously brutal civil war. It was the first war crimes conviction of a former head of state by an international court since the Nuremberg trials of Nazi leaders after World War II." Faith Karimi and Moni Basu, "Court Finds Charles Taylor Guilty of Aiding War Crimes," *CNN*, April 26, 2012, http://www.cnn.com/2012/04/26/world/africa/netherlands-taylor-sentencing/.

CRANE: It is a pleasure to be here, Michael.

SCHARF: So Dave, I understand that with you across the table in Washington, DC, is Paul Williams. Paul is from the Public International Law and Policy Group. He is a professor at American University. He has been with us before and it is great to have you back.

WILLIAMS: Thanks Michael, it is great to be here today.

SCHARF: Here in our studio, we have Shannon French who is the director of the Inamori International Center for excellence at Case Western Reserve. She came to Cleveland a few years ago from Annapolis where she was a professor at the Naval Academy. Good to have you here.

FRENCH: Great to be here, Michael.

SCHARF: Then our final expert is Milena Sterio, who is a professor of international law at the Cleveland Marshall College of Law.

STERIO: I am happy to be here, Michael.

SCHARF: We are all here together, ready to talk about some really controversial issues in international law. The last time we did one of these broadcasts,[33] we were having a spirited debate about the use of predator drones, which are these flying robots that are being used in Afghanistan and Pakistan and killing our enemies in the battlefield. Today, we are going to be talking about something even more controversial. We have just recently learned that these predator drones are now targeting Americans. Let me start with you, Dave. Dave, for thirty years, you were a lawyer in the department of defense in the army. So I think you have a really good sense of what is legal and what is not on the battlefield. The Obama Administration has now acknowledged that we're basically assassinating Americans abroad and that there is a hit list of U.S. citizens involved in al-Qaeda.[34] Doesn't that violate the international and U.S. prohibition on assassinations?

CRANE: Yes it does; and justices aside, not only was I a lawyer during those thirty years in the federal government, but I also was a special operations officer and a senior intelligence officer. Some of my clients, when I was a

---

33. Broadcast from March 1, 2012. (To hear recording of broadcast, see YouTube, *Talking Foreign Policy*, http://www.youtube.com/watch?v=PUvFvowWZmc&feature=youtu.be).
34. Shortly after the attacks on New York and Washington, DC, on September 11, 2001, the United States began its attempt to dismantle al-Qaeda as part of its global war on terror. The 9/11 Commission Report affirmed the attacks were driven by Osama Bin Ladin, a founder of al-Qaeda. (2004 WL 1846272, U.S. Senate).

judge advocate and a general counsel, were very special operations organizations that were very much on the pointed end of the spear. I am very much knowledgeable as to the parameters of how we can use very precise instruments such as special operations. To answer your question, the policy of the United States is we do not assassinate people under executive order 12333.[35] We only, for military necessary purposes, target lawful military targets; and if by chance we have another target that is going to be taken out by other assets within our national security apparatus, then the president can issue a special finding to allow that to happen. But then again, under the national security act of 1947,[36] he has to notify Congress to that affect.

SCHARF: So I guess that is the issue. We cannot assassinate people but we can engage them militarily. So let me ask you Paul, when you sat back and heard the attorney general give his speech where he was justifying the context in the situations when we can kill Americans abroad,[37] what were his justifications? What were his parameters?

WILLIAMS: Well Michael, there is three important parameters that emerged from Attorney General Eric Holder's presentation a few months back. The first is that is seems that the administration has found a legal basis for determining that the executive branch, quite frankly, can be the judge, jury, and executioner of American citizens abroad if they find it necessary to do so and there is an imminent threat to the United States. They also very cleverly have determined that since al-Qaeda is constantly looking to strike the United States, we are constantly under this imminent threat so it is essentially complete discretion of the executive branch to execute American citizens when they believe it is necessary to do so. The second important parameter, which is interesting, is that in order to get to this decision, they have blurred the distinction between constitutional protections and law of war. Earlier in

---

35. Executive Order 12333, the United States intelligence activities, was enacted in December 1981, giving more power and responsibility to United States intelligence agencies. Part 2.11 contains a prohibition on assassination. National Archives, Federal Register, Executive Order 12333, accessed October 21, 2012, http://www.archives.gov/federal-register/codification/executive-order/12333.html.
36. 50 U.S.C.A. § 413b. Available online, Cornell University Law School, "Presidential Approval and Reporting of Covert Actions," accessed October 21, 2012, http://www.law.cornell.edu/uscode/text/50/413b.
37. "Attorney General Eric Holder on [March 5, 2012] presented the Obama Administration's most detailed justification for armed drone strikes against Al-Qaeda leaders, arguing that the U.S. government doesn't legally need judicial review to kill terrorist operatives overseas—even when they're Americans." John Gerstein, "Eric Holder: Targeted Killings Legal, Constitutional," *Politico*, last modified March 6, 2012, http://www.politico.com/news/stories/0312/73634.html#ixzz29y3DqDjD.

the previous administration it was a global war on terror. This administration has rejected that approach and sought to criminalize it. However, traditional constitutional law limits the ability to go after American terrorists abroad so they have sucked back into the law of war and in doing so they have invoked this third element, that it is permissible to have collateral damage. We have a very perverted approach here where we are mixing constitutional provisions, limiting them by the laws of war and even permitting collateral damage when we carry out an execution of an American citizen abroad.

SCHARF: Now Paul, you just mentioned the constitutional approach in the United States. Let me ask our law professor, if we compared this to a situation in the U.S. where a police officer shoots a suspect, what does the constitution require in that context and how is it different than what the attorney general is saying we can do abroad?

STERIO: Under our constitution, there is a famous Supreme Court case called *Tennessee v. Garner*[38] which says that a police officer can shoot a suspect only if the suspect is engaged in a dangerous felony or is armed and represents an immediate threat to the police officer.

SCHARF: So just because they are a member of the mob or narcotics organization, we cannot just go and kill them on the streets, right?

STERIO: We cannot just go and kill them on the street just because of their status or membership in an organization; that is correct.

SCHARF: Okay, so now let's talk about what is going on in the field. Last September a U.S. drone attacked, in Yemen, an American named Anwar al-Awlaki.[39] He was a U.S. born cleric. He was suspected of being involved in al-Qaeda and was on the hit list that Paul told us about. Travelling with him was a journalist, who was not on any hit list. Both of them were killed. What would the constitution say about that?

STERIO: The Constitution would clearly not permit an assassination or shooting of someone like al-Awlaki in these circumstances. Al-Awlaki was driving in a car with a passenger in the middle of the desert. He did not represent an immediate threat. However, let me just come back to something that Paul mentioned. Under the current Obama Administration approach,

---

38. *Tennessee v. Garner*, 471 U.S. 1 (1985).
39. *See* Bob Dreyfuss, "Assassinating Awlaki: Obama Can Kill Anyone He Wants To," *Nation*, September 30, 2011 http://www.thenation.com/blog/163724/assassinating-awlaki-obama-can-kill-anyone-he-wants#.

basically we have defined al-Qaeda as a group that can strike against us at any time with no notice. Basically, we sort of defined the immanency requirement so that because we consider them to be able to strike against us at any point we say well basically any threat they pose to us is imminent.

SCHARF: Okay, so al-Awlaki and his friend, the journalist, are driving on a highway in a desert and a predator drone just blows them up and they say that he was somehow an imminent threat while he was driving his car in the middle of the desert and basically they are saying that because wherever he goes at any time he is always a threat.

STERIO: That is exactly right. You could make the argument that maybe he was in the car driving to an al-Qaeda training camp or maybe he was on his way to construct a bomb that he was going to be using against the United States. But that is essentially the approach, yes.

SCHARF: And it would not matter if it was ten hours away, this training camp or the bomb site, or ten minutes away?

STERIO: Correct. Under the Obama administration the approach would not matter, immanency requirements have basically has been defined away.

SCHARF: All right. So Mr. International Prosecutor, our military expert, let's get back to you. Dave, the attorney general's answer to this conundrum is that if an American joins the enemy in a war against the United States, he basically becomes a legitimate military target, the fourth and fifth amendments no longer apply. Does this mean that only on the battlefield, only in Afghanistan and maybe Yemen,[40] this theory works or would this apply anywhere in the world where members of al-Qaeda, who happen to be U.S. citizens are located?

CRANE: I think it is a matter of prospective. If we have an American who joins the enemy and is actively engaged in combat operations against the United States, then he is a legitimate military target and can be engaged. As we peel away from Afghanistan and broaden this alleged threat around the world, let's say in Yemen, then it becomes more problematic to hook this individual in as a valid military target because we have a bright red thread in international criminal law, which I prosecuted individuals in West Africa, you do not intentionally target civilians. But for certain rare or specific exceptions

---

40. *See* Jim Lobe, "U.S. Escalating Drone War in Yemen," *IPS*, April 26, 2012, http://www.ipsnews.net/2012/04/us-escalating-drone-war-in-yemen/.

such as their turnaround as a Libyan mass, or begin to target you, you have a right to self-defense or they become unlawful combatants taking up arms against you. So you can target them; but in this situation it becomes a very slippery slope I am very, very concerned about. Just like assassination, we go out and execute individuals for what they may do, be they American or not. I think that is very problematic and the wrong direction where we want to take the law and military operation.

SCHARF: Currently Dave, they are saying that not just in Afghanistan, where we are actually fighting a war, or Pakistan, where the war is spilling over, but in places like Yemen and Somalia—where else are they using predator drones around the world? Where else should we be concerned about this?

CRANE: Predator drones are the wave of the future. They are relatively inexpensive, very precise—which is good because you have to be precise when you use force. I think we are reaching for them without completely thinking through their legal use and ramifications. Listeners have to understand that if the military uses a drone, they have to follow the laws of conflict, military necessity, proportionality, unnecessary suffering, and discrimination. If other national security assets use it, those rules do not apply. I think it is really important for us to lay this on the table because, again, we have a different set of rules depending on who is flying that predator.

SCHARF: And back to Paul when you were describing the attorney general's justification, you mentioned that it is the CIA that is making these decisions here. Is that right?

WILLIAMS: I think David hit on the key point here, there has been a blurring of law because there are so many characters on the U.S. government side involved in executing individuals abroad including American citizens and the administration has been simply unwilling to simply say we are in a global war on terror and the laws of war apply. They have been mixing it with constitutional provisions, and quite frankly, Michael, they have been hallowing out our constitutional protections.

SCHARF: Paul, I am not going to let you get away with dodging the exact question. I am a little bit more comfortable with what Dave is describing as having a military officer control these drones maybe in a hot battlefield situation. What I am worried about is whether the CIA has control of this. What I want you to tell me is who has got control? Should I be losing sleep over this, Paul?

WILLIAMS: Michael, you should be losing sleep over this because you are one of the few people asking this question. And when it has been asked, the U.S. government has refused to answer. There is robust oversight. It is a serious and controlled process. Trust us. We have a death list and we are killing people without constitutional provisions.

STERIO: And the CIA is doing this. Shannon, do you agree with the proposition that the war on terrorism is worldwide and we can have the CIA kill, not just foreigners, but Americans may be across the border in Mexico or Canada or anywhere else in the world?

FRENCH: Absolutely not. It was raised before and I can't emphasize this enough that this blurring of the lines, absolutely undermines all of the core values that went into the principles in the first place. For example, the just war tradition[41] on which all military ethics is based is there precisely to try to limit the scope of war. When you do as the expression is used 'hollow it out' and take out all of these constraints, you are making it meaningless. You also have this problem that when they introduce a new technology, like the drones, they act like "Aha!"—it is a new technology, so that we can pretend the old rules do not apply. But, they do. I cannot say this strongly enough. The old rules, the principles that are behind the law of armed conflict,[42] the ethics behind it, they do not alter when you come up with a clever new way to kill people. There are still some people you can, in certain ways, and certain people you can't. I will also just point out that having a CIA director have the power to kill a U.S. citizen without due process, that is incredibly dangerous and it is nothing that you can find justification for in any of the principles of the founders of this country. Also, I would like to point out that no one man should have all that power. Yes, I am quoting Kanye West[43] when I say that.

---

41. The just war tradition is the institution of rules or agreements that have historically been established to apply to war. *See* George R. Lucas, Jr., "'New Rules for New Wars' International Law and Just War Doctrine for Irregular War," *Case Western Reserve Journal of International Law* 43 (2011): 677 (discussing the just war tradition application to the "global war on terror").
42. The international humanitarian law, also known as the law of armed conflict, is contained in treatises and customary rules between states limiting the effect of armed conflict. *See* ICRC Legal Fact Sheet, "What is International Humanitarian Law?," accessed October 21, 2012, http://www.icrc.org/eng/resources/documents/legal-fact-sheet/humanitarian-law-factsheet.htm?.
43. "No one man should have all that power," lyrics from American hip-hop singer Kayne West's lead single "Power," from his album *My Beautiful Dark Twisted Fantasy*, Roc-A-Fella Records, 2010.

WILLIAMS: Michael, I would like to jump in and agree with Shannon but take it in a slightly different direction. As Shannon has pointed out, when we have a new technology, the government sort of embraces it and thinks the old rules don't apply. But what is astounding is that the population also embraces that. For instance, 60 percent of those who identify themselves as liberals support executing American citizens abroad without due process. Only 49 percent support the death penalty after trial by jury.[44] That is astounding. Somehow, it is okay to execute American citizens by a drone without due process, but is not okay once they have been through a trial by jury.

CRANE: Let me ask a question here. Take the al-Awlaki scenario, instead of it being in Yemen, that it is on I-40 heading West just near Ashville and we find him doing the very same thing and we have got a predator drone. What happens then?

SCHARF: Relating to that—let me ask you, isn't it true that Congress just passed a law[45] that allows us to have predator drones in the United States now?

CRANE: There you go, it is just the beginning.

SCHARF: We are first going to start seeing surveillance, but who knows where it goes? Let's say it is not just al-Awlaki, let's say there is a drug bust, organized crime or something, that a predator drone happens to see. Does it have to call in the cops or can it just unleash a hell fire missile as it did against al-Awlaki in Yemen?

CRANE: Imagine this, the FBI seeking from a judge probable cause to kill because we have Awlaki on I-40 heading west.

SCHARF: Well, let us talk about the due process angle. Dave, some experts are now suggesting that there should be a special court established to decide when a targeted killing should be authorized so it is not completely in the discretion of the CIA director. What do you think of that idea?

CRANE: I think it is an excellent idea. I think we have already done it once before and we have decided to electronically surveil American citizens or U.S. persons, as the statue says, and the Foreign Intelligence Surveillance Act[46]

---

44. *See* The Field Poll, "Release # 2393," September 29, 2011, p. 3, http://field.com/fieldpollonline/subscribers/Rls2393.pdf.
45. Passed in February 2012, the bill makes it easier for the government to use drones in the United States. S. Smithson, "Drones Over U.S. Get OK by Congress," *Washington Times*, February 7, 2012, http://www.washingtontimes.com/news/2012/feb/7/coming-to-a-sky-near-you/?page=all.
46. The Foreign Intelligence Surveillance Act ("FISA") was passed by Congress in 1978, establishing the Foreign Intelligence Surveillance Court and laying out the procedure for

back in 1978–79. It was a compromise. The executive branch said we have got to have this capability to protect the country and Congress agreed, but said, we will compromise and let you have that authority, but we want to have our third branch of government, the judiciary, take a look at it to make sure that the constitution is not violated. So, I think we have a precedent. I think if we are going to go down this road, then I think we are going to need to have something like this or give the Foreign Intelligence Surveillance Act courts more power to review this. The system is already in place.

SCHARF: Let me ask Milena this, isn't it true that in all but one case out of thousands filed, this Foreign Intelligence Surveillance Act court has always approved the wiretap warrants?

STERIO: Yes, Michael that is correct. However, if you think about it, you could argue that the court here, the FISA court, does act as a barrier in a sense that only the well-written justified applications are submitted to the court. The fact that we have a court prevents anybody from submitting a frivolous application to the courts. So even if most of those requests have been approved, what about the thousands of requests that have never been filed? I agree with David that some sort of a judicial oversight is necessary because when the executive acts as prosecutor or judge, jury and, executioner in secret regarding the targeting of American citizens that is a very scary thought.

FRENCH: Well, there is a difference between wiretapping and killing someone. I would like to think that if there is (what you are talking about) a bit of a pause before even submitting a request for some wiretapping, there would be an even greater one before saying review this for permission to kill.

STERIO: Absolutely.

CRANE: I think that is an important point to bring up. I do not know the exact statistics. I used to write those and move those around for the Department of Defense on a particular issue. But the attorney general of the United States has to personally certify to the foreign intelligence surveillance court that there is probable cause to surveil you as a person. So the standard is so rigorous and the process is so reviewed by general counsels and judge advocates before it even goes to the attorney general; the point was well made here just now. I think it is important for your listeners to understand that

---

requesting judicial authorization for surveillance and collection of foreign intelligence information. It can be found online at http://www.law.cornell.edu/uscode/text/50/chapter-36 (accessed October 21, 2012).

they do not all actually go through the court because there is not enough probable cause. So I think that it would work. It is better than nothing.

SCHARF: Is there any proponent of this? Is anybody suggesting this on either side of the aisle?

CRANE: I just had a very bright student write about it in one of my papers which I just graded. It was simplistic, but yet perfect. You hear it in the academy and among practitioners over cocktails, but in reality, I personally know of nothing being formalized at the legislative level or being kicked around at the Departments of Defense or Justice.

WILLIAMS: This is what is sort of shocking. There is a weak accountability debate. When the war on terror was launched and drones were initially used, there was a fierce debate in the public and the media about whether we should be doing this. That debate no longer exists. For some of reason, as Shannon mentioned earlier, it is some new flashy technology, it has been embraced by the government and that is fine, but it also has been embraced by the general public and by the self-proclaimed watchdogs that are supposed to constantly challenge this type of activity. But there is deafening silence from the civil rights community, the civil libertarians. Quite frankly, Michael, it is stunning.

SCHARF: While we ponder the specter of the stunning robotic killing machines flying over our streets in the United States and abroad, let's take a short break and when we return, we will be discussing some of the challenges of bringing some of the world's most terrible tyrants to justice.

SCHARF: Welcome Back. So we have been having a really, really entertaining discussion that went way too long, but could not stop it discussing the legalities, pros and cons of targeted killings of Americans abroad. In our second segment today, we are going to be talking about the failed efforts to bring some notable tyrants to trial. David, I want to start with you. It is really amazing that we have you on this show, especially with this topic. A few weeks ago you were sitting in the courtroom when former leader of Liberia, Charles Taylor, was convicted by the special court for Sierra Leone. Dave, as the founding chief prosecutor of that tribunal, you were responsible for the indictment of Taylor back in 2003 and I understand that was somewhat controversial. What was your thinking at the time?

CRANE: As I walked through Sierra Leone and visited other parts of West Africa, I told the people of West Africa that no one is above the law and the rule of law is more powerful than the rule of the gun. I told them don't believe what I say, believe what I do. So when I decided to unseal the indictment of Charles Taylor, which I signed on the third of March of 2003, and then sealed it in June of 2003, my intent was to show the people of Africa that no one is above the law. So I wanted to bring down intentionally, Charles Taylor, before the world and let people know that the rule of law is more powerful than the rule of the gun.

SCHARF: And would you say that that was the signal that was sent two weeks ago?

CRANE: I think it was and, again, this is not about anybody but the people of Sierra Leone and I think that they now believe that the rule of law is more powerful than the rule of the gun.

SCHARF: But it sort of is about other populations as well because isn't it true that people like al-Bashir, the indicted leader of Sudan, are sort of looking over their shoulder and are sleeping a little bit less comfortably now?

CRANE: Indeed, but again at the end of the day, modern international criminal law is the bright red thread throughout all this. It is politics. We have the ability to prosecute. We have the rules, the procedure, the jurisprudence; it's going to be a political decision to hand over any head of state whether it be Charles Taylor, Melodich, Milošević, or Omar al-Bashir. So someday, someone is going to make the political decision to hand him over to the international criminal court.

SCHARF: Now Shannon, you taught for years and years at the Naval Academy. When you think about international prosecutions of these leaders, I am sure many people argue that it is important for deterrence to deter future war crimes. Is there empirical data or is there any evidence that there is any kind of deterrence?

FRENCH: I hate to say this, but the answer is no. There may come to be some level of deterrence, maybe it is a cumulative effect and the more that there is regularity and you can get a consistency of certain punishments coming down for these tyrants maybe there might come to be one. But the trouble is that you are dealing with people who are already risking their lives in the sense that they are obviously not making fans in the places where they are doing their war crimes and they risk getting killed if they lose power.

SCHARF: There must be something about being a tyrant where they are cost benefit analysis is not the same as an ordinary person.

FRENCH: Right, you are already dealing with people who are off the rail. So is the fact that, hey, you might be called in front of the Hague, really going to stop someone who already thinks it is okay to do the things that they are doing?

SCHARF: But someone like al-Bashir of the Sudan who has been indicted now for five years can continue to thumb their nose at international justice. Doesn't that send sort of an opposite signal? Doesn't it sort of say that you can get away with it?

FRENCH: Yes, I think it is more important from the justice perspective than from the deterrence perspective in the sense of what it says to the victims, what is says to the people who are judging the international community's resolve on questions like this, which is where it matters. But I am not convinced that anybody who was about to commit genocide goes, oh wait, I may get hauled in front of the international court.

SCHARF: Now speaking of Al-Bashir, let me bring Paul Williams into this conversation. Paul you were a peace negotiator between the Sudan and Southern Sudan. You were an arbitrator in the arbitration between those two countries. You know the situation in the Sudan. Tell us about Al-Bashir. What was he accused of and why is it important to bring him to justice?

WILLIAMS: What is so stunning about the continued existence of President Al-Bashir in power as the President of Sudan is as you said, over five years ago he was indicted by the international tribunal for genocide in Darfur.[47] That has not stopped a whole host of international envoys going to his door and trying to negotiate peace with him both in Darfur and now with the conflict in a place called Southern Kordofan in Blue Nile.[48] As David had mentioned, the rule of law is more powerful than the gun, but it is not entirely clear that the rule of law is more powerful than the political predisposition to accommodate and appease those individuals. Shannon mentioned that it might not change their mind, but quite frankly, it certainly should change the mind of the international community trying to negotiate peace deals or bring about peace. There is this delusion that you can dance with the devil and not get burnt, and I think that is the lesson that we have to start taking seriously and learning from when dealing with individuals indicted for war crimes.

---

47. Mai-Linh K. Hong, "A Genocide By Any Other Name: Language, Law, and the Response to Darfur," *Virginia Journal of International Law* 49 (2008): 235–41.
48. "Sudan: Crisis Conditions in Southern Kordofan," *Human Rights Watch*, May 4, 2012, http://www.hrw.org/news/2012/05/04/sudan-crisis-conditions-southern-kordofan.

SCHARF: Milena, Paul just mentioned that people are going to the Sudan. I guess they want Al-Bashir's oil, so you have diplomats going there, but he is just not hanging out in the Sudan, he is hopscotching all around Africa and nobody is arresting him. Don't they have an international law obligation to arrest him and send him to the Hague?

STERIO: Sure. Al-Bashir certainly is not travelling to places like France, England, and Italy, but he has been traveling around the African continent.[49] Other African states have been claiming that Al-Bashir has what is called 'head of state immunity,' which is an important principle and rule of international law.[50] So the question here is whether an outstanding warrant by the International Criminal Court trumps the principle of head of state immunity? There is a lot of argument to be said that yes, it does. Especially in this kind of situation where the International Criminal Court is actually investigating in Sudan because the situation was referred to the court by the UN Security Council.[51] So that arguably trumps any head of state immunity. However, African countries basically say that they are going to go to the international court of justice to ask for an advisory opinion before they decide what they are going to do.

SCHARF: David, let me turn back to you. I know you have been doing work on this issue. The countries of Africa are kind of losing their excitement about the International Criminal Court. They are becoming disenchanted and part of the reason is the situation involving their fellow head of state, Al-Bashir. What do you make of all that?

CRANE: Well again, I think it's wrong to think that the ICC is focusing on Africa, but I think that Africa is symptomatic of an attitude that is starting to permeate the court, and that is a bit of arrogance. From their perspective, they believe that they are the permanent international court that deals with these things. I think they have lost sight of the fact that they are a court of last resort and there is a great difference to the opinions and perspective of any country state's party as to how they would like to deal with the situation.

---

49. "Ethiopia to Host African Union Summit After Omar al-Bashir Malawi Row," *BBC*, June 12, 2012, http://www.bbc.co.uk/news/world-africa-18407396.
50. "Bringing Power to Justice: Absence of Immunity for Heads of State Before the International Criminal Court," *Amnesty International*, last modified December 1, 2010, http://www.amnesty.org/en/library/asset/IOR53/017/2010/en/9dd7f7ce-d531-486b-abe0-d873ad57287a/ior530172010en.html.
51. Sarah M. H. Nouwen and Wouter G. Werner, "Doing Justice to the Political: The International Criminal Court in Uganda and Sudan," *European Journal of International Law* 21 (2010): 941, 954–62.

I think that is a critical thing for us to consider because I think they have lost that perspective.

SCHARF: Well, speaking of a court of last resort, another situation involving the International Criminal court of last resort is Libya. They have indicted Muammar Gaddafi's son, Saif Gaddafi, and Libya says no, we want to prosecute him.[52] So Dave, why can't Libya prosecute him? Or Paul, what is your take on that?

WILLIAMS: Michael, let me pick up on that because I think this is an important lesson. We are learning an important lesson from Libya which answers the question you asked earlier about the African union and head of state immunity. The people of Libya are hugely in favor of accountability and justice. That is why they want to see Saif Gaddafi, the son of Muammar Gaddafi, prosecuted. They want to see him prosecuted in Libya because that is where he committed his crimes and it is important as far as the healing process. What we learn here is that the people of Africa are quite keen on justice. You hear a lot about the African Union not being interested in the ICC work or justice in Africa anymore and them being unfairly targeted. As Milena points out, they pick, oddly enough, head of state immunity because they are worried about themselves. Mike, a recent poll showed that 77 percent of Kenyans support justice mechanisms. 71 percent of Nigerians support these justice mechanisms and about 90–95 percent of the Libyans support these. So the people of Africa are very much behind this idea of accountability. It is just that the leadership is not quite as enthusiastic about that.

SCHARF: Shannon, I am going to let you have the last word on this.

FRENCH: I was just going to say that justice requires consistency and we, the U.S., but also the international community have been accused of inconsistency in places where we intervene and where we fail to do so. If there is inconsistency in terms of whom we haul before the court and who we still try to make deals with, we are just reinforcing the idea that it is not justice for all. That is a significant thing.

SCHARF: All right, it is time for another break. When we come back our experts are going to provide a critique of America's exit strategy from Afghanistan. Stay with us.

---

52. Bruno Waterfield, "International Prosecutors Back Demand Saif Gaddafi Stands Trial in Libya," *The Telegraph*, October 9, 2012, http://www.telegraph.co.uk/news/worldnews/africaandindianocean/libya/9597086/International-prosecutors-back-demand-Saif-Gaddafi-stands-trial-in-Libya.html.

SCHARF: We are back with *Talking Foreign Policy*. So we have been debating the policy of targeted killings of Americans abroad. We had a brief discussion of what to do about bringing tyrants to justice and in our final segment we are going to spend some time talking about Americas newly penned exit strategy from Afghanistan. David, I want to start with you. You spent 30 years in the military. To date, 1,900 American troops have died in the war in Afghanistan. There have even been 432 casualties from Ohio, where we are broadcasting from today. As a former special ops officer, a paratrooper and a senior executive in the DOD for 30 years, can you tell us why the United States has over 100,000 combat troops in Afghanistan? What are we doing there?

CRANE: I think we are there in fact to stabilize Afghanistan. We have already defeated Al Qaeda in Afghanistan and we have a challenge in Pakistan as well. The combat troops that are there are necessary for us to achieve our military objectives as we transition from a military operation to counter insurgency and then to essentially building a new country called Afghanistan. None of this happens in sequence A+B+C. There is blending and steps: one step forward and two steps back at times. You need the stability of combat troops not only to take on whatever threat it may be, but also to ensure they do not attack again until it is time for us to hand over the ability for the Afghan army and the Afghan police to keep Afghanistan stable.

SCHARF: Ten years ago when we determined that the Afghan government of the Taliban was partly responsible together with Al Qaeda in the attacks of 9/11, we attacked. We toppled the Taliban and they went into hiding. We have been there and you say we have been doing some nation building and we are trying to do counterinsurgency.[53] Are we winning? What are the measures of success here, Dave?

CRANE: In these situations, I have to tell you I honestly do not think that we are winning. There is no such thing as winning in situations like this. I started my public service career during the Vietnam era in a very interesting war. It is going to be up to the Afghan people as to what they want to do regardless of how hard we work to do it. I am certainly not belittling the sacrifice of American citizens, wherever they may be. That is not what I am saying. All I am saying is we have to be very careful in our objectives in what I call dirty little wars, and I think we have been there a bit too long. It is faded and at this point and time, we are not winning the war because we do not know what that is. But the Afghan people will eventually in the next couple of years.

---

53. Afghanistan, *New York Times* World News, last modified October 2, 2012, http://topics.nytimes.com/top/news/international/countriesandterritories/afghanistan/index.html.

SCHARF: So Shannon, David says maybe we are not winning. But if you read the newspaper account, the administration says we are doing just fine; we are making progress. What are the metrics that they are using?

FRENCH: You have heard them use some metrics that worry people because they reminiscent of the Vietnam War. We just heard the reference to that, in that they are talking about body counts.[54] However there is a difference and I think it is important difference in that when they do talk about having killed specific people it is named people within the Al Qaeda organization or in some cases Taliban leaders. It is not this really disturbing account that happened in the Vietnam War where they were simply tallying up numbers of dead on the other side and in some cases even blurring the line between whether they were civilian dead or combatant dead. So I think it is unfair to make the correlation that strong, and I would also point out from a just war tradition perspective that the war in Afghanistan has a much stronger reason to be there in the first place then say, Iraq did. But now all this time has gone by, do we still have a reason to be there? Are there better ways that we can do this moving forward?

SCHARF: We should be suspicious of the metrics that we hear the administration using. At the same time a few months ago, Afghanistan's people were outraged when U.S. soldiers burned copies of the Koran at a NATO base.[55] Then a couple of months ago, a U.S. officer went berserk. He went door to door on a shooting spree and killed sixteen civilians, including nine children.[56] There have been countless cases in the news where our predator drones, from our first segment, have killed a lot of innocent civilians that are collateral damage or maybe in mistaken airstrikes.[57] So are we losing the effort to win the hearts and minds in Afghanistan?

FRENCH: Well, I think that is one of those yes and no kind of questions. On the one hand you are absolutely right and a lot of this has led to what they

---

54. Mark Thompson, "Should the Military Return to Counting Bodies?," *Time*, June 2, 2009, http://www.time.com/time/nation/article/0,8599,1902274,00.html.
55. Kevin Sieff, "U.S. Probe of Koran Burning Finds 5 Troops Responsible, Officials Say; Afghans Demand Trial," *Washington Post*, March 2, 2012, http://www.washingtonpost.com/world/us-probe-of-koran-burning-finds-5-soldiers-responsible-afghan-clerics-demand-public-trial/2012/03/02/gIQAwJqYmR_story.html.
56. Ahmed Nadem and Ahmed Haroon, "Sixteen Afghan Civilians Killed in Rogue U.S. Attack," *Reuters*, March 11, 2012, http://www.reuters.com/article/2012/03/11/us-afghanistan-civilians-idUSBRE82A02V20120311.
57. United Nations Assistance Missions in Afghanistan, "Afghanistan: Annual Report 2011, Protection of Civilians in Armed Conflict," February 2012, http://unama.unmissions.org/Portals/UNAMA/Documents/UNAMA%20POC%202011%20Report_Final_Feb%202012.pdf.

call green on blue violence, meaning that some of the folks we are trying to train are partnering with, in Afghanistan some of the troops are attacking U.S. troops.[58] So obviously that is disturbing. It does not suggest that we are winning over the people in the country. At the same time, though, there isn't the urge to push us out immediately, at least in the kind of dramatic draw down that some folks would like to see; like us literally pulling everyone out immediately because there still is a reliance and there is an understanding that if we left immediately that people are not trained to replace the U.S. troops.

SCHARF: Well, the Afghan president, Hamid Karzai, certainly wants us to stay there. Let's talk about him for a minute. He is seen as corrupt. He is unpopular.[59]

FRENCH: That is because he is corrupt, Michael.

SCHARF: He is seen as contemptuous of the United States.

FRENCH: Some of the contemptuousness of the U.S. is playing to his domestic audience there and he has to, particularly when these horrible things happen. We have had these atrocities on our side, so of course he cannot turn around and say I love the U.S. after that happened.

SCHARF: But we have hitched our horse to his wagon, right?

FRENCH: There is no other horse.

SCHARF: What are the implications of that if we are taking our destiny and linking it with his?

FRENCH: I do think it is worrisome. I am not going to belittle that, but at the same time I think everyone understands that there is no other horse and that we are not linked so much to him as we are trying desperately to find some kind of stability in leadership. If a new leader came along that we had more confidence in, I don't think anyone expects that we would not ditch Karzai for this new and better prospect.

SCHARF: Now Paul, you have been in almost every war zone around the world, but I don't think you have been to Afghanistan yet, is that right?

WILLIAMS: No, and not any time soon.

---

58. Tucker Reals, "Afghanistan Police Officer Kills 2 U.S. Troops in Latest Green-On-Blue Attack," *CBS News*, August 18, 2012, http://www.cbsnews.com/8301-202_162-57495151/afghanistan-police-officer-kills-2-u-s-troops-in-latest-green-on-blue-attack/.
59. Skip Kaltenheuser, "Afghanistan: The Long Goodbye, Leaving A Failed State Crippled by Corruption," *IBA Global Insight* 66 (2012): 14–17.

SCHARF: Okay, so let's get you there in spirit anyway. With Osama Bin Laden dead and the Taliban ousted, is it still in American's vital interest to fight on in Afghanistan? Why not just pull out now?

WILLIAMS: Actually, Michael, you have hit on this. We have a very serious problem with our policy in Afghanistan and that is that we are delusional. We have lost this war and we are unwilling to admit it and, thereby, we are creating policies and commitments for the next decade that are going to tie us to this sinking stone. The military has done its job. They hunted down Osama Bin Laden and they shot him dead. They have pushed the Taliban out of the most important areas, they have cleared and they have held territory, and then they turn around and say, okay, we have cleared and we have held territory, let's get the Afghan security forces. As Shannon pointed out, there is just as much likelihood as green on blue violence as there is on actually holding territory from the Afghan forces' side. Politically, we have massively let down the people of Afghanistan and our military people who are in there fighting the battle. There was a recent interview on NPR, where a senior American official was asked the question, "What happens when all this international aid that is currently going to the country as part of the war effort, pulls out? Won't the bubble collapse?" And no kidding, he said "No, it won't because most of the money has been taken out as legitimate profits by international contractors or it has been brought out in suitcases of cash to points beyond Afghanistan. So the Afghans won't actually notice when the economic bubble supported by the war effort disappears." What kind of policy, what kind of strategy is that?

SCHARF: David, you used to teach at the judge advocate general school, you are a student of military history, and perhaps you have a different take on this. If we rapidly pulled out of Afghanistan what would be the risks?

CRANE: We are stuck. We are in it and we have to deal with it. I agree with my colleagues. We have got issues. We can't pull out. This has not been thought through completely. I agree with Paul. We have accomplished the military mission and now we just cannot pull out because it would be catastrophic. It would mean a weakened Pakistan. What we are really talking about here is Afghanistan/Pakistan or as they say over there in that part of the world 'Afpak.' That is how they are approaching it now because you have to. So if we have to pull out, it would be a sucking chest wound and there would be a black hole. Then we will start this all over again because someone is going to have to step in. We are in this. We will have to quote Richard Nixon as we pulled out of Vietnam, "We need peace with honor."

SCHARF: Well Milena, speaking of peace with honor, the president was just in Afghanistan, somewhere that Paul won't go. He made a deal with Karzai, a long-term strategic partnership agreement.[60] Can you tell us what the different provisions of that agreement are?

STERIO: The president recently just travelled to Afghanistan. It was a secret trip, unannounced for security reasons and, while over there, the president signed a pact with President Karzai. In the pact the United States promises to reduce troop levels of American soldiers in Afghanistan to sixty-eight thousand from one hundred thousand this fall. Then most American combat troops are to depart from Afghanistan by 2014. However, with all that said, the United States has pledged to keep military advisors, trainers, riot police, etc. in Afghanistan for as long as another decade. We also said we will no longer have any U.S. military bases, but we will use Afghan military bases over there. So that leaves the door open for the United States to use Afghanistan for continued drone strikes on the Taliban or Al Qaeda forces in Afghanistan or possibly Pakistan for as long as another decade. We actually will be there in somewhat reduced numbers, but we will still be there.

SCHARF: All right Paul, you have done twenty-four peace negotiations, help us break this down. What are the criticisms of this agreement? What should we be worried about?

WILLIAMS: The criticisms of this agreement are essentially that it is not an agreement. The obligations on the Afghan side are to fight corruption and Shannon can tell you why that is not going to happen. Then they commit us to pay the salaries of the Afghan security forces. David is right. We are stuck with this. We are swimming in a race with a stone tied around our waist. But we have to acknowledge that and embrace that and then craft a policy around that. Simply funding the Afghan defensive forces billions of dollars into the indefinite future is not a policy. We think we are winning, we're following the Afghanization approach, we turn to the Afghans because it has been successful; we have cleared, we have held. But we cannot just pump billions of dollars into the Afghan security forces and cross our fingers. We have to realize that we are stuck with a very difficult situation. We have to be more clear-eyed and, quite frankly, more realistic about how we approach the situation in both Afghanistan and Pakistan.

---

60. White House, "Enduring Strategy Partnership Agreement Between the United States of America and the Islamic Republic of Afghanistan," May 2, 2012, http://www.whitehouse.gov/sites/default/files/2012.06.01u.s.-afghanistanspasignedtext.pdf.

CRANE: The Vietnam War ended with Northeast tanks crashing through the presidential palace gates. We certainly do not want to see Taliban tanks crashing through presidential gates of Hamid Karzai's palace.

SCHARF: Let's say this worst-case scenario is what we see. Does that mean a return of Al Qaeda? Does that mean we will lose the war on terror, Dave?

CRANE: No, I do not think so. Again, it is going be up to the Afghan people as to how they want to be governed, if they have ever been governed, and that is the problem. We have to look back at history, speaking of military history. No one has ever actually turned Afghanistan into the country that we would all like to see it. Quite frankly, that is not what the Afghan people want anyway.

FRENCH: Can I just say, Michael, if Alexander the Great could not conquer a place, probably no one can.

SCHARF: Is there any possibility, then, Shannon that we can see a deal with the Taliban? If they are not the same as Al Qaeda, can they be rehabilitated? Can we join with them for the good of the country?

FRENCH: Possibly, temporarily if our interests align. I think that is about as cautious as I want to put it. But I think it is important to make a distinction between the Taliban and Al Qaeda because it is a question of huge difference between domestic concerns and a larger international strategy.

SCHARF: Milena?

STERIO: On the other hand, aligning ourselves with a regime like the Taliban basically is counter to all of the human rights obligations and principles that we believe in as a country.

FRENCH: So is that realistic? Would they ever agree to human rights points enough for us?

SCHARF: And are they the Taliban that they were ten years ago?

STERIO: Who knows if they are the same people. Probably some of them are still the same. The problem is, as they pointed out earlier, that Afghanistan has basically been a war zone for a long time, and before that the Soviets were in for ten years, and before that it was pretty much civil war and chaos. Nobody really knows who is aligned with whom. The other thing is that there is not really any unity in Afghanistan. There are all these huge tribal areas where the different tribes just govern themselves. It is extremely difficult to say who we can align ourselves with or what we can do there.

FRENCH: You cannot use western principles when dealing with the tribes.

SCHARF: Explain that to our listeners.

FRENCH: Well, it is just the idea that we are treating a nation state like a unified sovereign power and it isn't. There are a series of tribes in many cases that have more of a bond with people over what we see as borders, than otherwise.[61]

SCHARF: All right, but when we left Vietnam it took a big toll on Americans; on its foreign policy, on its interest run in the world. If we are seen as losing and abandoning Afghanistan, what are the implications worldwide, Dave?

CRANE: Well, I do not think that I agree with Paul. If we are just honest with the American people and the world and say here is where we stand and here is our plan and where we are going, it is not a defeat. It is a political circumstance that we must face and we must make the best of it. We do not have to pull away from that part of the world. We just need to make sure we work with partners in the area to at least keep that particular group of clans stable enough that we don't see Al Qaeda or the Taliban come back in. Quite frankly, I do not think Al Qaeda is going to stick around that area. They are moving southwest toward Yemen and Somalia.[62] I think that is our next major area that we need to be concerned about is Yemen. I think that Al Qaeda has realized that this is just not going to happen there. They do not need to be there, nor do we.

SCHARF: Paul, let me ask you this. You have been talking about polls all day. In 2009, opinion polls in the U.S. showed that 56 percent of the American people felt the Afghan war was worth fighting. Now we have had polls the last couple of months that have shown that the number of Americans who support the war has sunk to only 35 percent.[63] Is this going to be a major campaign issue in the presidential election? Do people care about the outcome of this?

---

61. Ruhullah Khapalwak and David Rhode, "A Look at America's New Hope: The Afghan Tribes," *New York Times*, January 30, 2010, http://www.nytimes.com/2010/01/31/weekinreview/13rohde.html.
62. Peter Baker, "Obama Acknowledges U.S. is Fighting Groups Tied to Al Qaeda in Somalia and Yemen," *New York Times*, June 15, 2012, http://www.nytimes.com/2012/06/16/world/obama-admits-us-fight-of-al-qaeda-has-extended-to-somalia-and-yemen.html?_r=1&gwh=8BE8252293F7D01A5F51352BC51C88DA.
63. Lucy Madison, "Poll: Support for War in Afghanistan Hits All-Time Low," *CBS News*, March 26, 2012, http://www.cbsnews.com/8301-503544_162-57404807-503544/poll-support-for-war-in-afghanistan-hits-all-time-low/.

WILLIAMS: Yes, I think of course this is going to be a major campaign issue and in fact, because it is a campaign issue, it is going to contribute to our delusional approach to Afghanistan. The president doubled down on Afghanistan. It was at a point and time when he first came in that he could have picked a different path, but for whatever reason he doubled down and decided to fight this war and now he has lost this war. But he cannot say that, so he is going to have to pretend he has won it. Of course, Mitt Romney is going to make the argument that the president doubled down and lost the war and now cannot find a way; a clear-eyed way to deal with it. I think what the Americans are realizing a little bit quicker than some of our government officials that we are not stuck in the Cold War. You do not lay out a map and then color code all the countries blue or red, us or them. It is much, much more complicated than that. Afghanistan, four years from now, is going to be a hybrid with territories controlled by the Taliban and other territories within Afghanistan will be controlled by other groups. It is going to be highly complicated. We should be thinking about how we manage our relationship with that intensely complicated and volatile country and not pretending that we are going to pump thousands of dollars in to the National Guard and hope it stays in the blue category and does not go to the red category.

CRANE: Success is a regional approach. We should look at the area regionally. Look at the Indian Ocean as a lake with a whole bunch of partners around it and look it that way. Afghanistan is a small part of it versus focusing all our energy just on Afghanistan.

SCHARF: Shannon, once again the last word on this?

FRENCH: I am just going to say, I do not think it is going to be a major campaign issue and that is because domestically the trouble is that people lost interest after Bin Laden was killed. That is a problem for many other reasons, but I do not think it is going to be a major campaign issue. I think the focus is going to be on the economy and that some of these subtleties are going to be lost. Michael, well, I do not want to bet on the air, but I think I would bet against you if I were.

SCHARF: Today, we have been looking at three very thought-provoking issues ripped right from the headlines; CIA assassinations of Americans using predator drones, indicted tyrants that are still on the loose and now America's Afghan exit strategy. We hope that some of our conversation has shed some light where before there was only heated debate. If you want to weigh in on this discussion or suggest a topic for an upcoming broadcast, please send an email to: talkingforeignpolicy@case.edu. That is talkingforeignpolicy@case.edu. Thank you again to our panel of experts, former international prosecutor David Crane, President of the Public and International Policy Group, Paul Williams—both in Washington, DC, and also our experts in studio—Director of Case Western's Inamori Center, Shannon French and Cleveland State Law Professor, Milena Sterio. I am Michael Scharf, Director of Case Western Reserve's Cox International Law Center. *Talking Foreign Policy* has been brought to you by Case Western Reserve University in partnership with WCPN 90.3 Ideastream.

Talking Foreign Policy—September 27, 2012

Participants:
Michael Scharf
Jack Goldsmith
Baher Azmy
Milena Sterio
Mike Newton

SCHARF: The Roman philosopher Cicero famously declared that in times of war the law falls silent. In his classic novel *1984*, George Orwell envisioned a future in which the government claims to be in constant war in order to justify repressive measures against its own population. Are there parallels to post-9/11 America? With the presidential election just a month away, in today's broadcast of *Talking Foreign Policy*, our expert panel will be discussing the timely question of presidential power in a war without end. I'm your host, Michael Scharf. We'll begin our conversation with Jack Goldsmith, who had been assistant Attorney General in charge of the Office of Legal Counsel during the Bush administration. He's the author of the new book, *Power and Constraint: The Accountable Presidency After 9/11*. But first the news.

SCHARF: Welcome back to *Talking Foreign Policy*, produced by Case Western Reserve University and WCPN 90.3 FM Ideastream. I'm your host, Michael Scharf, the Associate Dean for Global Legal Studies at Case Western Law School. I'm talking today with Jack Goldsmith, the author of the new book, *Power and Constraint: the Accountable Presidency After 9/11*. Jack, thanks for being with us today.

GOLDSMITH: Thank you, Michael, for having me.

SCHARF: So, Jack, in a recent presentation on CSPAN Book TV, which I happened to catch, you said that in this endless war on terrorism you worry as much about the excess powers of the president as you do about the terrorist threat. In this regard, can you tell us what keeps you up at night?

GOLDSMITH: In terms of presidential power, the thing that keeps me up at night most, generally, is the excessive secrecy of the executive branch. It is that the executive branch secrecy bureaucracy is broader than it's ever been. Millions and millions of people have access to classified information which is illegal to disclose to the public except through very circumscribed means and the executive branch gets to determine what gets classified as secret.[64]

---

64. Laura A. White, "The Need for Governmental Secrecy: Why the U.S. Government

And so I worry that in this endless war so much being classified and the president is determining the scope of the classification. That's what I worry about. Let me just say that the secrecy bureaucracy is more porous than it's ever been but it's also larger than it's ever been, so there are reasons to think that lots of stuff is leaking out, but there's also reasons to think that a lot of stuff isn't leaking out.

SCHARF: So when it comes to our concerns, yours are not about the warrantless wiretaps, or the assertions of extraordinary interrogation methods or black sites, or military commissions or targeted killings, it comes down for you to what they're not telling us.

GOLDSMITH: I think that the substance of almost all of our counterterrorism policies is in a pretty good place. I think the substance of the counterterrorism policies have been largely blessed by Congress and/or the courts and largely have the approval of the American people. So based on the contours of what we know about our counterterrorism programs I'm pretty satisfied. I've got quibbles at the margins. But the thing I worry about is that there's a lot we don't know and that a lot of mistakes happen in secret.

SCHARF: Now, the thesis of your new book is that the biggest surprise about President Obama is that he's actually continued President Bush's controversial counterterrorism policies without much change at all, even practices that President Obama specifically criticized in his presidential campaign. Which policies in particular do you see this as a continuation?

GOLDSMITH: There are a lot of them. The main ones are, I would say, military detention without trial, military detention, and the broad assertion of the state secrets privilege. He's continued the warrantless surveillance, which was approved by Congress in 2008,[65] but he criticized it and has continued that. He's ramped up targeted killings outside the United States from the baseline of the Bush administration, and again, this is not his fault, I think he wanted to do this, but he's failed to close Gitmo.

SCHARF: All right, so the claim of continuity is not one that the Obama supporters are too crazy about. They would like to see the Obama administration as being different from the Bush administration, in particular with

---

Must Be Able to Withhold Information in the Interest of International Security," *Virginia Journal of International Law* 43 (2003): 1071.
65. Eric Lichtblau, "House Approves Power for Warrantless Wiretaps," *New York Times*, September 29, 2006, http://www.nytimes.com/2006/09/29/washington/29nsa.html; *see also* Ellen Nakashima, Joby Warrick, "House Approves Wiretap Measure; White House Bill Boosts Wireless Surveillance," *Washington Post*, August 5, 2007.

respect to respect for the rule of law. So how do you explain this continuity, the fact that two different presidents of two different parties, who have such different approaches, could end up with the same policies?

GOLDSMITH: So this is one of the burdens of my book is to explain that paradox: how did two such different presidents end up in about the same place. However, there are lots of reasons for it. The main one that I argue for and that not everyone agrees with is that they ended up in the same place because there are larger structural forces outside of the preferences and inclinations of the presidents that led them to that place. So, courts and Congress, with the help of NGOs and the press, did an extraordinary job of pushing back against some of the excesses of the Bush administration; pushing him through law, through politics, through persuasion, through force, to a place that by the end of his term was a much more moderate set of counterterrorism policies and they had much firmer legal blessing. And then Obama inherited those policies and they turned out to be a lot more legitimate and when he got into office there was a lot more need for them than he had known as a candidate on the outside and then in the areas when he actually did try to push away, most notably on Guantanamo Bay and closing Guantanamo Bay[66] and having criminal trials, the very same forces that pushed back against Bush, pushing Bush to the center, pushed Obama to the center, and they didn't allow him to do that. So I think that the story of the continuity is really a story of these larger structural forces. I would call them constitutional forces pushing back against the presidents.

SCHARF: And would you add to the list of forces the lawyers on the inside; for example, yourself and the folks at the State Department Office of the Legal Advisor?

GOLDSMITH: Absolutely. A big part of the story that I tell that I didn't mention just now is not just lawyers on the inside, but all sorts of institutions that have grown up since the 1970s inside the executive branch to watch and check and vet what the executive is doing. These forces are hard to see. They're hard sometimes to convince people that they have any effect, but I think there's no doubt that they were, inspector generals, lawyers, ethics monitors, no doubt that they were consequential in watching what the president was doing and pushing back against him.

---

66. Carol Rosenberg, "Why Obama Can't Close Guantanamo," *Foreign Affairs*, December 14, 2011, http://www.foreignaffairs.com/articles/136781/carol-rosenberg/why-obama-cant-close-guantanamo.

SCHARF: And so to be clear—if you look at the Obama policies, they're very different than the Bush administration policies in the first two years?

GOLDSMITH: Yes.

SCHARF: But very similar to the Bush administration policies in the last two years?

GOLDSMITH: That's right.

SCHARF: Now, you were a high level Pentagon lawyer and then later the assistant attorney general in the Bush administration in charge of the Office of Legal Counsel. In your previous book, *The Terror Presidency*, you wrote that the Bush administration felt overly constrained by the law. Did President Bush succeed at all in expanding the powers of the presidency, which I know was one of his goals in the post 9/11 years?[67]

GOLDSMITH: So as you say, that was certainly his goal to expand the powers of the presidency. It's a very hard question to answer because obviously after 9/11 when there's a war, an authorized war by Congress, there's going to be an expansion of presidential power. But along many dimensions, I think Bush, his attempts to expand presidential power, ended up being self-defeating because some of his unnecessarily broad assertions and proclamations of executive power I think invited, worried people, and invited the pushback from Congress, the courts, the press, NGOs, and the like that led to a whole array of constraints, small and large, on the presidency now and the conduct of the War on Terror.

SCHARF: And picturing this as a pendulum that swung in the early years to the right and has swung back, are you suggesting that it's about in the right place now, that the constraints are just about right?

GOLDSMITH: That's not quite my claim, I try hard in the book not to make that claim and I'll explain why. I do think that what's happened is that we can be pretty confident that the institutions of our government and of civil society are watching the presidency closely and can push back if he goes in the wrong direction. Whether we're in exactly the right place on counterterrorism policies I think is an impossible question to answer. We'd have to know a lot more about the threat. We'd have to know a lot more about the efficacy of various counterterrorism techniques. I don't know personally whether the broad surveillance powers the president's using is

---

67. Warren Richey, "Bush Pushed the Limits of Presidential Power," *CSMonitor*, January 14, 2009, http://www.csmonitor.com/USA/2009/0114/p11s01-usgn.html.

necessary. I don't know if every single person needs to be detained at Gitmo. I don't need to know if we need a more aggressive policy. So I would say that I'm comfortable with where we are. The American people and courts and Congress seem comfortable with where we are, but I wouldn't say we've got exactly the optimal policies.

SCHARF: And when you mention that the American people are comfortable. Opinion polls have changed over the years. Some opinion polls ten years ago showed a much higher degree of discomfort with extraordinary interrogation or torture and some of the other things. The American people, according to the polls, are very much in favor of the targeted killing that some academics like myself still feel are controversial.[68] Would you say that this is because of the legislative and judicial responses that have legitimized these policies? Is that your theory?

GOLDSMITH: That's my basic theory. I think it has to do with a couple of things, but the main point is that the policies that were controversial and that had less support were not the same policies as we have now. The policies have been changed and when the courts say that a detention in Guantanamo is lawful, that sends a much different and much more comfortable signal to the American people than when the president just says it on his own. And when Congress steps in and says certain interrogation techniques aren't allowed and the people know that the interrogation techniques that are going forward now are taking place within those constraints, they can have more confidence in them. So I think you have to look at what kind of broad political and legal support the policies have and I think, this is a broad generalization but, the American people's comfort with these policies largely tracks those other institutions' comfort with them.

SCHARF: So would you say that the institutional legitimacy has created a new normal where, right after 9/11 the American people weren't quite ready to embrace some of these techniques that were necessary for national security but now that they've been constrained and blessed, the American people now find it comfortable?

GOLDSMITH: I do think that's not the way I would put it, but I think that's an accurate description. I think that we do. I guess I do use the phrase new normal in a slightly different sense in the book, but I do think we are now, after eleven years, where there was, as always happens in war, an aggressive reaction

---

68. Adam Serwer, "Poll: Americans Approve of Targeted Killing of American Terror Suspects," *MotherJones*, February 8, 2012, http://www.motherjones.com/mojo/2012/02/poll-americans-approve-targeted-killing-terror-suspects-americans.

by the president right after an attack, the pendulum has swung back. The other institutions have engaged, We've had debates, very open public debates, lots of leaking of information, and all these issues have been debated. They've run through the mill of Congress and the courts and public opinion and I do think we've got an equilibrium now. I would call it where people are generally comfortable about where we are. Now it could change at any moment and I don't think everything is settled, but I think things are largely settled for now.

SCHARF: Now do you think there was also a role to be played by some of the policy makers in their rhetoric? So, for example, Vice President Cheney spent eight years in office telling the American people that, if we didn't do extraordinary interrogation techniques, we couldn't stop the next terrorist offense against us, and also making the claim, which turned out to be false, that the evidence that was used to locate and kill Osama bin Laden came from these extraordinary interrogation techniques; these things that some people call torture.

GOLDSMITH: So some of the rhetoric of the Bush administration I do think invited unnecessary criticism and I do think sometimes they exaggerated their criticism. I don't know if they exaggerated their claims about the nature of the threat. I think that if you generally look at what the Bush administration said in the last four or five years about the nature of the threat, it's pretty similar to what President Obama says now. But I do think some of their rhetoric was overcharged, and especially their rhetoric about presidential power and the need for it was largely self-defeating.

SCHARF: All right, so we've set the stage for an interesting discussion, we're going to bring in some other experts. It's now time for a short break. Not everyone agrees with Jack's argument that there isn't much difference between the foreign policy approaches of the two candidates. So when we return, we'll bring in the legal director of the Center for Constitutional Rights, a former high-level State Department official, and an international law professor that will all jump into the conversation and we'll try to ferret out what the American people need to know as this election looms. You're listening to *Talking Foreign Policy*. Back in a moment.

SCHARF: Welcome back to *Talking Foreign Policy*. I'm Michael Scharf and I've been talking with Harvard Law professor Jack Goldsmith, the author of *Power and Constraint: The Accountability Presidency After 9/11*. Let's widen the discussion now by bringing in our panel of experts. At the top of the program, I mentioned the phenomenon of war without end. Let me introduce Milena

Sterio, she's been on the program before, she's an international law professor at Cleveland State's Marshall College of Law. Milena, good to have you back.

STERIO: Thank you, it's a pleasure.

SCHARF: From the standpoint of an international law professor and from the standpoint of U.S. constitutional law as well, would you say that the war on terrorism has become a sort of war without end that has shifted the power balance between Americans and their government?

STERIO: Yes, I agree with that assessment. Essentially, under the Bush administration and now under the Obama administration, the approach to some of the policies, for example the targeted killing policy, the drone strikes, has been that the executive makes the decision as to who can be targeted. We have to trust the executive with what the policy is, when it will end, and if it will end. There's really no sort of check and balance on the presidential power to do that. So I think—and the other thing is we don't really know if the war on terror will ever end, what the parameters of that war are, and for all we know, it could be another hundred-year war.

SCHARF: George Bush was the one who coined the phrase 'The War on Terror' and I believe the Obama administration has modified that to be the War on Al Qaeda, but it's still a war in both the administrations' views, right?

STERIO: It's still a war. Under the Bush administration, we were engaged in a global war on terror. Now we're engaged in a war against the Al Qaeda, the Taliban, and associated forces. So if you think of that phrase 'associated forces,' that can be just about anyone.[69]

SCHARF: And you think this rhetoric of war changes the way that the Americans perceive the government and the free range that the government has in taking actions?

STERIO: Yes, because I think if you were to poll…our citizens, I think everyone would agree that at a time of war, things change. Civil liberties can be curtailed. I think that's a relatively well accepted premise and so if the rhetoric is we're at a war, we're engaged in an armed conflict, that, I think, gives a lot of liberty to the executive branch to craft all sorts of policies.[70]

---

69. Joseph I. Lieberman, "Who's the Enemy in the War on Terror?," *Wall Street Journal*, June 15, 2010, http://online.wsj.com/article/SB10001424052748703509404575300420668558 244.html.

70. Adam Liptak, "Civil Liberties Today," *New York Times*, September 7, 2011, http://www.nytimes.com/2011/09/07/us/sept-11-reckoning/civil.html?pagewanted=all&_r=0.

SCHARF: Now we're also joined today, in studio, by Mike Newton. Mike was a former military attorney who served as the deputy to the ambassador at large for war crimes issues at the State Department and now he's a law professor at Vanderbilt. Mike's been on with us before. It's good to have you back, Mike.

NEWTON: Thanks, Michael.

SCHARF: Now Mike, you were also a former JAG colonel for many years. Do you agree with Milena's conclusions from that point of view?

NEWTON: Well, from a military perspective for any military operation, the job of a commander in chief is to proscribe a wartime objective.

SCHARF: And are we at war?

NEWTON: Well, in the sense that there's an active enemy that's trying to harm American interests and kill Americans, yes we are; remembering, of course, that it's also an armed conflict, to use the legal sense of the term, that is authorized by both the United States, and UN Security Council, and the Congress of the United States. The problem, of course, being that the scope and the definite military objective is much more vague and uncertain than has ever been the case in American history, I think. And the other paradox is the statistic—the last statistic I saw is that only 0.5 percent of the American people have been directly involved in that. So we're at war in the sense that people conceive of it, as this very distant, very dim, and yet for the American military service members and women on the ground it's very real and very dangerous.

SCHARF: All right, so would you say that the Iraq part of the war is over now? I know that we still have troops there, but Obama says the war is over.

NEWTON: Well, it's true both legally and politically. The sovereign independent state has stood up and therefore they are a sovereign equal like any other. We no longer have the right to simply invoke the wartime law and the flag to do anything we want to do.

SCHARF: Now, in Afghanistan, we're still in war, but there's an agreement between the United States and the Afghan government that we're supposed to be out of there in two years. So, at that point, the war is over in Afghanistan?

NEWTON: In the sense that it changes the legal regime applicable, yes it is.

SCHARF: So will there still be a global war against Al Qaeda that exists after the two geographic wars are over?

NEWTON: Well the issue is then how the United States Congress goes back and reshapes the authorization for the use of military force. I think scholars—and I know Jack has written about this and talked about this—is how you define the enemy and more particularly, when in the context of interrogation policy, how do you define the instate, because at the moment the conflict is over, any articulable legal authority—you've got to hold somebody in the absence of a conviction—ends immediately. And so that's why the lawyers in among us really care about that, and in particular, that's why the military people care. Remember, the military, from the institutional perspective, wants to win the war and go home. They don't want to stay deployed for the next hundred years.

SCHARF: But the politicians are saying that this is a war that may last generation after generation.

NEWTON: And the military will dutifully follow the orders of the commander in chief.

SCHARF: Well, the final member of our panel of experts today is Baher Azmy. He's the Legal Director of the Center for Constitutional Rights in New York City. Baher, thanks being with us today.

AZMY: Thanks for having me, Michael.

SCHARF: So, Baher, you've litigated a number of the leading cases arising out of the so-called War on Terror, including those related to indefinite executive detention, extraordinary rendition, and torture. Do you believe that the so-called War on Terror has led to a diminution in our civil liberties?[71]

AZMY: Oh, I certainly do. I think that just to underscore one of the points in Jack's book, some of I think the most egregious practices of the Bush administration from the first term, like extraordinary rendition, secret black sites, incommunicado military detention in Guantanamo, were largely constrained during the Bush administration. But still other, I think, deeply controversial practices have endured across the administrations as Jack describes, and that includes the idea of an indefinite preventative detention regime based on military law principles. For people in Guantanamo, this includes the use of military commissions instead of civilian courts and the dramatic expansion of the targeted killing program.[72]

---

71. *Supra* note 7.
72. Detlev F. Vagts, "Which Courts Should Try Persons Accused of Terrorism," *European Journal of International Law* 14 (2003): 313–26.

SCHARF: Now let me follow up with you on that. I once testified before the House Armed Services Committee about the new Military Commissions Act.[73] One of the things I said and I want to get your take on it, is that even if somebody is prosecuted at a military commission and acquitted or let's say prosecuted and given a short sentence and the sentence is over, it is unlikely that they will be released. They, in fact, will be detained even after they're acquitted the rest of their life.

AZMY: Yeah, I think this is a really problematic feature of the Obama administration's description of their justice system. So the way that they initially articulated it is if there is overwhelming evidence of guilt, then we'll put them in the Article 3 civilian trial box because we're certain there will be a conviction. If there's insufficient evidence that would support conviction beyond a reasonable doubt, then we can put them in the military commissions' box and, if there's not enough evidence for any of those two, we'll just indefinitely detain them. And I think that's a really distorted system of justice where the prosecutor shifts the game.[74]

SCHARF: Under the law, Baher, this would only apply to non-American citizens, right? We're not comfortable having American citizens detained forever in Guantanamo.

AZMY: That's—I mean, I think that's somewhat of an open question. Under Supreme Court precedent I think there's—I'd be optimistic that a U.S. citizen could not be detained, but I think the law is not settled on that question.

SCHARF: But there are no U.S. citizens now at Guantanamo.

AZMY: There are no U.S. citizens now in Guantanamo.

SCHARF: But you're saying in the future there could be?

AZMY: Or the question of whether or not a U.S. citizen could be detained in a military brig as Jose Padilla was, which was never was conclusively resolved by the Supreme Court.[75]

SCHARF: And that was in South Carolina?

---

73. James B. Staab, "The War on Terror's Impact on Habeas Corpus: The Constitutionality of the Military Commissions Act of 2006," *Journal of the Institute of Justice and International Studies* 280 (2008).
74. *Supra* note 7.
75. Abby Goodnough and Scott Shane, "Padilla Is Guilty on All Charges in Terror Trial," *New York Times*, August 17, 2007, http://www.nytimes.com/2007/08/17/us/17padilla.html.

AZMY: That's right.

SCHARF: And what about people who have dual citizenship, who are they? Foreigners or U.S. citizens for the purposes of this?

AZMY: I think they retain the rights of U.S. citizens in that circumstance, yes.

SCHARF: Okay, so now, does this mean that you agree with Jack Goldsmith's characterization that President Obama has continued President Bush's national security policies and practices pretty much without change?

AZMY: Yes, I would agree with that…mindful again the distinction that Jack himself makes between the early Bush administration practices and the sort of Bush two practices which I do agree have carried over.

SCHARF: And you're troubled by that, I assume.

AZMY: I am, yeah.

SCHARF: And Jack Goldsmith says there are these checks and these checks have succeeded, but to say that there are some checks is not the same thing as saying that they're sufficient checks. Would you say that Jack is overstating the efficacy of the checks that have constrained presidential power?

AZMY: In general, yes. I mean, I don't think that Congress has played a particularly constructive role here, particularly in relation to closing Guantanamo. They've made it impossible for the president to try the 9/11 conspirators in New York.[76] They've made it impossible to resettle—or at least extremely difficult to resettle detainees in the United States or even resettle them abroad, I think because of narrow political considerations and some amount of grandstanding. And I think the courts have not been as effective, aside from some sort of blockbuster cases at the Supreme Court. At a kind of retail level I don't think the courts have been dutiful in checking the president's actions.

NEWTON: Can I—

SCHARF: Just hold on a second, Mike, because I'm going to jump in and ask you the follow-up question. I want to focus us a little bit on what the courts have done with Guantanamo Bay. So Mike, this will be a question for you. In 2008, the Supreme Court held that Guantanamo Bay detainees are entitled to judicial review, a process us lawyers know as habeas proceedings.[77]

---

76. Scott Shane and Benjamin Weiser, "U.S. Drops Plan for a 9/11 Trial in New York City," *New York Times*, January 29, 2010, http://www.nytimes.com/2010/01/30/nyregion/30trial.html?pagewanted=all.
77. Richard Brust, "As D.C. Circuit Weighs the Future of Guantanamo Inmates, Some Say

Now the district courts have actually ruled in a number of cases that these detainees have to be released because there's insufficient evidence of guilt or insufficient evidence that they are a continuing threat to the United States. Those cases have been appealed to the Court of Appeals of DC and the DC Court of Appeals has done what, Mike, with these cases?

NEWTON: For the most part, in every case that I know of, they've reviewed the standards of detention and the reasons for detention brought forth by the executive. They've then done what's called a de novo review of the evidence. They've looked at all of the evidence, which is very difficult because you remember some of these statements now at this point are a decade old. In some cases of corroboration where people are dead and they have affirmed those so that, no detainee has been released under the order of the DC Circuit Court of Appeals.

SCHARF: Okay, so just to be clear, the district court says you've got to release them. Who's appealing it to the Court of Appeals? Who's bringing these appeals?

NEWTON: The Justice Department.

SCHARF: The Obama administration?

NEWTON: Yes, yes.

SCHARF: So the Obama administration, who says they believe in habeas and that these people if they're proven to be innocent or not to be a threat need to be released, are taking these cases and they're asking the court to keep them in prison in Guantanamo.

NEWTON: Well, this is a really important point that you're getting at which is the balance between the executive obligation to protect Americans, as long as there's a continuing threat and somebody needs to be held—this gets back to what Jack was saying about more than 600, the last count I saw was 602, detainees have been released from Guantanamo Bay, which began early in the Bush administration, accelerated during the second Bush term, and so, the people at that point that they're litigating—

SCHARF: But these are discretionary releases.

NEWTON: Yes. But the ones that they're litigating at that point have been through multiple, multiple filters of review and at that point the executive

Judicial Review Can Harm Military," *ABA Journal*, October 1, 2012, http://www.abajournal.com/magazine/article/detention_dilemma_as_d.c._circuit_considers_guantanamo_inmates_can_judicial/.

branch in the form of the Justice Department really feels like that, for whatever reason, they don't need to be released. And remember that there's about a 28 percent recidivism rate of the ones that have been released.[78] And so…these are not just sort of theoretical, legalistic kinds of determinations; they're determinations where American lives and property are in some threat of continuing risk.

SCHARF: Now this is in the DC circuit's opinion; the district court, the fact finders think not. And the DC circuit, which is known as a conservative court, has in every single case that's been appealed to them, reversed the district court and held these people for the rest of their lives in detention in Guantanamo.

NEWTON: That's true, although I don't know that you can simply derive from that that there's this rubber stamp process. I mean, these are federal judges who—I don't think it's appropriate to just to sort of impugn the integrity of and say, well they're all just sort of doing whatever the executive asks them to do. You know, they're federal judges who are really going over the evidence to the extent that they can. And maybe we can quibble about the degree of deference and the processes which they're following, but I just saw a decision just issued just yesterday where the Justice Department argued that—that the rights to counsel terminated at the end of a successful habeas—or, I'm sorry, an unsuccessful habeas petition and the DC circuit ruled otherwise, meaning that even if you lose your habeas petition you have the continuing right to counsel.[79] So they're not just sort of rolling over and doing what the executive branch asks them to do.

SCHARF: Well to me it sounds like habeas, which was promised by the Supreme Court decision has become sort of an empty promise for these detainees. Baher, what's your take on that?

AZMY: I agree completely, and it wasn't the DC circuit that issued that decision, it was the district court, and we all, the detainees lawyers, are terrified that the government will appeal to DC circuit, get a stay and reverse it, because that is the last court we want to be in. And I think…of course we can impugn the court. They're generally fair-minded people, but I think if you unpack what the DC circuit has done they have ensured that the government will prevail in every case by crediting—giving the government's evidence a presumption of accuracy, expanding the detention standard far broader than

---

78. Mark Hosenball, "Recidivism Rises Among Released Guantanamo Detainees," *Reuters*, March 5, 2012, http://www.reuters.com/article/2012/03/06/us-usa-guantanamo-recidivism-idUSTRE82501120120306.

79. "The Right to Counsel at Guantanamo Bay," *New York Times*, August 16, 2012, http://www.nytimes.com/2012/08/17/opinion/the-right-to-counsel-at-guantanamo-bay.html.

what the district court would have wanted to do, in some cases far broader than what the administration would have argued for, and reviewing factual findings by the district court de novo, which a court of appeals shouldn't do. And so, I think Boumediene[80] is not the law of the land anymore and I think—

SCHARF: That being the Supreme Court case from 2008.

AZMY: The Supreme Court decision guaranteeing a meaningful habeas review by courts that is at least somewhat skeptical, or skeptical enough to uphold the purposes of the Great Writ. And so that for me has been an area of great disappointment about the role of the courts.

SCHARF: Well Milena, let me ask you to clarify something that Mike had said about recidivism. He said that there was some percentage—what did you say, Mike, 8 percent?

NEWTON: It's about 28 percent.

SCHARF: 28 percent that are recidivists. Isn't it true, Milena, that the definition of recidivism is quite broad and that even people who have made speeches against the United States count the same as people who joined the battlefield for purposes of that statistic?

STERIO: Yes, it's entirely unclear as to...we've...under the Obama administration, even the press, we've used these terms of jihadist, Islamist...all sorts of terms and it's unclear as to what roles, what kinds of acts, a lot of these individuals have committed against the United States. And so, yes...we catch somebody making statements against the United States and we say, aha, recidivist.[81] One additional point I would make regarding that is that if we are to detain somebody and it turns out that person actually hadn't done much against the United States, the likelihood then of, after we release them, that person hating the United States and wanting to engage in all sorts of bad activity against the United States is higher, I would argue, and the likelihood that that person's family member will also hate the United States and want to hurt us is also higher. So I think—

SCHARF: What you're saying is if they weren't a security risk when we took them in, after we've kept them in custody down in Flor—in Cuba for eight years, they kind of get angry at us and then they become a security risk?

---

80. Center for Constitutional Rights, "Legal Analysis: *Boumediene v. Bush / Al Odah v. United States*," http://ccrjustice.org/learn-more/faqs/legal-analysis%3A-boumediene-v.-bush/al-odah-v.-united-states.

81. *Supra* note 13.

STERIO: Yeah, I think the likelihood is they don't like us very much and all their family members really don't like us very much either. So I think it gets back to being very careful in the first place as to who we detain, who we target, who we go after.

NEWTON: And this is actually the problem with what the DC circuit has done. Now, our basis to hold people under military law and the federal habeas structure rests entirely upon the premise that this person, if released, poses a danger and imminent threat to U.S. interests. That's really the evidentiary standard. And so what Milena is really saying is there's a lot of cases where that's really a difficult case to make and yet we have seen courts that have erred on the side of simply accepting at face value claims to that even in the absence of or the presence of very, very shaky evidence.

SCHARF: Now Baher, when I was researching some of your statements I saw one where you said that President Obama's hands have been tied, not by Congress or the courts, but by the previous actions of the Bush administration, and in particular you said that because they used torture during the interrogations, it's made it impossible for the president to take these cases to ordinary courts. Can you explain that?

AZMY: So I'm not sure when I made that statement but I think it's—I would revise it because I think the Obama administration did try and set a number of cases for criminal trial and then set up a procedure of the Justice Department, the FBI, to send down what they called 'clean teams' and to build a case that was independent of any interrogation statements and that those cases could, in fact, proceed to trial and Attorney General Holder said he was confident we would get convictions as a result of that independent evidence. So it made it harder, but they were able to do it and then ultimately the 'but for' cause, I think, was Congress's decision to withhold funding for any trials that would happen in New York in addition to some, I think, some public and political opposition to bringing terrorist suspects into New York City.[82]

SCHARF: Now Jack Goldsmith, author of *The Accountable Presidency*, haven't forgot about you there. Let me ask a follow-up about this concept of torture and accountability, which is in the title of your book, and in particular look at the case of John Yoo. John Yoo was the lawyer who had written the so-called torture memos, and when you got into your position, you actually

---

82. *Supra* note 13.

rescinded those.[83] So in the case of John Yoo, he seems to have gotten a pass. How did you see that?

GOLDSMITH: I don't think that John has gotten a pass, and I think that he's been subject to—in fact, he hasn't gotten a pass at all. He's been subject to extraordinary scrutiny, unprecedented scrutiny, I would say, inside the executive branch, in federal court, in the public. You say—by getting a pass I assume you mean that he hasn't been criminally prosecuted. But I don't consider that the only means of accountability and I don't know of any definition of accountability that limits it just to criminal prosecution.

SCHARF: And so you think the story of John Yoo does send a signal for future lawyers to be a lot more careful?

GOLDSMITH: There's no doubt that it does. Ask any national security lawyer in the government about whether they're significantly more careful with what they do and more cautious as a result, not just with what happened to John, but there are a lot of lawyers and they will say absolutely yes.

SCHARF: Well, that's a silver lining in the story. It's now time for a short break. When we return the panelists and I will be talking about the most controversial issue of all; the president's power to order the killing of suspected terrorists, including U.S. citizens, without any judicial review. We'll be back in a moment.

SCHARF: Welcome back to *Talking Foreign Policy*. I'm Michael Scharf, the Associate Dean at Case Western Reserve University School of Law and with me in our studio today are Jack Goldsmith, author of *Power and Constraint: The Accountable Presidency After 9/11*, Baher Azmy, the Director of the Center for Constitutional Rights in New York City, Colonel Mike Newton of Vanderbilt University, and Professor Milena Sterio of Cleveland State University. We've been talking about the president's powers during an endless war on terrorism. Now, I want to look specifically at one of the most controversial aspects of that: the policy of using predator drones to kill suspected terrorists, including American citizens, outside of the battlefield. The issue was discussed in previous broadcasts of *Talking Foreign Policy*, but we have a new collection of experts and I want to begin this segment with a question for Jack Goldsmith. Jack, who was the assistant attorney general of the United States during the Bush administration. Jack, the ACLU brought a lawsuit about the targeted

---

83. Dashiell Bennett, "John Yoo Granted Immunity for 'Torture Memos,'" *Atlantic Wire*, May 2, 2012, http://www.theatlanticwire.com/national/2012/05/john-yoo-granted-immunity-torture-memos/51836/.

killing policy and the court held that it was blocked from reviewing it by the political question doctrine.[84] You've described this, I believe, as judicial approval of the drone policy, but isn't it more accurate to describe it as a judicial dodge?

GOLDSMITH: I don't think it was—I don't think I quite described it as judicial approval of the drone policy because the judge didn't remark on the policy[85]—he didn't approve the policy but in fact, he didn't even say that it was lawful. What he said was that the Constitution—he interpreted the Constitution—that the Constitution left the issue of the legality of those strikes to the Congress and the president, to the political branches that's what the political doctrine, political question doctrine, means in that context. So I don't think—you can call it a dodge if you'd like. That judges took his obligations very seriously. He interpreted the Constitution on the merits and he said, he held, and I think correctly so, that the Constitution left that issue, that difficult issue about targeting an American citizen in war, to the president and the Congress.[86]

SCHARF: So, in the end the plaintiff lost, the president won, and the perception, at least for the American people is that there has been some kind of judicial—

GOLDSMITH: That's true, and I would say that—that I agree with that. I think that I would even go further, that the *New York Times*' headline is "President Wins Drone Case." And more broadly, I think that President Obama is in a much stronger legal position as a result of that case than he was before that case brought because now he can at least point to one precedent that says, look, the Constitution has been interpreted by an independent branch of the government, a federal judge, who said that this was an issue that was not for courts to decide, it was an issue for the president and Congress to decide.[87]

SCHARF: Now that was a case, I believe, of a plaintiff going in when there was some kind of a rumor that his son was on the kill list and he wanted to

---

84. Louis Michael Seidman, "The Secret Life of the Political Question Doctrine," John Marshall Law Review 442 37 (2004): 442.
85. American Civil Liberties Union, "Targeted Killings," http://www.aclu.org/national-security/targeted-killings.
86. Charlie Savage, "U.S. Law May Allow Killings, Holder Says," *New York Times*, March 5, 2012, http://www.nytimes.com/2012/03/06/us/politics/holder-explains-threat-that-would-call-for-killing-without-trial.html.
87. Jonathan Ulrich, "The Gloves Were Never On: Defining The President's Authority To Order Targeted Killing In The War Against Terrorism," *Virginia Journal of International Law* 45 (2005): 1029.

get information about that to save his son. Let me ask Baher Azmy, do you think that courts should be able to review targeted killing after the fact? Is that different than this case? So it would be more like a wrongful death action taken against police for excessive or unjustified use of force?

AZMY: We do, and put money where our mouth is because the Center for Constitutional Rights along with the ACLU has filed such a wrongful death action challenging the legality of the targeted killing of Anwar al-Awlaki who was specifically on a kill list,[88] another U.S. citizen, Samir Khan, who wasn't on a list but was presumably collateral damage and Anwar al-Awlaki's sixteen-year-old son who was killed at an open-air restaurant in a strike two weeks later, and—[89]

SCHARF: And the sixteen-year-old is also an American citizen?

AZMY: He's also an American citizen and was not targeted, was part of a strike at an open-air restaurant that killed a half dozen civilians. And so this litigation argues that any citizen, any civilian, is entitled to the protections of due process; that is, a charge or a trial unless they're directly engaged in hostilities. And your analogy of a wrongful death action is a correct one; that is, a criminal suspect should be apprehended and tried unless he poses some imminent threat to law enforcement. In that situation lethal force can be applied.

SCHARF: I actually didn't know that this case had been filed. What court is that in?

AZMY: That's in the district court in DC.

SCHARF: So you're back in the same court that we were talking about earlier.

AZMY: We're familiar; it's our favorite court.

SCHARF: And the reason these cases all go to that court is because?

AZMY: Well, it's typically where we can get personal jurisdiction over all the defendants.

SCHARF: And the defendants being Obama, the Department of Justice, the folks that are in the federal government in DC?

---

88. Mark Mazetti, Eric Schmitt, and Robert F. Worth, Two-Year Manhunt Led to Killing of Awlaki in Yemen, *New York Times*, September 30, 2011, http://www.nytimes.com/2011/10/01/world/middleeast/anwar-al-awlaki-is-killed-in-yemen.html.
89. Peter Finn and Greg Miller, "Anwar al-Awlaki's Family Speaks Out Against His Son's Death in Airstrike," *Washington Post*, October 17, 2011, http://www.washingtonpost.com/world/national-security/anwar-al-awlakis-family-speaks-out-against-his-sons-deaths/2011/10/17/gIQA8kFssL_story.html.

AZMY: Primarily CIA individuals and the individuals who run the program that identifies who should be put on the list.

SCHARF: Now I want to get back to Milena Sterio, our international law professor, who has spoken and written a lot about this issue. What is the standard that the administration is now using to decide who to kill with these predator drones?

STERIO: So is your question regarding American citizens who are being targeted, or is it just anybody?

SCHARF: Is it a different standard?

STERIO: It is a different standard. Our Attorney General Eric Holder gave a much-anticipated speech in March of this year where he announced what the policy would be regarding targeted killing of American citizens.[90] Now this only applies to American citizens. It does not apply to non-American citizens. So American citizens can be targeted if they're located abroad, if capture is not feasible, if they're engaged in hostile acts against the United States, if they pose an imminent threat to the United States; so all of these 'ifs' have to be satisfied in order for an American citizen to be targeted. For—

SCHARF: And then who's making this decision?

STERIO: Well, the decision is being made by the executive branch and it's not being checked by anybody before and hopefully—

SCHARF: And when you said the executive branch, I know there were some news reports saying that President Obama himself has these cards that he reads and decides who to say yes to kill and who to say no to kill.[91] Is that accurate?

STERIO: That's a pretty scary account, but the problem, I think, with the drone problem in general is that there's all this secrecy surrounding it because, for the most part, the drones have been operated by the CIA, and so there are no public documents really telling us about how these decisions are made as to who can be targeted. Eric Holder announced what the policy is, but how that's being applied we don't really know.

---

90. Charlie Savage, "U.S. Law May Allow Killings, Holder Says," *New York Times*, March 5, 2012, available at http://www.nytimes.com/2012/03/06/us/politics/holder-explains-threat-that-would-call-for-killing-without-trial.html?gwh=51C913503E2445108F32F25E619EC51C.
91. Jo Becker and Scott Shane, "Secret 'Kill List' Tests Obama's Principles," *New York Times*, May 29, 2012, http://www.nytimes.com/2012/05/29/world/obamas-leadership-in-war-on-al-qaeda.html?pagewanted=all.

SCHARF: And that gets right back to what you were saying at the top of the hour, Jack, that what should keep us up at night is what they're not telling us.

GOLDSMITH: I agree, and, while I'm generally supportive of the legality of the drone strikes as they've been conducted, I also think that the administration is keeping too much information from the public. They could do a much better job of disclosing information, especially about the processes and criteria by which these decisions are made.

SCHARF: And how can we get that information? As lawyers, what can we do? File Freedom of Information Act?

GOLDSMITH: There are all sorts of things going on. The truth is—is that the ACLU's and the CCR's first lawsuit against al-Awlaki, the one that failed on the—it succeeded in many respects; it raised the profile of the issue, people in Congress were interested, now there have been tons of leaks to the press, there have been disclosures, there are FOIA cases going on.[92] We actually know quite a bit more now about what's going on than we did when the first ACLU/CCR case was brought, but the problem is—the thing that really bothers me the most is the level of nondisclosure, combined with what's the obvious level of manipulation by the administration of the secrecy system. They disclosed all sorts of facts through leaks to the press, putting them in a good light and—but then they take this hardcore stance in court, which they say went to state secrets or it's—we can't disclose it.

SCHARF: And if they've said something publicly, they can then turn around and go into court and say I'm sorry, we can't disclose it?

GOLDSMITH: They've walked a very fine line in which they have—in an official capacity winked and nodded but never said, yes, we've done this. They've been very careful with their language not to, quote unquote, confirm the program. But there have been tons of leaks to the press, obviously, with high level officials not named. And in court they argue that the program is still officially classified and it can't be revealed. That gamesmanship is what I think is really appalling about the secrecy policies and the drones. And there's no reason why they can't disclose, in my opinion, a lot more information, and they should.

SCHARF: Baher, has your organization been arguing these cases as well?

---

92. Center for Constitutional Rights, "Torture *FOIA: ACLU, CCR, et al. v. Dept. of Defense, et al.*," http://ccrjustice.org/CCR-v-DOD-torture.

AZMY: Yes, yes, we're involved in a second litigation challenging the legality of the killing. We have some Freedom of Information Act requests to try and surface some of the justifications for the policy. And just to underscore Jack's point about the CIA's position, in one Freedom of Information Act lawsuit brought by the CIA—sorry, brought by the ACLU—the CIA has taken the official position that it will not confirm or deny the existence of a targeted killing program in court. And the same targeted killing program that Jack talks about in his book that we're all talking about in an Alice in Wonderland way, actually exists.

GOLDSMITH: And that the administration talked about every day, publicly and through leaks.

AZMY: That's right.

SCHARF: Now I just read in today's newspaper that Congress has authorized the use of drones in the United States,[93] and there's a debate going on about whether those drones can be armed and potentially do targeted killings or whether they only can be used for surveillance. But that decision hasn't been made yet. Mike Newton, is this something that should also keep us up at night?

NEWTON: I've spoken a lot in public, as Jack has, about the need to be forthcoming. But just to be clear, on the other side is the executive obligation to protect Americans, and in particular, in the context of what Jack calls the 'security bureaucracy,'…there really are sources and methods that don't need to be talked about, either in an open court case or in the *New York Times* that really do have implications, not only for the narrow context of a case, but for the larger, longer term effort in this war without end, if we want to call it that, to protect Americans. I mean, in the case of al-Awlaki there's clear communication between him and the Fort Hood shooter, and that comes out after the fact.[94] How many other situations are out there like that? Who else is being tracked? What other American lives might be saved? I'm not sure that the administration needs to talk about that, but I think after the fact they absolutely need to talk about as much as they can. And more

---

93. S. Smithson, "Drones Over U.S. Get OK By Congress," *Washington Times*, February 7, 2012, http://www.washingtontimes.com/news/2012/feb/7/coming-to-a-sky-near-you/?page=all.
94. Rehab El-Buri and Mark Schone, "Fort Hood: Hasan Asked Awlaki If It Was Okay to Kill American Soldiers," *ABC News*, December 23, 2009, http://abcnews.go.com/Blotter/FtHoodInvestigation/fort-hood-hasan-asked-awlaki-kill-american-soldiers/story?id=9410718#.UJ2i5GiE9UQ.

importantly, for our purposes, the legal criteria, these are real fuzzy kinds of legal criteria that should be talked about.

SCHARF: Now speaking of that—now Milena, you started to tell us that there's one criteria for U.S. citizens and another criteria for non-U.S. citizens. Can you finish that thought?

STERIO: Sure. So regarding U.S. citizens, there's this immanency requirement, which really comes from international human rights law, where you can go after someone only if it's absolutely necessary; only if they're an imminent threat. Regarding non-American citizens, they can be targeted as enemy combatants. Now there's also this term of unlawful enemy combatants, but unlawful and lawful enemy combatants can be targeted equally, and the approach has been that they can be targeted by virtue of their membership in these terrorist organizations. So they do not have to pose any kind of an imminent threat. They just basically have to be a member of Al Qaeda, the Taliban, and the associated forces.

SCHARF: Now I guess I'd feel okay if we were the only ones with the drones, but there's a lot of countries that are getting this technology. It's not even that high tech. And in fact, in Las Vegas there was a drone convention with all the manufacturers and people from all over the world were bidding on the latest drones.[95] So there's this notion of blowback; can you describe how that might affect us?

STERIO: So here's the problem, we're not—I think the initial assumption, I think what a lot of people don't understand—I think the original assumption might have been we're the only ones that have drones, we're the only ones that are going to use them, nobody else has them, right? Well that's not true. There are many other countries including—well, Israel has been the only other country that's been really forthcoming, but there's Israel, there's other countries, so other countries have them.[96] We don't know how they're going to use them, and so to the extent that those other nations look to the United States for policy guidance, for moral guidance, I think we'd be much better off with a much more careful drone policy and that policy could be public. We wouldn't necessarily have to disclose in each particular

---

95. Ben Wolfgang, "Las Vegas Convention Puts Drones on Big Stage," *Washington Times*, August 5, 2012, http://www.washingtontimes.com/news/2012/aug/5/convention-puts-drones-on-big-stage-debate-still-r/.
96. Stephen R. David, "Israel's Policy of Targeted Killing," *Ethics and International Affairs* 17 (2003).

case what the surveillance information was, who the person was, but I think we could announce a policy. And I think Israel, for example, has been a lot more forthcoming with their policy.

SCHARF: Mike?

NEWTON: Well, I just want to—I think Milena touches on something critically important. Jack alluded earlier to the shift as the Bush administration went along after the first couple or three years. In part that was driven certainly by the policy bureaucracy and by the intervention of other U.S. government actors, but it was also driven by this dramatically demonstrated need to consult with allies. This idea in the early days that, well, we've got a special mission to protect Americans and it's great if other countries agree with us, but we really don't want that, we really don't need that. I think that's a fundamental watershed. So Milena's exactly right, we really do need to be working with our allies and with other states, to be as transparent as we can, but also to shape the legal regime in a way that going forward long-term really is effectual.

SCHARF: The use of the drones began in the Bush administration but it has accelerated greatly in the Bush—in the Obama administration. Let me return back to Jack Goldsmith. You've written and said that if the Bush administration were doing this, they would get all kinds of pushback, but because it's Obama there's a different response. Can you describe?

GOLDSMITH: Yeah, I think that's right, but I think it works both ways. President Obama is not as much criticized as President Bush when he does aggressive things against terrorists, like targeted killing and ramps up targeted killing. He gets much more criticism than President Bush when he acts softer; when he tries to close Guantanamo Bay and have criminal trials. George W. Bush did those things and he wasn't criticized at all. When Obama does those things, he's severely criticized. So I think there is a symmetry there in our politics that Democratic presidents get more of a free ride when they do aggressive things and much less of a free ride when they do what I call quote unquote, softer things. And it's just a flip mirror image for Republican presidents.

SCHARF: So you're basically saying that there's some segment that votes on the policy and some segment that votes on the person.

GOLDSMITH: Right, and that's especially true in Congress, I think.

SCHARF: Well, we're getting to the end of the program; I want to ask two last questions of this group while you're here. The first one is, if Barack Obama had been president at the time of 9/11, do you think he would have done things differently? And the second one, and you can answer either of them, is do you think that Mitt Romney, his national security policy, would differ in any significant way from Barack Obama? Let's just go around starting with Milena.

STERIO: Sure, and I'll keep my remarks brief. I'm not exactly sure that President Obama would have done things drastically differently than President Bush did...remember...President Obama is the one who accomplished the mission of killing Osama bin Laden and on a lot of these issues President Obama has really been to the right of center...really in line with the Bush administration policies. Regarding—

SCHARF: The New Republic says that he has a classic Republican foreign policy. Is that something you would agree with?

STERIO: Right, I do. And regarding Mitt Romney, my answer is just going to be, who knows?

SCHARF: Okay, very quickly because we're running out of time, Mike?

NEWTON: With respect to President Obama, a previous President Obama in 2001, it's very difficult to go back and imagine what the country was like in those days and what it was like in Congress. I think maybe policies would have been similar, and in fact, the speed with which those decisions were made and had to be made would have been almost identical. It's very difficult to then predict the precise outcomes from that.

AZMY: I should hope his policy would have been different, of course we can't know. I think one thing I should imagine that would have been different is that he would have listened to the military's advice and applied the Geneva conventions.

SCHARF: And former Assistant Attorney General Jack Goldsmith, the last word on this?

GOLDSMITH: I'll just say, I'll answer the second question, the same reasons that—structural reasons that led Barack Obama to be very much like the late George W. Bush, will in my opinion, if Mitt Romney's elected, lead him to be very much like Barack Obama.

SCHARF: Great way to conclude. You've been listening to *Talking Foreign Policy*. We hope that this program has shed some light on the national security issues that will be debated in the presidential candidate debates in the coming weeks. I want to thank again author Jack Goldsmith and our panel of experts Director of the Center for Constitutional Rights, Baher Azmy, who has come all the way from New York City, former State Department official Mike Newton who came to us from Vanderbilt in Nashville, and international law professor Milena Sterio, who came about two blocks to be with us today. Thank you all. I'm Michael Scharf, Associate Dean of Case Western Reserve School of Law. Thank you very much. Talking Foreign Policy is a production of Case Western Reserve University and is produced in partnership with 90.3 FM WCPN Ideastream.

Talking Foreign Policy, Feburary 4, 2013 Broadcast

Participants:
Michael Scharf
Mike Newton
Shannon French
Milena Sterio

SCHARF: President Obama has selected three very different men to lead his second term foreign policy team. He's picked John Kerry, a Democratic senator from Massachusetts, to be secretary of state, Chuck Hagel, a Republican former senator from Nebraska, to be secretary of defense, and John Brennan, a career intelligence officer, to be director of the CIA. I am Michael Scharf, the host of *Talking Foreign Policy*. In this hour, our expert panel will discuss what the appointments of Kerry, Hagel, and Brennan will likely mean for U.S. foreign policy during the next four years. In the first part of today's program we'll examine their backgrounds, and the next, we'll look at their likely legislative agendas, and in our final part, our experts will forecast where these men are likely to stand on the most important foreign policy issues facing the United States. First, the news.

SCHARF: Welcome back to *Talking Foreign Policy*. I'm Michael Scharf, the Associate Dean at Case Western Reserve University School of Law. Today, our experts will be discussing America's new foreign policy team: John Kerry, Chuck Hagel, and John Brennan. If you're joining this program for the first time, the format we use is sort of a radio version of the McLaughlin Hour.[97] Our panel consists of a military expert, Mike Newton, an ethicist, Shannon French, and an international law professor, Milena Sterio. Let's start our conversation with Milena Sterio. Milena, you're a professor at Cleveland Marshal College of Law, you've been on the program before, and it's great to have you back.

STERIO: Thank you. It's a pleasure to be here.

SCHARF: Can you give us some background about the three positions: secretary of state, secretary of defense, and director of the CIA? What does each do and which is the most powerful of the trio?

---

97. Richard Sandomir, "At Lunch With: The McLaughlin Group; Just Another Talk Show? Wronnnggg!," *New York Times*, December 16, 1992, http://www.nytimes.com/1992/12/16/garden/at-lunch-with-the-mclaughlin-group-just-another-talk-show-wronnnggg.html.

STERIO: So all four positions are extremely powerful. The secretary of state and the secretary of defense positions are officially among the four most prominent cabinet positions and in terms of an official hierarchy of positions when you look at the presidential line of succession, The secretary of state position is number four and the secretary of defense is number six. The CIA director is not mentioned but, of course, I think everybody understands how powerful this position is.

SCHARF: And you've mentioned four positions, we're focusing on three, but of course, the fourth is the national security advisor.

STERIO: Exactly. Now, in terms of what they do, The secretary of state heads the State Department, and is basically in charge of foreign relations and diplomacy. The secretary of defense heads the Defense Department, is the head of our army, navy, and air force, The director of the CIA heads all of our intelligence operations. All are extremely powerful positions.

SCHARF: So we're about to have a new foreign policy leadership and it could really make a difference in the direction of our country. Mike Newton, you have joined our program before, it's good to have you back. Mike is a former Colonel in the Judge Advocate General's Corp.[98] He's now a professor at Vanderbilt. Mike, let me start out with a question for you.

NEWTON: Shoot.

SCHARF: You personally know Susan Rice?

NEWTON: Yes.

SCHARF: You worked with her back when you were at the State Department. She is currently the U.S. Ambassador to the United Nations. And she was President Obama's initial choice to replace Hilary Clinton as secretary of state. Why did Ambassador Rice withdraw her name from the nomination last month?

NEWTON: Well, she's done yeoman's work in the position in New York. The position at the U.S. delegation to the United Nations is an extremely difficult job and she has, by all accounts, done an incredible job behind the scenes, brokering fractured coalitions, and handling very difficult issues. A promotion to secretary of state would have been something that, I think, would have been very much in her personal desires and career interests. But, she politically she had no real choice but to withdrew in the aftermath of

---

98. U.S. Navy Judge Advocate General's Corps, http://www.jag.navy.mil/.

the Benghazi Controversy.[99] The day after the attack, she went on several talk shows, as the face of the administration, not just to the American people but to the world with what were demonstrably false facts, but from her perspective, she says, "I was using the information that I was provided," which is actually true. So, the short answer is that I think she withdrew two parts prudence, one part policy. To really keep the focus on advancing U.S. policy interests, knowing that a long drawn-out confirmation battle would detract from our interests at a very critical point in our relations with all of the other things going on in the world.

SCHARF: And that seems to be playing out. It seems that John Kerry is not having a problem with his confirmation. But let me ask you since you know Susan Rice, you know her background as someone who has risen up through the State Department and has fought these battles, from that point of view, whereas John Kerry has come from the legislative side, how do you think Kerry would compare with her in terms of his approach, especially to human rights?

NEWTON: I think that on the human rights portfolio it's important to remember that because we're not seeing a huge change in administration—there will certainly be a number of people at the second and third tiers that are moving in and out, but the structure of the bureaucracy is going to remain in place. On the particular human rights portfolio, in the first term there were some things, such as intervention in Libya, that are potentially very significant for the looming crisis Syria. What Senator Kerry will bring, if he's confirmed, I think is the ability to really engage with Congress in much the same way that Secretary Clinton did. She [Clinton] knew the senators and congressmen and women, they were many of her friends, and that's critically important.

SCHARF: Now, let me go back to Milena. You were telling us about the different roles that these officials play and you mentioned the national security advisor. There are reports that Susan Rice could be named the next national security advisor when Tom Donilon, who currently holds the post, steps down in about a year. How would her appointment to that position affect John Kerry's effectiveness as secretary of state and his access to the White House?

STERIO: Well, I don't think that John Kerry would be undermined in his position in any significant way because in the Obama Administration the

---

99. Joshua Hersh, "Libya Attack Controversy Becomes Full-Fledged Political Football," *Huffington Post*, October 28, 2012, http://www.huffingtonpost.com/2012/10/28/libya-attack-john-mccain_n_2035396.html.

positions of secretary of state and national security advisor are distinct positions with different areas of responsibility and authority. Susan Rice, if she were appointed National Security Advisor, would have to work very closely with the president and by all accounts she does enjoy a very close relationship with the president, so that might be a good thing. And from what Mike Newton mentioned earlier, it might be a good thing that we have someone like John Kerry, who has been the chairman of the Senate Foreign Relations Committee and knows the senators and congressmen well; who will be able to work closely with both houses.

SCHARF: Well, I'm thinking back to history, you had a strong national security advisor with Henry Kissinger, and that made all sorts of problems for his secretary of state at the time, William Rogers. Condoleezza Rice, a more recent example, seemed to have more power than the secretary of state, Colin Powell. Let me ask Shannon French. Shannon, you taught at the Navy Academy in Annapolis before coming to Case Western to head the Inamori International Center for Ethics and Excellence, what do you think the relationship would be if someone like Susan Rice is closer to the president in proximity than the secretary of state?

FRENCH: Well, I think one of the points that Milena has already highlighted for us that's significant is that it is not as though John Kerry is not tightly linked to this administration in other ways too. I think the long history that Kerry has established in Washington gives him great respect and he will command that respect with a president as well, so I also think that Susan Rice's relationship won't interfere with John Kerry and he's a heavyweight in this role and he's got big shoes to fill.

NEWTON: Can I disagree slightly with that, though?

SCHARF: Go ahead Mike.

NEWTON: Because the problem in Washington always, and we've seen it lately in the macro, is the paralysis in the policy-making functions. So any time there's a new cadre of top officials, there's always going to be shifting organizational roles and, from my experience in Washington working with the NSC and working with the highest levels of the State Department, that relationship is not just a monolithic relationship, it's always in flux depending on the issue. So it really does come down to a question of here's a disagreement between the upper levels, who has the access, who has the funding, who has the expertise, who has staff to win the day? And the trick is that an effective national security advisor can really move mountains to move the bureaucracy or, conversely, lock us into bureaucratic gridlock.

SCHARF: All right, now we're sort of starting to psychoanalyze John Kerry and let me ask you, Shannon, as an ethicist, the defining moment in John Kerry's early life was his return from the Vietnam War. And as we know from press accounts, what he did is he threw away his military decorations and protested at the Capital and then he testified before Congress in 1971 and accused his fellow soldiers of systematic atrocities. Do those actions suggest that John Kerry might be more of a pacifist secretary of state than the previous occupants of that office—people like Hillary Clinton, Condoleezza Rice, Colin Powell, and Madeleine Albright?

FRENCH: Well, I mean the moment that you're alluding to is very important, historically, we're talking about over forty years ago now, the young John Kerry, in a similar committee, but in this case speaking about his personal experiences, the horrors that he had seen, and very famously saying this line that has definitely had some traction since then. The quote was, "How do you ask a man to be the last man to die for a mistake?" And that…was John Kerry's point in this hearing. So if you think of that as part of his formative experience, I think it does at least suggest that he would be a cautious secretary of state in terms of committing, particularly ground troops, boots on the ground, to various conflicts. However, having said that, he's not a pacifist. It's one thing to have felt that a particular conflict was unjust or to think that particular tactics and strategies are inappropriate but overall, he's not a pacifist and I don't think that he would shy away from taking military measures. He's going to lean to diplomacy but arguably all secretaries of state lean towards diplomacy.

SCHARF: Well, since we're talking about people who returned from Vietnam, Chuck Hagel, the appointment for the secretary of defense, has a similar background and let me turn to Mike. Mike, you're our military expert. You, yourself, have served in Iraq and Afghanistan. Chuck Hagel, like John Kerry, served in the Vietnam War but unlike Kerry, Hagel felt that the Vietnam War was justified and he blamed the leadership for failing to win a winnable war. Mike, how do you think Hagel's experience in Vietnam will shape his approach to foreign policy and the use of armed forces?

NEWTON: Well in the big picture, the lesson of Vietnam, which I think people who were there—as was my father—learned intimately, and anybody in any other military organization would echo this—is to understand the innovation and comradery and the teamwork that's essential down at the lower levels, that you're the ones that bear the hardships, bear the greatest burden, and having experienced that personally, I think that Shannon's right. The secretary of state will tend towards diplomacy. That's part of the job description of secretary of state. But the critical lesson out of Vietnam is that the leadership comes from the secretary of defense—both the advocacy for the defense position, but also the ability from on high to give clear guidance and the resources, the time, and the full support of the bureaucracy because that's the frustrating thing from the ground looking up. And what we're really talking about in military terms is someone who can create a fusion between the operational and the strategic level all the way down to the tactical level.

SCHARF: And it's not just the leadership side,; it's also the political leadership. Let me ask Shannon this question. Senator Hagel reluctantly supported the 2003 invasion of Iraq, and then he ended up being one of the few Republican critics of the Iraq war, and then he opposed the so-called surge.[100] What does that tell us about him? Is he going to have the kind of leadership, politically, that Michael Newton says is so important in the position?

FRENCH: Well, I think it's interesting that we're drawing out these parallels with Kerry and Hagel and the strongest parallel that I see is this concern about our actual troops, about the individuals on the ground, what we send them off to do on our behalf, and I think something we haven't mentioned, which is relevant on the biography side with Hagel, is he will be the first person who held an enlisted rank to become a secretary of defense. That's significant to me because this is someone who has seen war from that enlisted person's perspective, very low on the totem pole but doing a lot of the very hard work and facing the wars squarely on. So I am interested to see how he does this. He's also been described as very thoughtful. That he's a reflective person and the seeing both sides and going back and forth on judgment isn't always a sign of weakness. Sometimes it's a sign of getting more information and amending your previous judgment based on the new knowledge. So I'm not negative on him for those points, but he was arguably wrong about the surge, and I think people might highlight that and say this is a case where the reluctance may have prevented something that did in fact prove effective.

SCHARF: We're starting to peel the onion on these individuals, but it's time for another short break. When we return, we'll continue our discussion on America's new foreign policy team. Stay with us.

---

100. Jesse Singal, Christine Lim, and M. J. Stephey. "January 2007: The Surge." *Time*, March 19 2010, http://www.time.com/time/specials/packages/article/0,28804,1967340 _1967355_1968027,00.html.

SCHARF: Welcome back to *Talking Foreign Policy*, brought to you by Case Western Reserve University and WCPN 90.3 Idea Stream. I'm Michael Scharf and I'm joined in studio by Shannon French, the Director of the Inamori International Center for Ethics and Excellence, Professor Milena Sterio of Cleveland Marshall College of Law, and Colonel Michael Newton of Vanderbilt Law School. We've been discussing the backgrounds of the three men who have been selected to head America's Foreign Policy team for the next four years and we were just looking at what Chuck Hagel would mean as head of the Department of Defense. Mike Newton, you said you wanted to jump into that discussion.

NEWTON: Well, I did want to pick up on Shannon's point. I think that one of the subtle things in Chuck Hagel's background as an enlisted man having served on the ground, remember and people forget this, is that the surge was really a ground-up tactical initiative developed from the bottom percolating to the top. People think now in hindsight, oh it was General Petraeus,[101] it was the thinkers, it was Washington. No, these were tactical innovations that were done from the ground up, and to the extent that Hagel opposed the surge, what it meant was he had forgotten that basic lesson—that the keys to victory, or in military terms 'mission accomplishment,' are best understood by the people on the ground having to do it and then you've got to listen to them, you've got to empower them, and more importantly, you have to resource them. And if he's forgotten that basic lesson, he'll be a disaster as secretary of defense.

SCHARF: Milena Sterio, you wanted to add something?

STERIO: I just wanted to bring back Susan Rice in the conversation. We had been talking about her earlier and to just sort of wrap this up with bringing her name up again. We've been talking about how Hagel and Kerry, both of their experiences seem to have been shaped by the fact that they both served in the Vietnam War. Well, Susan Rice did not. She is a generation younger than they are and she has actually been quoted as saying, "You know, why do we keep talking about Vietnam? Now we're dealing with completely different issues. Let's just forget about Vietnam." So it is going to be very interesting to see if she were to become the next national security advisor how she deals with Kerry and Hagel on these kinds of issues.

---

101. Scott Shane and Sheryl Gay Stolberg, "A Brilliant Career with a Meteoric Rise and an Abrupt Fall," *New York Times*, November 10, 2012, http://www.nytimes.com/2012/11/11/us/david-petraeus-seen-as-an-invincible-cia-director-self-destructs.html.

SCHARF: You know this reminds me of something that was in that new movie, *Lincoln*. Have any of the three of you seen that?

FRENCH: Yes.

STERIO: Yeah, I saw that movie.

SCHARF: Okay, you both have. Milena, then let me ask you this question. So the movie, *Lincoln* is based on the book *Team of Rivals*, by Doris Kearns Goodwin, which is getting a lot of attention along with the movie. Some people have likened Hagel's appointment to the cabinet appointments of Abraham Lincoln. What do you think about that comparison?

STERIO: About Hagel and Lincoln?

SCHARF: Yeah, a team of rivals, someone who is a Republican coming into the democratic fold. How is that likely to work? How often has that happened in the past?

STERIO: It has not happened that often, but I think in this instance it can work because Hagel, on many different occasions, has taken positions more like to the official Democratic Party line than the Republican Party line. I don't see him becoming a source of paralysis. And I don't see a major conflict between him and the president.

SCHARF: So I'm reminded back to the last time we had a Republican secretary of defense during a democratic administration that was during the Clinton administration with Bill Cohen. Mike, you were at that time part of the U.S. delegation negotiating the international criminal court statute. Wasn't the fact that you had the Defense Department headed by a Republican opponent of the ICC something that made it very hard for the Democratic administration to break a log jam and have a good negotiating position?

NEWTON: Well it did create policy paralysis but the problem was lack of presidential leadership. In Lincoln's *Team of Rivals*, they were all of the same party. They were personal rivals and that had as much of an impact as if they were from different political parties. But President Lincoln overcame that. So I don't attach much to labels, the personal rivalries, and the animosities, but the important point to remember is that these are the heads of huge organizations. The secretary of defense, because of the power and the reach and the funding of the Pentagon, is always going to have essentially a disproportionate share of that power. When the State Department wants to do something, they go to the Pentagon, for security, for funding, for transportation, etc. So here's the problem, it takes presidential leadership and that's the key. There will be inevitable frictions and it takes presidential leadership to both set policy but more importantly to move the bureaucracy and that will in the end determine the success of all three of these new appointments.

SCHARF: And speaking of leadership—well Shannon, that is what you teach, right? So tell us your take is on this.

FRENCH: I just want to add that the point of the *Team of Rivals* was to actually put people in the room who would disagree with President Lincoln and so a lot of this is about what President Obama expects, and what he will tolerate, and what he's going to encourage from his new foreign policy leadership team. It only works if he is, in fact, sincerely inviting challenge and cordial dispute. Otherwise, it really doesn't matter if they are from different parties, if they're all either cowed in some way, or not willing to challenge one another. It doesn't create that healthy atmosphere that you really need for ethical decision making.

NEWTON: And let me just add quickly that there are very troubling signs. The recent reports, for example, that General James Mattis was pushed out prematurely from the central command indicate that President Obama does not in fact tolerate that healthy exchange of ideas vigorous debate regarding military policy.

SCHARF: Well, let's take our microscope which has been looking at Senator Kerry and former Senator Hagel and now let's focus in on the third important new nominee, and that's John Brennan, who's been nominated to be the new director of the CIA. Now let me ask Shannon this question. The press has reported that Brennan wasn't put forward for the position of the CIA four years ago because of the role that he may have played during the Bush administration in approving some of the extraordinary interrogation techniques, which have been so controversial. Those are the things for our listeners that you may have seen in the movie *Zero Dark Thirty*, like waterboarding for example. So what does this mean for his confirmation this time around? Is it going to be a problem for him? Should it be?

FRENCH: I have to admit, of the people we're looking at in our conversation here, Brennan is the one who gives me the most pause and you've shot right to the reason. It's not only the enhanced interrogation, which I don't like those euphemisms, we're talking about torture. It's not only that he's also been associated with leaks and other problems that suggest and I don't know the full truth I am not enough on the inside to know how much he's involved with decision making there, but it suggests that he is at least associated in people's minds with an era that eroded some of the core values that our military depends on. And I definitely remember, I was teaching at the Naval Academy during the Bush administration, and understanding the effect that it had on the military at many different levels. To be hearing about this gradual chipping away of the rules and to hear it authorized from the highest quarters, this is a corruption of the command climate and we saw many horrible things come out of that, Abu Ghraib, Black Sites, and so forth, and you could pin a lot of harms to that. So I feel like he is a tainted choice. I am not myself on board the Brennan train. I could be convinced otherwise but I need more information.

SCHARF: Now the controversy about Brennan is not just about things that happened in the Bush administration because he was a carryover. In fact President Obama gave him a big promotion to the position of White House counterterrorism czar.

FRENCH: He's also the drone guy.

SCHARF: Yeah, let's get to those questions. Mike, you have held several sensitive positions in the army, JAG, at the State Department. You know how important it is to really have a certain amount of good judgment and discretion in these types of situations. Let me ask you about John Brennan and something that Shannon said. He has sort of a reputation for shooting his mouth off, right? Right after the takedown of Osama Bin Laden, he was reportedly the guy that said Osama Bin Laden came out firing like Butch Cassidy and the Sundance Kid, which we later learned was not true. He was the guy who told the press that the Seal Team had captured Osama Bin Laden's personal stash of porn videos, which we later learned had nothing to do with Osama Bin Laden. And then finally, with respect to use of predator drones, he's the one who said that in the years of their use in Pakistan not a single innocent civilian casualty could be blamed on the use of the predator drones, which apparently is far from the truth. So do you think Brennan has the right temperament for the CIA's top position?

NEWTON: Who in Washington doesn't have a habit of shooting their mouth off? I mean let's be real. I think there is a bigger problem, and in fact I'm going to push back on Shannon just a little bit on this. In terms appointing a new director of the CIA—if not John Brennan, then whom? This is a critically important time in the life of the agency having just been through the scandal that they've just been through, having just had a forced change of leadership, you've got to have somebody that comes in like Brennan that knows the organizational structure, that knows the mission, and that really can rebuild the role of the agency in a time of transformation. So the public statements you're talking about, some of the allegations about to me are very troubling. Not so much because the initial reports from the killing of Osama Bin Laden were inaccurate but because they signal this desire to use policy processes and intelligence processes for political advantage—that's a huge problem. In fact, that's a trend.

SCHARF: Are you saying that Brennan was doing this as the mouthpiece for President Obama?

NEWTON: I think those are questions that will come up during his confirmation hearing and to be an effective director of CIA he needs to clearly rebut those and say, look, it is the job of the intelligence community, headed by the director of Central Intelligence, to be neutral, to be apolitical, to be diligent in providing the very best advice. We are not the political pawns of this administration or any other administration.

SCHARF: Well, another issue that is almost certainly going to arise in his confirmation hearings is about his very aggressive advocacy for the use of predator drones. And Milena Sterio you have written extensively about predator drones and their use, and their legality, and the politics of that. Tell us what it means to have the CIA director to be somebody who has gone on record as being such a forceful advocate of expanding use of drones—not just abroad, but even in the United States.

STERIO: As we all know, under the Obama administration, the use of drones has increased for both surveillance purposes as well as for targeting operations, and John Brennan has really been the key person to President Obama's drone policy. So, for example, in an April 2012 speech, John Brennan argued that drone strikes are legal both under domestic law as well as under international law, and that there's nothing in international law that would prohibit the use of drones. He also claimed that drone strikes are ethical because of "the unprecedented ability of remotely piloted aircraft to precisely target a military objective while minimizing collateral damage"—these are his words. I don't think that everybody would agree with that assessment of the drone technology. And I have to say that I am with Shannon on this one that I also am a little bit troubled by the choice of John Brennan to head the CIA because of his very aggressive stance on drones and also it's been reported that he has been an advocate for using drones not just in areas like Afghanistan and Pakistan but for using them in Yemen, and in countries like Mali. So, for some of us that would be a somewhat troubling development.

SCHARF: I think that one thing the hearings will do is give the American people and the Congress the ability to have that detailed discussion, which we haven't really had. We've crept up on the use of drones without having that very public debate. Now let me, speaking of the legislature, ask you Milena to tell us a little bit about the treaty process. The President is very powerful but he can't ratify treaties without the Senate. He can't get executive agreements implemented without the Congress. So what are the treaties that are awaiting approval that have been sort of stacked up during the last four years that are likely to be at issue in the coming years?

STERIO: So, just very briefly, there are three different ways in which the United States can enter into international agreements. If you're talking about treaties, those are authorized by Article Two of our Constitution and there the president needs a supermajority of two-thirds of our senators. Historically speaking, very few of our international agreements have been entered into via the treaty Article Two route. Just to give you a number between 1946 and 1999, the United States completed almost 16,000 international agreements and only 912 of those agreements were treaties. So the other ways in which we can enter into international agreements are congressional executive agreements where the president needs a majority of both houses, the House of Representatives and Senate, to authorize or implement the agreement or sole executive agreements where the president unilaterally enters into international agreements pursuant to his inherent power as commander in chief. So, over the last four years, not many treaties have been approved using that Article Two clause where you need a supermajority of two-thirds of our senators.

SCHARF: But there's a bunch of agreements that are Article Two treaties that are stacked up right now. Some of the ones that come to mind are the Law of the Sea Treaty, some disarmament treaties, and several human rights treaties. Let me ask the panel at large to chime in. Which ones do you think are the most important that will possibly now get a fresh start under the foreign policy team?

NEWTON: Well, understand that this is the process that doesn't just happen with a change of administration and a change of people. Every year the State Department prepares its master priority list and the president approves this. So there's a backlog, a huge backlog, of those treaties. There's an important principle here, which is when the United States goes out and negotiates an agreement like the Law of the Sea Treaty in good faith, and parties make concessions to obtain our support, and then afterward the Treaty gets locked up in the Senate for decades, this is going to have an effect when we try to negotiate other treaties, whether they're trade agreements or human rights agreements or security agreements. Our treaty partners will say, why should we compromise with you when you're not going to accept the legal obligations? This was a problem in the International Criminal Court negotiations. And it's why I hope the new team can to unlock some of those treaties, particularly the Law of the Sea Treaty.

SCHARF: All right, so several administrations have wanted the Senate to approve the Law of the Sea Treaty. Why is that treaty so important? What are the practical things that we need it for?

NEWTON: Freedom of navigation through the straits of Hormuz, freedom of navigation of U.S. Naval Forces to enforce embargos, freedom of navigation in and around the South China Sea.

SCHARF: What about Russia's claims to oil on the floor of the melting Arctic?

NEWTON: Yes, and Russia's claims up in the Arctic.

SCHARF: So this is a treaty we absolutely need and it's just stuck in the Senate?

NEWTON: The argument has been that we can assert our rights without the treaty under customary international law. But the status of some of the provisions of the treaty as customary law is in dispute, and that approach doesn't give us the benefit of using the treaty's dispute resolution procedures. And I have to say, for me, and my experience negotiating treaties, the United States gets the Law of the Sea Treaty thrown in our face routinely. When other countries say to us, why should we negotiate in good faith when the promises that you have made us you can't keep because your Senate will never approve the treaty? And that's a serious diplomatic problem for the United States.

SCHARF: Shannon?

FRENCH: I just wanted to throw out a related point. You and Mike were talking about the Arctic and, of course, one of the reasons that this is becoming an issue is some of the melting that is occurring because of global climate change is actually opening up new routes that were not available before and those are becoming points of contention. And that relates to something else that I think we ought to at least put in the mix here that came up already in John Kerry's hearings, and that is that the secretary of state has a role to play in issues regarding climate change, including negotiating and getting the Senate to approve a climate change treaty. I think people are really trying to take his temperature on that and figure out where he stands. There are some environmental groups that are very optimistic that he's going to, for example, try to block the Keystone XL Pipeline that crosses the Canada-U.S. border—it's a State Department issue because it's an international pipeline. And there are others who are concerned that he may seem too squishy on that or they can't tell for sure where he's going to ultimately come down. So there a lot of core environmental related treaties in which John Kerry is going to play an important role.

SCHARF: Do you think as somebody who has actually been the chair of the Senate Foreign Relations Committee, who's been on that committee for three decades, that he will somehow be able to do what Hillary Clinton and President Obama were not able to do the last four years, and that is to break the logjam and have some of these treaties move forward?

FRENCH: Possibly, I mean he has often been reported to have a very good relationship with John McCain, so there's a team of rivals in a way who are in fact good friends and have a background together. So that gives him a position, again, of respect, which I mentioned earlier that might allow him to move some of these treaties forward. I know, also, in his hearings they brought up the concerns about nuclear disarmament. And as always happens, you have people with particular interest in their districts who are worried about if this happens, local jobs will be lost because there are materials and systems that are produced in my state. And Kerry seemed to have the finesse to deal with that and to talk about the practicalities, saying, look, this wouldn't happen overnight, you'd have time to adjust. He would understand what language to give to some of these legislators in order to allow them to speak to their constituencies and make this argument to them. So I think that's something we haven't seen in a while.

SCHARF: Okay, now let's assume that part of the reason that John Kerry was selected was because he might have this ability with his old friendships to get things moving again in the Senate Foreign Relations Committee. Let's go back to the question of what Chuck Hagel brings to the table. And my question for Mike Newton, an army guy from West Point, is this: what do you think Chuck Hagel's role will be in American military policy in an era of austerity, where there may need to be deep budget cuts for the Department of Defense?

NEWTON: Well, the cynical answer is to be a political weasel. It is a political appointment and so the idea is that you're just the mouthpiece of the president. But remember, in our constitutional structure under a civilian controlled military, he's also the critical liaison between military forces in the field and regional commanders, theatre commanders, and the White House. There's a critical policy role he must play. There's a deep seated fear in the military that Senator Hagel will simply become the mouthpiece of the White House to superimpose, to cram down people's throats in a way that's dismissive of the military professionals, and in doing that will undermines military effectiveness. Clearly it's an area of shrinking resources, but the trick is to get control of the bureaucracy and to make smart cuts. And the great fear is that they won't do that, that it'll just become a political process.

SCHARF: Well, in many ways that's more challenging than even the things that face the secretary of state. It's time for another break, when we come back our experts will discuss how the members of the new Foreign Policy team are likely to respond to the most important foreign policy issues facing the United States in the next four years. Stay with us.

SCHARF: We're back with *Talking Foreign Policy*. This is Michael Scharf, the associate dean at Case Western University School of Law. With me in the studio are ethicist Shannon French, military expert Colonel Michael Newton, and international law professor Milena Sterio. We've been discussing America's new foreign policy team, John Kerry, Chuck Hagel, and John Brennan. In our final segment today, our expert panel will forecast where the new team members are likely to take American foreign policy in the next four years. Shannon, I'm going to begin with you. There have been all sorts of reports about where these people stand. Some people believe that both Kerry and Hagel are two guys who will always error on the side of not intervening; we've heard some of that in our discussion earlier. What do you think this means for humanitarian intervention in places like Syria?

FRENCH: First, the point that needs to be clarified is that the kind of intervention they are most likely to be hesitant about is the actual ground troops type of intervention, a large scale intervention, and one that puts a large number of our troops in peril. I don't think that it is a fair assumption that they will be against interventions by other means, such as the kind of aerial campaign that the United States led in Libya last year. But second, if you look back to the 1990s, Senator Hagel, himself, called for ground troops in support of the intervention of Kosovo. And I think that John Kerry has made it clear about Syria, that he's had conversations with John McCain about the issue of whether some kind of support for the forces against Assad is appropriate and when and what that support would look like. And he seems very open to at least exploring that. He's talked in the past about trying to negotiate with Assad, but he has made very strong statements that that is no longer possible. He's been quoted as saying that Assad's actions are inexcusable and reprehensible and so forth. So, he's said that the time for talk has passed, and that the clock on his leadership is ticking. These are not the words of someone who is against intervention.

SCHARF: Milena or Mike, do you want to weigh in on this?

STERIO: I really agree with that, and Shannon said earlier how John Kerry isn't really a pacifist. So I agree with the assessment that the question is going to be whether we commit ground troops, probably not unless we really have to but I do think that he would be willing to support other kinds of intervention and in many ways both Kerry and Hagel seem to be tilting more towards a counter terrorism strategy where you use, for example, drones and you really go after the bad guys, neutralize the bad guys, rather than engaging in a ground kind of offensive strategy where you're going to try to protect the good guys. So it is just the question of how it's done, but I don't really see him as a pacifist either.

NEWTON: Yeah, but there is this sensitivity, and Shannon alluded to Kerry's famous quote, "How do you ask a man to be the last man to die for a mistake?" Well, it's only a mistake if the mission fails, and the military is going to have to be put in danger to succeed. So there's a larger issue, which is if you're going to do something in Syria, define a mission, define the terms of success, generate the political support, let the military go in and do their job, resource them properly, give them rules of engagement that are sufficient to accomplish the mission, and let them go in, every military person in the world wants to go in, do their job, secure victory, accomplish the mission, and go home. They're not troubled by being put into harm's way, that's why they're in the all-volunteer force.

FRENCH: You know, that quote that I gave earlier from Kerry about not dying for a mistake is what you're highlighting and I think that there may even be a reluctance with both men to be put into a position of judging whether this is a mistake or not because of their tie to Vietnam, which you were highlighting would not have necessarily been the case with Susan Rice.

SCHARF: Shannon, let me put this into the context of Afghanistan. I mean those words of Kerry could just as well be said of our exit strategy in Afghanistan. What do you think Kerry and Hagel are likely to do in their approach to our exit from Afghanistan? Are they going to want to quickly pull out all the troops? Are they going to want to leave some? How do you ask someone to be the last man or woman to die in Afghanistan?

FRENCH: Well, I think the strategy we've seen supported so far suggests that we are never going to pull out every last man and woman. That hasn't been President Obama's approach and nothing I've heard from any of these new leaders suggests that they are going to radically change that. So that does mean that we are going to leave people in harm's way, though radically fewer numbers than we have now. But I think we're going to quickly see a clash of this idealistic concept of not letting anyone die for a mistake and recognizing that we're going to have to leave people in these countries even if you do feel it was a mistake to go there in the first place. And I'm not sure how they're going to reconcile that with their own histories.

SCHARF: And our troops are extremely vulnerable in these countries.

FRENCH: Clearly.

SCHARF: Milena, what would you add to that?

STERIO: So, President Obama had announced that basically the United States would withdraw combat troops, would withdraw from any combat role in Afghanistan, by the end of 2014 and right now we have about sixty thousand troops in Afghanistan. So the real question then is come January 2015, how many troops are left there? Do we withdraw fifty-five thousand and leave five thousand, or do we withdraw fifty-seven thousand and leave three thousand? I think Shannon is absolutely right, there are going to be some troops left and there's going to be some danger to those men and women, but the question really is, how many will be left? And it seems like Kerry and Hagel are pushing towards withdrawing more than what President Obama had originally suggested.

FRENCH: They may even push harder on our partners as well, to try to supply some of those remaining troops; I mean that's certainly been another point of contention all along in these conflicts, the vast numbers of U.S. troops versus those of our allies. We do have some excellent strong partners around the world.

SCHARF: They're going to have to be good salesmen because they've got some swamp land to sell.

FRENCH: That's true.

NEWTON: To me, it's not a question of how many people are there, it's a question of what they're doing, and that's the big strategic $64,000 question. After a decade of war in Afghanistan, we know where we are, and in fact, we know where we would have wanted to be. We are not nearly where we would have wanted to be. For example, there are many, many Afghan forces that simply will not go on patrol without U.S. forces. And frankly, there are many coalition forces that won't go on patrol without U.S. forces or U.S. air cover. So the challenge is to shape a role where we have a designated number of troops but that are resourced appropriately that actually does some good.

SCHARF: Mike, let me draw on your military expertise in another area. In the *Plain Dealer*, which is the local Cleveland newspaper, we have this column that's called "Whatever happened to?" And this is that sort of question. Whatever happened to the Strategic Defense Initiative, which Ronald Regan called Star Wars?[102] I think what happened is that they've continued to be researching it and building it. And the question I have for you is, while they're trying to find places to cut the budget, is Senator Hagel likely to be somebody who is going to be in favor of drastically cutting the SDI? And is that something that is in our interests? Is that something in our allies' interests?

NEWTON: Star Wars is a term I haven't heard since the 1970s in terms of defense policy. But it did understand it did lead to some very important strategic results. You think of the Israelis using the iron dome system,[103] you think of the fact that the North Korean's just came out several days ago and said we are going to intentionally target our intercontinental ballistic missiles on the United States. So missile defense capacity is clearly, clearly an important U.S. and, frankly, NATO interest. The big problem that will be encountered will be in Eastern Europe, the fate of the deployment of a missile defense system in Poland, which was designed to address a whole range of threats from Iran to North Korea. This is a critical element to the so-called Russian Reset. The reset, the desire to start with a clean slate with the Russians, is not turning

---

102. Mark Thompson, "Why Obama Will Continue Star Wars," *Time*, November 16, 2008, http://www.time.com/time/nation/article/0,8599,1859393,00.html.
103. William Broad, "Weapons Experts Raise Doubts about Israel's Anti-Missile System," *New York Times*, March 20, 2013, http://www.nytimes.com/2013/03/21/world/middleeast/israels-iron-dome-system-is-at-center-of-debate.html?pagewanted=all&_r=0.

out so well. The problem is that the Poles are sitting there having spent a great deal of political capital to support the United States and we've made promises to them, which we may not be prepared to keep. I think beyond just the narrow issue of whether we can defend places with a missile shield or not, there's a larger issue of the credibility of U.S. commitments and the credibility of statements that we make to our friends and allies around the world. And to the extent that people say we cannot trust the United States to keep its word, we have a much bigger strategic problem.

SCHARF: Well, speaking of trusting us to keep our word and what our word means, let me ask Milena about the situation in Iran, which Mike Newton just mentioned. Chuck Hagel has said that preemptive strikes against Iran's nuclear program would be counterproductive. Recently, John Kerry said our policy in Iran is not containment, it's prevention. I don't know, it sounds like those are two things that are in mutual contradiction. So what do you think this means in terms of our approach to Iran in the next couple of months?

STERIO: Well, first of all, if in fact John Kerry thinks we should do something about Iran preemptively, and Chuck Hagel doesn't, I just want to reiterate one point that I think Mike Newton mentioned before—it's going to be up to President Obama to show strong leadership to bring his team together to make sure that we have an effective policy. Chuck Hagel doesn't seem to believe that Iran is such a significant threat that would warrant intervention. John Kerry may seem slightly more in favor of intervening in Iran. Personally, I do not see the United States intervening in Iran over the next three or four years, unless something exceptional were to happen where all of a sudden we found information that Iran is about to do something extraordinarily dangerous.

SCHARF: Now, Shannon, let me ask you. Chuck Hagel is not an empty vessel. He actually is a professor at Georgetown and he's been writing books. One of his books is titled *America: Our Next Chapter*. And in it, he surprisingly emerges as a huge supporter of the United Nations. What will that mean for U.S. foreign policy going forward—to have a secretary of defense, a Republican no less, who is a strong supporter of the UN?

FRENCH: You could see I was sort of chuckling there a little bit because our relationship with the UN has been so uneven in recent years. We have had people in leadership positions, Bolton comes to mind, who have said deeply insulting things about the UN and its existence.

SCHARF: You are referring to John Bolton, the former U.S. Ambassador to the UN?

FRENCH: Right. And he's someone who once stated that the world would be better off without the UN, and now we're talking about a new secretary of defense who has praised the UN and extols its benefits for the United States. I do think, as someone who is an expert in military ethics, that going forward the support for international institutions and international law will positively affect military policy. But at the same time you always run into the issue of whether the UN has any teeth, whether it can enforce international law, and it's not clear to me that Hagel is or will be in any position to significantly strengthen the UN in the way that would make it a more important force.

NEWTON: In this regard, go back to the issue of Iran. Consider the question from the point of view of Israel, which faces an existential threat from a nuclear armed Iran, which has said our goal is to eliminate those Jews from their territory. There are some things the UN does very, very well—delivering medicines, water, humanitarian relief, election monitoring, a whole range of things. But acting in a decisive, expeditious basis to protect sovereignty and lives at risk is not one of them. And if you're the Israelis, you cannot depend on the United Nations, which in the past adopted numerous anti-Israeli resolutions. So in that sense, it's great to talk about what the UN does, but Senator Hagel and Senator Kerry are going to have to focus on the precise line between what the UN is capable of doing and what it is not capable of doing.

SCHARF: And in saying that, I recall during the presidential debates, both candidates said that the UN had been very effective in its crippling sanctions on Iran, and that that was driving Iran back to the table. Milena, do you have thoughts on that?

STERIO: Yeah, so obviously Iran is a very, very difficult issue and I absolutely agree with Mike Newton, that for a country like Israel, Iran poses a direct threat, and I think that it's sort of easy for us here in the United States to debate what that means when we're not the targets of such a direct threat. On any kind of intervention on Iran, with respect to the United Nations, there's always going to be paralysis within the Security Council. The Security Council is the only body that can authorize military action against a country like Iran. It's very likely that countries like Russia or China would veto any kind of proposed military action against Iran. So if Iran were to take it up another step in the development of nuclear weapons and we were to find out that there's really even more of an existential threat against Israel, we may be in a situation where Israel would have to do something drastic and in that sense, it would be up to the United States to really show whether then we would provide a sort of unilateral support to Israel if the UN were paralyzed.

SCHARF: And speaking about these potential conflicts between the secretary of state nominee and the secretary of defense nominee, John Kerry is known as one of the most pro-Israel members of the Senate, whereas, Chuck Hagel has been criticized as being too tough on Israel for opposing the expansion of Israeli settlement on the West Bank. So they're going to be debating it out on that issue as well. Well, we're almost out of time. Today's program has provided a fascinating look at the Obama administration's new foreign policy team. As always, we hope that we have shed some light where before there was just heated debate. If you want to weigh in on the discussion or suggest a topic for an upcoming broadcast of *Talking Foreign Policy*, just send an email to talkingforeignpolicy@case.edu. Thanks again to our panel of experts, Shannon French of Case Western Reserve University, Mike Newton of Vanderbilt University, and Milena Sterio of Cleveland State Marshal College of Law. I'm Michael Scharf, thank you for joining us. Talking Foreign Policy is a production of Case Western Reserve University and is produced in partnership with 90.3 FM WCPN Ideastream.

Contributors

David L. Cooperrider is the Fairmount Minerals Professor of Social Entrepreneurship at the Weatherhead School of Management, Case Western Reserve University. Past chair of the National Academy of Management's OD division, he has lectured and taught at Harvard, Stanford, University of Chicago, Katholieke University in Belgium, MIT, University of Michigan, Cambridge, and others. Cooperrider is founder and chair of the Fowler Center for Sustainable Value. The center's core proposition is that sustainability is the business opportunity of the twenty-first century, indeed that every social and global issue of our day is an opportunity to ignite industry leading eco-innovation, social entrepreneurship, and new sources of value. Cooperrider has served as advisor to a wide variety of organizations, including Boeing Corporation, Fairmount Minerals, Green Mountain Coffee Roasters, McKinsey, Parker, Sherwin Williams, Wal-Mart, as well as American Red Cross, American Hospital Association, Cleveland Clinic, and World Vision. He has published fifteen books and authored over fifty articles.

Martin L. Cook is the Admiral James Bond Stockdale Professor of Professional Military Ethics at the United States Naval War College. Dr. Cook serves as coeditor of the *Journal of Military Ethics*, and as a member of the editorial board of *Parameters*, the scholarly journal of the US Army War College and the *Journal of Military Medical Ethics*. He has authored or co-authored several important books on military ethics and more than forty-five scholarly articles. He has lectured on topics of military ethics in the United Kingdom, Australia, Singapore, France, the Netherlands, Hong Kong, and Norway. His book, *The Moral Warrior: Ethics and Service in the US Military* was published in 2003 by the State University of New York Press, and a new volume, *Issues in Military Ethics: To Support and Defend the Constitution*, also with SUNY Press, was published in March 2013.

Gregory L. Eastwood is University Professor at the State University of New York (SUNY) and Professor of Bioethics and Humanities and Professor of Medicine at SUNY Upstate Medical University, Syracuse. Eastwood teaches bioethics and is a member of the University Hospital Ethics Consultation Service. He has authored over 130 articles and book chapters and has written or edited several books. Eastwood received his M.D. from Case Western Reserve University and trained in internal medicine and gastroenterology. Subsequently, he was on the faculty at Harvard Medical School and the University of Massachusetts Medical School, where he was Director of Gastroenterology and Associate Dean for Admissions, and then became Dean of the Medical College of Georgia. Eastwood was President of SUNY Upstate Medical University from 1993 to 2006. He served as Interim President of Case Western Reserve University from 2006 to 2007, and then directed the Inamori International Center for Ethics and Excellence from 2007 to 2008.

Shannon E. French is the Inamori Professor of Ethics, Director of the Inamori International Center for Ethics and Excellence, and a tenured member of the Philosophy Department at Case Western Reserve University. Prior to starting at CWRU in July 2008, she taught for eleven years as an Associate Professor of Philosophy and Associate Chair of the Department of Leadership, Ethics, and Law at the United States Naval Academy in Annapolis, Maryland. French received her B.A. in philosophy, classical studies, and history from Trinity University in 1990 and her Ph.D. in philosophy from Brown University in 1997. Her main area of research is military ethics, and she is widely published in this field, including the book, *The Code of the Warrior: Exploring Warrior Values, Past and Present*. Her scholarly interests also include leadership ethics, organizational ethics, moral psychology, bioethics, and environmental ethics. She has been a featured speaker at professional gatherings in the U.S. and in France, England, Italy, Norway, Canada, Japan, Australia, and the Netherlands.

Duncan Gaswaga is an Ugandan expatriate Judge with the Supreme Court and Constitutional Court of the Republic of Seychelles. He also heads the Criminal Division and has written more judgments on maritime piracy committed by Somali pirates on the Indian Ocean than any other judge in history, thereby contributing to and developing a unique type of jurisprudence which is cited internationally. In 2012, Judge Gaswaga was appointed Distinguished Jurist in Residence at the Case Western Reserve University, School of Law and served as a Visiting Professional at the International Criminal Court (ICC), The Hague.

David Hassler is the director of the Wick Poetry Center at Kent State University and the author of two books of poems, most recently, *Red Kimono, Yellow Barn*, for which he was awarded Ohio Poet of the Year in 2006. With photographer Gary Harwood, he is the author of *Growing Season: The Life of a Migrant Community*, which received the Ohioana Book Award, the Carter

G. Woodson Honor Book Award, and was a finalist for the Great Lakes Book Award. He is coeditor of two anthologies, *Learning by Heart: Contemporary American Poetry about School* and *After the Bell: Contemporary American Prose about School*, as well as *A Place to Grow: Voices and Images of Urban Gardeners*. He received a B.A. from Cornell University and an M.F.A. from Bowling Green State University. His poems have appeared in *Prairie Schooner, The Sun, DoubleTake/Points of Entry, Indiana Review*, and other journals. He speaks widely at state and national conferences on issues of poetry and education.

Michele Hunt, of DreamMakers, is internationally known for her work as a change catalyst and 'thinking partner' to leaders of organizations and communities on leadership development, organizational transformation, and organizational effectiveness. She works with leaders and their teams to help transform their organizations to higher levels of participation, teamwork, and performance. Her work is rooted in the principles of shared vision, values, alignment, and continuous learning. Michele launched her firm in 1995. Her clients have included leadership teams of IBM, Motorola, Swiss Reinsurance Company, Popular, Inc., EVERTEC, Banco Popular of North America, Bright China Management Institute, Banco Do Brazil, BHP of Australia, the US Veterans Administration, the Food and Drug Administration, the National Park Service, the Chicago Public Schools, Junior Achievement of New York City, World Vision International, the Episcopal Divinity School at Harvard, and the Aruba Quality Foundation.

Chris Laszlo is an Associate Professor, teaching sustainability, strategy, and organizational behavior at the Weatherhead School of Management, Case Western Reserve University, where he is also the Faculty Research Director of the Fowler Center for Sustainability Value. He is the coauthor of *Embedded Sustainability: the Next Big Competitive Advantage*. His earlier books include *Sustainable Value*, and *The Sustainable Company*. His work over the last decade has helped launch mainstream management approaches to sustainability for value and profit. Chris is also the managing partner of Sustainable Value Partners, a sustainability strategy consulting firm he cofounded in 2002. In 2012, he was selected a 'Top 100 Thought Leader in Trustworthy Business Behavior' by Trust Across America.

Duncan Morrow is a Lecturer in Politics at the University of Ulster. He was previously the Chief Executive of the Northern Ireland Community Relations Council, which was responsible for supporting the development of community-based initiatives for reconciliation across Northern Ireland and for developing policy ideas to support peace building. He is also Director of Community Engagement for the university.

Peter Neergaard is Professor in Corporate Social Responsibility (CSR) and Supply Chains at the Centre for Corporate Social Responsibility, Copenhagen Business School. He holds a M.S. from Copenhagen Business School and from University of Wisconsin and a Ph.D. from Copenhagen Business School. He has been partner in many EU-funded projects. The last one—RESPONSE—researched how CSR were perceived and managed by a large number of multinational companies. He has published intensively in the areas of quality management, supply chain management, and CSR. In 2009, he received the outstanding paper award for the best paper in Measuring Business Excellence from Emerald.

Louise Rosenmeier is a consultant at Climate Change & Sustainability Services, KPMG, near Copenhagen, Denmark. She has a graduate degree from the Copenhagen Business School, where she studied International Marketing and Management. She also received her undergraduate degree from the Copenhagen Business School, with a focus on Business, Language, and Culture, and earned a Certificate in Business Studies from the Grenoble Ecole de Management in the Grenoble Graduate School of Business in Grenoble, France.

Michael Scharf is the John Deaver Drinko – Baker & Hostetler Professor of Law and Associate Dean for Global Legal Studies at Case Western Reserve University School of Law. He is also President of the Hague-based International Criminal Law Network (ICLN). In 2005, Scharf and the Public International Law and Policy Group, a non-governmental organization he co-founded and directs, were nominated for the Nobel Peace Prize by six governments and the Prosecutor of an International Criminal Tribunal for the work they have done to help in the prosecution of major war criminals, such as Slobodan Milosevic, Charles Taylor, and Saddam Hussein. During the elder Bush and Clinton Administrations, Scharf served in the Office of the Legal Adviser of the U.S. Department of State, where he held the positions of Attorney-Adviser for Law Enforcement and Intelligence, Attorney-Adviser for United Nations Affairs, and delegate to the United Nations Human Rights Commission. During a sabbatical in 2008, Scharf served as Special Assistant to the Prosecutor of the Cambodia Genocide Tribunal. A graduate of Duke University School of Law (Order of the Coif and High Honors), and judicial clerk to Judge Gerald Bard Tjoflat on the Eleventh Circuit Federal Court of Appeals, Scharf is the author of seventy-five scholarly articles and sixteen books, including *The International Criminal Tribunal for Rwanda* which was awarded the American Society of International Law's Certificate of Merit for outstanding book in 1999, and *Enemy of the State: The Trial and Execution of Saddam Hussein,*" which won the International Association of Penal Law's book of the year award for 2009. His latest books are *Shaping Foreign Policy in Times of Crisis: The Role of International Law and the State Department Legal Adviser* (Cambridge University Press, 2010), and *Customary International Law in Times of Fundamental Change: Recognizing Grotian Moments* (Cambridge University Press, 2013). Scharf produces and hosts the radio program *Talking Foreign Policy*, broadcast on WCPN 90.3 FM (Cleveland's NPR station), available at: http://www.youtube.com/watch?v=PUvFvowWZmc. Scharf is also the first professor in the world to offer an international law MOOC, available at: https://www.coursera.org/#course/intlcriminallaw.

Charlene Zietsma is an Associate Professor, and the Ann Brown Chair of Organization Studies at Schulich School of Business, York University. Zietsma's research focuses on multiple pathways to social change, including the processes of institutional change, especially in the context of stakeholder conflicts; intra-organizational processes of learning and change; and the effects of cognition and passion on entrepreneurial opportunity recognition and start-up decisions. She has published in *Organization Science*, the *Journal of Business Venturing*, *Business & Society*, and *Corporate Reputation Review*, among others, and has received several research awards. Zietsma has also served on a number of boards and committees for nonprofit, professional, and government organizations and she consults with entrepreneurial organizations.